MARSHALL

THE PROMISE OF SILENCE

ISBN: 9781973323242

For Philippe... My eternal love...

The Promise Of Silence

The Promise Of Silence

1

The Immortalisation of Sufferance

What if I came out of that dark dusty closet and confided everything to you without restraint? Will the judgement of humanity have the compassion to tread softly on my dreams? Will there be a glorious resurrection to liberate me if I unearth my sufferance forever or will I be destroyed by a sensation of despair if I confront my forgotten tears again? Perhaps I will empower the past to resurface with a vengeance, but I must disclose my tragedy overtly if I want to be truly free. Since the beginning of my creation ungodly thoughts were deeply embedded in my mind. I struggled not to sin, I battled to silence my difference forever, but the brutality of time denuded me. Corruption invaded, contaminated and conquered me. It tore my flesh and devoured my soul without remorse. It made me become unworthy in the eyes of the catholic god and banished me from the eternal kingdom of heaven. I was born to be crucified in a prison of judgement; intolerance punished me for my catholic crime, but without hesitation I would live that war a million times again.

This is the reality of the battle of my life and the hard consequences of an invisible difference. The passing of time has changed me, the natural ageing process has rendered me strong and my current flow of thoughts liberates me to journey into the unknown. Since the beginning of time I was condemned to be an eternal sinner. I survived with an ocean of despair in my eyes as the solitude of my unholy difference destroyed me. I faded away in the agony of my sufferance alone as the brutality of silence slaughtered me more and more. I learnt by the intolerance of the holy sermons that there was no compassion in catholic Ireland for "a fucking queer". I needed to repent for my silenced sin, but the corruption of my erections betrayed me and in the changing colours of the seasons I fell in love with men. I was aroused by what was socially immoral and religiously forbidden; hence it was proclaimed by the almighty god of Ireland that Irish Catholics were to rightfully crucify me. The savagery of their pious

7

judgement certainly punished me and I lived the sufferance that no gay man should ever taste. This is not my revenge or my coming out, but the immortalisation of my plight. If you taste the emotions of my sufferance, smell the colours of my dreams and touch the sounds of my fallen tears, perhaps you will not dehumanise homosexuality further? If I give you a harmonious voyage into the horizons of tolerance, perhaps the cycle of social brutality against gays will come to an end? If I resurrect the forgotten silence, perhaps my dream of homosexual liberty for others can rise from the ashes of my destruction?

God created my homosexuality, but I was raised to be a straight boy in the prison of rural catholic Ireland. I really wanted to conform to my mother's dreams, but the road of my life went in a completely different direction. I was an Irish man that declared the beauty of love to men, I was a sinner that seduced and denuded virile men, but the crime of being homosexual was not my choice despite the social myth that was firmly entrenched in the morality of Ireland. I didn't want the glances of disgust in holy eyes to judge me, but the catholic god of Ireland banished me from the kingdom of heaven and the Catholics of Ireland punished me for my innate sin. I absolutely didn't want my pious mother to forsake me, but the sermons of god enriched her with such strong disdain. I prayed to the almighty god to hetero-sexualise me, but gay erections corrupted me more and more. I battled to graciously become a heterosexual man, but my ungodly desires devoured and conquered me with the temptation to taste naked men. I belonged to the social and religious belief that homosexuality was a contamination, but I kissed men passionately and liberated my Irish crucifixion. The world became a prison of silence, solitude, sufferance and tears as the eternal brutality of catholic Ireland slaughtered me. Why did the restraining catholic world that I belonged to fear my difference with so much hate? Why did so many Irish hypocrites have a venomous distaste for the freedom of the gay religion? Why did it make such a bloody difference that a man belonged to the homosexual culture or not? I struggled to survive in the narrow mindedness of rural Ireland. Society retarded my natural evolution, religion impeded my self-acceptance and humanity humiliated queers without remorse. I wanted to be a normal boy and certainly not "a fucking queer", but the inborn homoerotic feeling deep inside me made me different. There was no pity in the eyes of my oppressors as they crucified me, no catholic compassion to wipe away my tears, but the hardships of life definitely made me become a better man.

From an early age I learnt that homosexuality was forbidden by my religion. The sermons certainly preached about compassion, but it was made clear that there was no catholic forgiveness for homosexual immorality. The world of my catholic childhood was a complicated and lonely place of immense solitude and brutality. I was a very frightened and over-sensitive boy. On each catholic Sabbath day I feared the wrath of god and prayed in repentance, but my prayers to become straight were always silenced. I grew up in a hostile world that judged homosexuality as ungodly. The church doctrines fuelled society to believe that queers denuded men in sin and the holy heterosexuals of Ireland condemned me. My mother thoroughly believed in the myth of god, in the righteousness of heterosexuality and in the dehumanisation of queers. She slaughtered me a million times without remorse because homosexuality was forbidden in the discoloured gilded pages of her aged bible. She had no tolerance for homosexuals and her tears implored the almighty catholic god to hetero-sexualise me. I believed that her sufferance was a stepping stone on the road of acceptance, but her love for god contaminated her more and more with the passion to forsake me forever. I craved for her eternal love, but rather than taint her catholic reputation she crucified and slaughtered me. I closed my eyes and tasted the desolation that should never be inflicted on a queer son. Did she want my blood on her hands? Her rancour certainly almost destroyed me. I wanted to walk through the shadows of the valley of death. I wanted to die rather be "a queer fucker". I wanted the love of god to liberate me for eternity. I really thought that if death seduced me and not the passion of homosexuality that the kingdom of heaven wouldn't banish me, but then I learnt that suicide was also envisaged as a mortal sin. Somehow in the darkest moments of solitude and despair I had the strength and serenity to battle for the liberation of my reveries, but thoughts of death resurfaced to devour me again and again.

I battled to silence my homosexual desires, but I was too queer to be a righteous Catholic. The compassion of god didn't have any forgiveness for gay immortality, but I fell in love with men rather than believe in the intolerance preached by my religion. The first step of my homosexual freedom was my own self-acceptance. I was gay. Indeed I needed to denude men and become a homosexual sinner, so I abandoned the love of god and liberated my forbidden erections forever. That was my first coming out and such self-sincerity was ultimately the hardest part. Catholic Ireland was not contaminated by a gay disease; there wasn't a queer in the length and breadth of rural Ireland other than me. I even thought that I was the only living homosexual in the world, but step by step I began to

understand that the social judgement of gay immorality silenced all queers to live in the closet. I survived with the passion and vitality of a boy that knew absolutely nothing about the real sufferance of the gay culture. In my crucifixions I became a homosexual survivor. The holy judgement of Ireland destroyed me, but I believed in the resurrection of my dreams from the ashes of destruction and when despair completely devoured me I somehow always found a vision of hope again.

What provoked and nurtured such vile perversion within me? What traumatic experience overly influenced my choice to be different? Why did I fall in love with men and rebel against the heterosexual laws of nature? Was non-conformity a fashionable trend or a deliberate intent to cause provocation within the core of my catholic family? Did I choose to be tragically punished by human judgement for my ungodly sin? Was I really contaminated by the corruption of Satan? Since biblical times the main function of humans was to maintain the purification and survival of the race. Irish men were created to copulate and to reproduce an abundance of catholic heterosexuals, but in gay promiscuity there was certainly no reproduction. Being childless was my eternal damnation and the authentic proof that the homosexual disease was clearly an abnormality. Was it possible to exterminate homosexuality before it exterminated the purity of righteous religious values? The almighty god believed in the genocide of homosexuals and certainly needed to create homophobia to liberate catholic Ireland of queer immorality. My difference was innate; homosexuality was engrained in me from the moment of conception. God had created me barren to love men and catholic sinners crucified me with their intolerance. The holy judgement of Ireland slaughtered gays and the wrath of pious Catholics condemned Irish homosexuals to suffer another pink triangle holocaust. "In the name of the Father, and of the Son and of the Holy Spirit", the Trinitarian formula offered absolute deliverance from homosexual discrimination in the Sacrament of Penance. If gays were the forbidden fruit of heterosexuals, why was homosexuality created in the passion of heterosexual love? Why did heterosexuals give birth to homosexual vermin rather than miscarry such undesirables? Why was sexuality such an important social identifier in catholic Ireland? Was destruction the strongest of all human emotions? Was homophobic Ireland the creation of an almighty god or was the homophobic god created by the Irish? Why did the homosexual culture need to battle for the freedom and the right to love?

2

The Liberation of Catholic Hypocrisy

In the beginning god created the sin of homosexuality. I was born in rural Ireland in 1976. I had the affliction of being catholic and homosexual. I was drowned in baptism to save me from original sin. I was dictated cannibalism in the Sacrament of Communion. I was given the grace of the Holy Spirit and further contaminated by god's righteousness in the Sacrament of Confirmation. I was devout to god's love in the profoundness of my catholic education, but despite all the measures taken to purify me the almighty god wasn't powerful enough to eliminate my gayness. The church was enriched by Irish sinners that feared the wrath of god and abided by the obsolete beliefs of a dying religion. There was no social liberty in Ireland, no sexual intercourse before marriage, no contraception, no abortion, no divorce, no ungodly crime of homosexuality and absolutely no freedom of choice. Religion dominated all Irish lives in the sufferance of prayer and penance. Abortion was sinful and immoral because no man-made barrier had the right to interfere with the intent of god, which led to the deplorable silence of illegal backstreet abortion. The 1967 United Kingdom Abortion Act was a greatly welcomed English solution to silence the abundance of Irish problems. The Catholic Church systematically refused to contaminate Irish women with contraception, but tolerated that unwanted pregnancy forced six thousand socially judged "Irish whores" to take the abortion boat to England ever year. Irish homes enforced the high catholic principles and social moral values of Ireland. Some pregnant women were rushed up the aisle to be wed before god, because real Catholics didn't give birth outside of wedlock. The Sacrament of Irish Marriage silenced their illicit heterosexual sins and they accepted the solemn pledge of eternal obedience. "Premature births" were widespread in the immediate days after some Irish marriages, but there were no bastard children to pollute catholic Ireland with immorality. There was no harmony between the love of god and the savage treatment of women in catholic Ireland. Others were consigned to the state funded religious run homes to liberate catholic families from the shame of sexual sin. God

silenced their screams as their new born babies were forcibly seized by catholic nuns for adoption. The catholic culture of secrecy and self-preservation silenced that holy sin. The last Magdalene asylum in Ireland closed in 1996. An estimated 30,000 Irish women had been judged for their immorality, incarcerated in the punitive prison of religion and enslaved in repentance. They were brutalised emotionally, physically and spiritually in the cruelty of the catholic institutions. They were methodically dehumanised because they had fallen from the grace of god. That was the inhumane treatment that the Irish catholic religion practiced. Such was the sufferance and the tears of the silenced women that the almighty god had destroyed. The laws of god were enforced with brutality and not with love in catholic Ireland. I endured monotonous sermons in freezing cold churches. I dreamed of being free from the constraints of religion. I counted the marble pillars rather than listen to the words of the divine god. I observed the devotion of the hypocrites around me, but they did not share my scepticism about the love of god. The destruction of famine and the injustice of war plagued the world. I had the vague impression that god didn't hear my prayers to save the starving babies in Africa, that religion had encouraged human slaughter since the beginning of time and that god equally ignored my implorations to save me from the contamination of homosexuality.

The almighty god enforced the social moral value of heterosexuality on all Irish men and it was a catholic victory to offer everlasting life to the queers that surrendered to the sufferance of heterosexuality. The grace of god granted eternal forgiveness to the homosexuals that forsook their immorality and many by miracle became straight. The intolerance of holy judgement certainly believed that if Irish homosexuals were silenced that the sin of homosexuality didn't exist in Ireland. Some homosexuals became prisoners in the Sacrament of Marriage and swore their fidelity to the solemn promise of heterosexuality, but they also enriched the pink market in silence and betrayed the Seventh Commandment by secretly denuding men. Beneath their heterosexual appearance was their innate desire to taste the freedom of homosexual promiscuity. They led straight lives not really because they believed in the myth of the kingdom of heaven, but because catholic Ireland was heteronormative and they needed to conform to a righteous culture. They survived in the pretext of heterosexuality that the catholic god of Ireland imposed on them, but they fucked their wives with distaste and concealed from the world that they fucked men with pleasure too. The catholic religion banished all practicing homosexuals to the love of Satan. Hell was the perpetual punishment for

the catholic queers that did not pray in repentance to god, but if Satan's compassion was the sanctuary for all the homosexuals of Ireland, perhaps I wanted to seek asylum in that paradise of queers? Perhaps hell liberated homosexuals to sin without any social judgement? In rural catholic Ireland a holy resurrection after a crucifixion seemed plausible, so the Irish also naively believed in god's battle to save Ireland from the immorality of homosexuality. In the abstinence of sodomy god was compassionate to the remission of the gay sin, but the homosexual sub-culture in the core of the Roman Catholic Church was widespread.

Homosexual priests were silenced by the prayer of salvation, heterosexual priests were silenced by the prison of celibacy, but behind the closed doors of the sacristy there was an abundance of gay and straight promiscuity. Homosexual and heterosexual acts were common in the sexual practices of the Catholic Church, but the profound hypocrisy of Irish religion silenced the naturalness of such human behaviour. Annie Murphy sought spiritual peace in Ireland in 1973, but there was romance in the penis of a holy man rather than compassion in words of the bible. The saintly man of god that read the sermons from the pulpit kissed her. The devout servant of god that tasted the blood of Christ directly from the chalice denuded her. The holy hands that distributed the body of Christ from the altar fondled her naked breasts. The pious catholic devotee that had taken the solemn vow of celibacy fucked her, but the catholic culture of secrecy and self-preservation enabled Bishop Eamonn Casey to silence that his sperm fecundated her ovule. The virtuous man of god forgave Irish sinners in the Sacrament of Confession, but did god grant Casey total absolution for his sins? In the bible the rooster crowed as the apostle Peter disowned Jesus three times, but in Ireland the tabloids exulted that Casey had disowned his son Peter for eighteen years. There was no truth that the blood of the covenant was poured for the forgiveness and the remission of sins, because the religious hypocrite that raised the Eucharist to god in front of the congregation did not abide by the catholic laws that he passionately preached. Silence was not eternal in Catholic Ireland. Revelations of their sexual relationship became one of the greatest scandals ever to befall on the Catholic Church in 1992. The Roman Catholic hierarchy began to lose its considerable influence over society and politics. In my mother's humble opinion it was not problematic that a holy man had had sex, but some strong minded Catholics reacted by their desertion of the church. Others believed that Annie was a harlot and that Casey had been enticed into sin. Annie Murphy published "Forbidden Fruit" in 1993; but was it her

dignified revenge on god or her real need to reveal the truth about the brutality of catholic silence?

My mother was a fragile minded catholic that feared the wrath of god and the sin of homosexuality. She certainly lived in strict accordance to the doctrines of the Catholic Church and supplicated in prayer for my salvation. Being homosexual was demonic. I was not made in the image and likeness of her divine god. She implored, begged and besought the compassion of god to change me, but the almighty god of catholic Ireland shunned her prayers and my homosexuality destroyed all of her dreams. Much against my inclination, my holy mother proclaimed that my vocation was to become a priest, but my devotion was not to her saviour. I completely believed in the promiscuity of the gay culture, the fundamental rights of queers and the liberation of homosexuality. I certainly did not believe in the intolerance that was practised by her religion. My catholic mother completely believed in the resurrection of Jesus and the assumption of Mary and she longed to believe in the promise of everlasting life if I repented for my sin. Ashes to ashes, dust to dust; I did not believe in heaven, purgatory or hell. She worshiped god with total awe, knew all the scriptures off by heart and recited her prayers in mass with such reverence. She lived abiding by the rules of the Ten Commandments and in total accordance to the myths that she read in her holy bible. She attended a monthly prayer group and never questioned the non-existence of god even in the darkest moments of her life. I had tears in my eyes when she zealously abandoned me to attend her annual pilgrimage in Knock and every year she bought me another religious souvenir to decorate my shrine. I didn't understand why she punished me to be alone with that righteous man; I clearly didn't want to stay alone with my father. Even at an early age I didn't have a sensation of love for him. I utterly worshipped my mother. I felt the profoundness of her love in the gentleness of her soft kisses. I really thought that she would always love me with the same devotion that she loved her catholic god, but the bitter taste of my homosexuality destroyed her love forever.

My mother was a holy woman that prayed to god with utter devotion to begin each day and the discoloured gilded pages of her aged bible also turned in prayer before closing her eyes every night. She abstained from meat on Ash Wednesday and Good Friday and implemented strict prayer, penance, repentance and almsgiving during the period of Lent. I hated the feeling of contamination when she sprinkled me with divinity from the

holy water font by our front door and all the church candles that she burnt to hetero-sexualise me. She crucified me for my queerness, but was it homosexuality that contaminated me with the passion to become atheist or her total allegiance to god's intolerance of queers? I was catholic, Irish and homosexual. I learnt about the compassion and forgiveness of god, but nourished to believe in the sin of homosexuality. Certain values in the sermons undoubtedly made me into a compassionate man, but it was the catholic brutality against homosexuals that made me become a strong man. Religion was a prevailing part of my youth. I had an ornate shrine of holy relics in my bedroom containing two prayer books, a rosary bead from Lourdes, hundreds of miraculous medals and a million statues of the saints. I feared the wrath of god against me and prayed with despair in my eyes not to be homosexual. I kissed those inanimate holy objects with reverence and my tears implored the almighty god to purify me. I did not want to be a homosexual sinner, but my prayers were silenced by god. It was certain that my pious mother had eternal salvation in the kingdom of heaven, but it seemed that god had always wanted to condemn me to suffer in the burning fires of hell.

For a Catholic in rural Ireland it was strange that I read a Jehovah Witness bible, but Caroline had discreetly given it to me before my mother banished her from our home. My mother always had an aggressive tendency of destroying people that refused to submit to her desires. There was no compassion in the catholic religion; one day it was Caroline's turn to be repudiated and like many others I never saw her again. Father O' Brien anointed the walls of our home as part of the ritual of his annual visit. My mother graciously served him with coffee and double-sided chocolate biscuits. A cloud of smoke distended from his cigarette. He smiled in corruption as she generously placed a money filled envelope in his hand. It was feasible to buy a place in heaven when you lived in rural Ireland, but definitely not possible to love a homosexual son. I worshiped god without understanding why. Like all the sinners in Ireland I regurgitated my sins in the confession box on a weekly basis, but I cunningly silenced my gay thoughts. I created innocent sins that I had not committed rather than have nothing to confess. I methodically admitted that I had lied to my parents, that I had stolen sweets from my brother and that I had cursed in the street. My penance was always one Glory Be, one Hail Mary and one Our Father, except the time that I disclosed that I had smoked a few puffs of a cigarette in the fields after a football match. The bastard, who smoked like a trooper, gave me 3 supplementary Our Fathers. For the petty sin of my adolescence I had been severely punished, so of

course I concealed my homosexuality in fear of reprisal. Would I have been obliged to recite the Rosary a million times? Would he have simply exiled me from the church or denounced me to be crucified by my holy parents immediately? Did my silence betray the catholic god or did the profound silence of homosexuality ensure my survival in rural Catholic Ireland? By being omnipresent god certainly knew that I was a queer, but didn't punish me. Perhaps homosexuality wasn't a real sin? Perhaps the semi-naked man on the crucifix above my bed wanted me to be gay? Perhaps Jesus Christ had been judged and crucified for his promiscuity with the twelve disciples?

All children in public national education in Ireland systematically prayed to god without effort, thought or choice. Prayers flowed from our lips as we were enslaved in the catholic religion. Irish teachers were paid to be religious fanatics. They poisoned me incessantly with biblical incoherence since an early age. When I was four years old Miss Barry nominated me to be Jesus in the school naivety play. It didn't matter that I had a severe speech impediment, because the role didn't require me to utter a single word. My overly possessive mother verbally disputed with the social welfare speech therapist, who informed her that I would never speak like a normal child. The profoundness of my mother's love refused to abandon me to that sore. She walked the wet streets of Cork City savagely and energetically knocking on all doors without despair, until she found me private elocution lessons with Miss Daly. With the eyes of a child I saw a highly sophisticated old woman near the age of death. The gentleness of her efficient method empowered me to control my voice and step by step she conquered my inability to communicate with the world. That was the era of my life when my mother loved me the most, but in time I tasted her hate in the awakening of my homosexuality.

I attended a catholic boys' school for my primary education. When I was seven Mrs. Kennedy implored me to be the Virgin Mary in the school naivety play. She must have been a gay rights activist or a revolutionist for transsexuals because she wanted to feminise me. I gladly seized the opportunity that all the other boys for some strange reason had zealously declined. Stewart played the dominant masculine role of Joseph and as a biblical submissive woman I had only the right to declared "Ta ocras, tart agus tuirse orm freisin". Humanity had silenced and liberated women, humanity had silenced and liberated slaves, humanity had silenced homosexuality, but the war for gay liberty had just begun. There was no

tolerance of Irish queers in puritan Ireland and the catholic world that I grew up in was savagely inhumane and barbaric in the judgement of homosexuals. There were definitely no gay rights among the hostile structure of the catholic religion. The death penalty for homosexuality had become completely forgotten in holy Ireland, but homosexuals were still liable for penal servitude. Homophobia was certainly tolerated by the almighty catholic god, the pulpit sermons brutalised Ireland into believing that homosexuality was a crime and absolution was even given for the brutality of gay bashing. The suppressed community of Irish queers denuded and fucked in silence, but was homosexual freedom a coming battle or an eternal dream? Perhaps Mrs. Kennedy's acuteness had understood the subtlety of my homosexual tendency and wanted to martyr me by outing my sufferance to the world? Perhaps she really believed that my pious catholic mother would be proud that I was different from all the other boys? Perhaps it was my instigation to taste the sublime drag queen culture in the limitations of rural Ireland? It was apparent by my gentle disposition that my emotions did not conform to the heterosexual behaviour of my peers, but I still didn't know that the politically correct term was homosexual.

Like all gays in 1986 I idolised Samantha Fox, especially her audacity to defend the human right of sexual freedom and the acceptance of alternative lifestyles. I made a hole in the ass of my jeans to be just like her, but such fashion was immoral for a virtuous Catholic. I implored my holy mother to have more tolerance in her judgement, but she silenced my tears and ripped it into rags. She disapproved of my ungodly distaste in pop music and completely detested that I frivolously mouthed and danced to "Touch me I want to feel your body". She really desired to believe that Fox's voluptuous breasts had conquered me to be straight thinking, but I certainly didn't have a breast fetish. I was force-fed that gay men were "fucking queers" and I survived with sufferance in the prison of catholic prayer knowing that I was different. The A-Team was my devout religion every Saturday and with my blue eyes devouring Face I fell in love with a man for the first time. In the silence of my thoughts I fantasised about kissing the virile, black leather jacketed, casual cigar smoking man. I did not understand what an erection was, but I knew that the bulge in my pants was a sin that I had to silence. His seductiveness strongly influenced my definition of masculinity and even impacted my attraction to certain lovers along the road of my promiscuity, but in the passing of time I discovered that the real value of love was more profound than the surface appearance of physical beauty.

In both third and forth class Miss Collins brainwashed me with the rich values of her almighty god. She was even more catholic than my mother and completely deprived me of chocolate, sweets, cakes, biscuits, crisps and fizzy drinks during the long period of Lent. My mother had more of a heart because she permitted me to eat a bar of Cadbury's after Sunday mass and sometimes I found a surprise treat when I opened my lunchbox. One day Miss Collins shrieked "Begone Satan" and grabbed a biscuit from my mouth. Jesus had fasted in a barren desert for forty days and forty nights, but I had displayed great irreverence for the son of god, who had died for my salvation. There were tears in my eyes because I had shamed my religion. The wrath of god judged me and Miss Collins condemned me to copy 500 lines from the bible. I was isolated in purgatory until I fulfilled the totality of my penance and nobody had the right to speak to me until my mortal sin had been remitted by her. Why was her imposition given with such catholic vengeance and not for my betterment? Would she have crucified me for my homosexual sin, if my gay thoughts had betrayed me? I silenced my homosexuality and learnt to imitate the catholic heterosexual behaviours that I saw around me. Was I a sinner in the eyes of god or was hypocrisy the key to victory in the catholic religion? We systematically recited grace before lunch, so every day I thanked god for the jam, cheese, corn beef, ham, Tayto or banana sandwiches that my mother's hands had delicately made for me. If laughter interrupted the prayers of thanks giving the culprit was punished by starvation. Miss Collins deafened my ears with daily bible studies. She had a really high pitched voice that screamed when she prayed to Padre Pio, which gave the impression that she suffered in prayer. She certainly worshipped the catholic god with the purest veneration and reverence that I have ever seen. I was forced to memorise the same prayers as Bearla agus as Gaelga. I learnt reading, writing and arithmetic, but I especially learnt how to pray and how to face the wall in meditation of my sins.

I sincerely don't remember praying in fifth class, perhaps Mr. McCarthy was part of a secular cult, but in sixth class I became a devout follower of Christ again. I feared the wrath of Mr. Breatnach, who overly displayed his veneration to the almighty god and imposed his catholic beliefs upon me. I memorised Latin prayers off by heart and learnt all about the graces that the Holy Spirit was destined to bring upon me in the Sacrament of Confirmation. I was also enriched with the moral values of the Pioneer Abstinence Association of the Sacred Heart. James Cullen had founded it in 1898 in response to the widespread problem of intemperance among Irish Catholics. It was a measure that "encouraged" Irish Roman Catholic

children to pledge allegiance to teetotalism until the age of eighteen, but such a dream was too idealistic in the social binge drinking culture of catholic Ireland. Some of the boys in my class had even tasted their first hangover before the age of twelve. Patrick Dillon had done things that I had never dreamed of and when he disclosed to Mr. Breatnach that he didn't believe in god, Father O' Brien was summoned to come immediately. Patrick fuelled the priest's wrath further by not consenting to be confirmed, but such a rebellion was not tolerated and the brutality of holy Ireland silenced his freedom. The hands of the Bishop did anoint him with chrism oil and he was contaminated forever with the Holy Spirit.

In rural Ireland Irish sinners feared the wrath of god and believed in all the biblical parables that resounded from the church chancel. The congregation struggled to afford pints of Guinness every night in the local pub, but generously enriched the collection box at weekly mass in the belief that their coins ensured their place in the kingdom of heaven. The priest openly denounced and deplored gay perversion during the sermons from the pulpit. Nobody contested such an injustice, which dehumanised and discriminated against catholic queers. My tears fell in prayer beseeching god to make me straight, if a holy man had walked on water my hetero-sexualisation for such an almighty god should have been possible, but there was no salvation for me. The more that my homosexuality manifested itself the more I believed that god was a man made myth. I begged with all my strength not to be a queer, but god condemned me to be homosexual and the catholic judgement of Irish sinners crucified me. Perhaps the catholic culture of secrecy and self-preservation silenced the real truth about homosexuality? Perhaps Jesus had two queer fathers and a surrogate mother called Mary? Perhaps the relationship between the twelve apostles wasn't platonic but sexual? The doctrines of the Catholic Church were an influential part of my life since the beginning of time, but the more I became gay the more I hated religion. In despair I wanted to believe in the love of god, but god's perpetual intolerance against queers liberated me.

In the beginning there was a mere corporal flaunt that should have been silenced, but it was soon followed by an overly friendly smile and a flirtatious compliment. The virile novelty of such attractiveness intensified into a subtle touch, a seductive word, a stolen kiss and then my father's erection gave rise to seven years of forbidden sex with a factory woman. He venerated god with reverence, but behind his saintly piety was the destructiveness of his adultery. He was a charitable catholic righteous

moralist compulsive liar that liberated his heterosexual desires and betrayed the Seventh Commandment without feeling a sentiment of culpability. He fondled the breasts of his female lover, with gentle kisses he denuded his fucking whore, but did his sperm really fertilise the fruit of their passion? Time destroyed silence, that night in 1987 I learnt about his promiscuity and the innocence of my childhood was tainted by my mother's eternal tears. There was no holy judgement to punish him for his immorality, but catholic Ireland certainly crucified me for being a queer. I wanted to forget his sin, but the profound emotions of sufferance that fell from my mother's blue eyes were engrained in me forever

"The Late Late Show" was like a second religion in Ireland and Raidió Teilifís Éireann was systematically watched in the majority of Irish homes every Friday night. I cherished that moment alone with my mother and the routine of my father's absence clearly did not affect me. I understood that carrying out maintenance on the industrial machines in Mallow was part of his catholic duty to provide for his family, but in reality his absence was a pretext to be with his whore. He kissed her naked body, fondled her breasts and his erections fucked her, while I laid asleep beside my mother in their electric blanket heated double bed. My mother didn't know of his betrayal and none of the factory workers that frequented her had the catholic compassion to tell her. Rather than free her from the prison of loving him in despair they silenced his adultery in hypocrisy. The next morning I always awoke to the familiar sight of the semi naked man on the crucifix above my single bed. After having fucked his lover, the hands that had sinned contaminated me by lifting my sleeping body from my mother's bed and transferring me into mine. In the changing colours of the seasons I didn't want to have a father. I hated him for my mother's sufferance and for his eternal devotion to a religion that severely judged me. I never felt like his son; I struggled so hard to be loved by him and on the rare occasions that he granted me some affection I was enriched with a feeling of repulsion. I only knew the profound coldness of his emotions and his surfaced jealously because my mother cherished me so much. Perhaps he understood that I was gay since the very first moment he saw me or perhaps my mother hadn't been so catholic and I wasn't really his biological son?

I did not grow up in the sufferance of Irish poverty, but enriched in the affluence of a consumption society. My father was a good man that battled hard to cater for all our needs, but he didn't display any emotions for me. I

should have gratefully loved him in the silence of his sins, but I hated him with all my passion and strength instead. I hated the industrial machines that he forced me to clean; the oily smell always reminded me of the licentious factory women that he fucked. I hated the way he looked at me with disdain and the perpetual tears that glittered in my mother's eyes. There was an abundance of brutality in catholic Ireland. My mother was a gay basher and my pious father witnessed in silence as she crucified and slaughtered me. I beseeched and implored him to save me, but he abandoned me to my hardship and did not protect his queer son from her potent blows. He courteously held the door open for an elder in a catholic fashion, knelt with reverence before his mythical god in prayer, generously tossed a coin to the beggar on the church steps and created the sign of the cross every time he passed a cemetery, but I was forsaken to the sufferance of her catholic punishment alone. Why did he gloriously forget me in the tearful hours of my need? Was there really no love for queers in holy Ireland and in the kingdom of heaven?

The Promise Of Silence

3

The Brutalisation of Humanity

I am totally unable to visualise the exactitude of that forgotten night due to a huge lapse of time and the erosion of my memory. I vaguely remember the insignificant details of colours, shapes and sounds of that tragedy in 1987. I did not understand why that woman declared her undying love for my father. She had abandoned her husband in a drunken rage and her intrusive knocks on the door were intentionally to destroy the love that flourished in the catholic home of my happy childhood. All she wanted was to destroy my mother and she didn't care that my precious world shattered in her revenge. The noise of hysterical screaming awoke me from my sleep. I descended the carpeted stairs to see my fragile mother crying. She turned towards me with a river of tears falling from her blue eyes. Suddenly the sufferance in those fragile eyes was engrained in my mind forever. I fear that I don't have the strength to relive all that destruction again, but such sufferance is too deeply enrooted in me be ignored for eternity. It is certain that I will discover more than I want to find if I journey into the forgotten past, but I believe that there will be a glorious resurrection from the tears I cry. I know that sometimes it is the forgotten suppressed sufferance that destroys even more as it resurfaces with a vengeance, but I must unearth the brutality of the past in order to liberate my emotions forever.

For an ample time my mother had deliberately chosen to ignore the telltale signs of his infidelity. Certain unwanted truths gave less credibility to my father's blatant lies, but my mother still silenced her sufferance. He enhanced the attractiveness of his appearance to carry out the maintenance on the industrial machines in Mallow every Friday night, but such dirty work didn't really require such cleanliness. I heard her say that the strong smell of cigarette smoke was always embedded in his impeccable clothes and hair when he returned, which was strange for a non smoker coming back home from an oil smelling factory. It was confirmed several times

that my father danced flirtatiously with some woman in a club, but the gossiper that had started that rumour was a reputed compulsive liar. Her story wasn't plausible and enraged my catholic mother, who rightfully justified that he hated socialising and music. The pink coloured lipstick I found in his van didn't correspond to the pale red coloured lipstick that my mother occasionally used. She informed me that it belonged to Paula. That seemed rather strange to me; being gay I was attentive to things that straight boys didn't ever remark. Paula was more into natural beauty, so I figured out that that pink lippy definitely wasn't hers. Rather than return it, my mother binned it with a rage in her blue eyes that I hadn't seen before; perhaps her suspicions were aroused further? The perfume that repulsed my mother when my father kissed her was the fragrance of another woman, but she silenced that too. It was inevitable that my mother was to suffer, but she never thought that she would come eye to eye with my father's philandered whore. Nothing was ever to be the same again. She had always been a strong survivor, but I saw her human fragility for the first time.

There was total confusion in my sleepy eyes, not understanding what was happening. I initially thought that someone had attacked her on the street and that she sought refuge in our catholic home. The sound of vulgarity terrified me as that women cursed words that I had not heard a woman ever say before. It was clear that she did not appreciate that my mother revolted by calling her a whore. A forceful push of aggressiveness ensued; I clearly remember that as my mother staggered to survive from it, there was the smashing noise of a vase that had fallen to the floor. An ocean of tears rolled down my face. Terrorised I stood in front of my mother to protect her from her aggressor. All I wanted was to intercept the physical force of the blows, but my father pulled me away immediately. I implored him to shield my mother from such brutality, but there was absolutely no reaction on his behalf. Then, there was the horrible vociferation of two babies crying in fear. It was only at that point that my attention was attracted to the children in the corner of the room. I heard the woman screaming that they were the fruit of his adventure, but I didn't understand the impact of those words for many years. I wiped away my mother's delicate tears. I consoled her woe with tender kisses. I held her hand gently with the promise that nothing would ever destroy her again, but it was the tragedy of a promise that I was unable to respect. I was merely an eleven year child unable to quench my mother's suffering. I was lost in the turmoil of an adult war. I was unable to cope with the onus of calming my mother's tears alone. Aunty Mary had always been tender and affectionate towards me. She had spoiled me with penny sweets and cream donuts from her small

grocery shop. In her smile I knew that there was always love and I mechanically dialled for her help. It was the only phone number that I knew off by heart. It had been memorised for emergencies and I was almost certain that that qualified as being one. There wasn't a real necessity for me to explain why; she had certainly heard the rumours too and the screams she overheard in the background justified that we needed her immediately. Without hesitation she crossed the dark fields of rural Ireland under a starless sky. On her arrival she consoled my mother, but I genuinely don't remember anything that happened after that. All I know is that my emotions subconsciously blanked out the sufferance of that night and that the profoundness of my eternal hate for my father was born. Under the surface of my innocence I hated him forever after that. I was not able to forget the tears that had destroyed my mother. God did not punish catholic men for the adulterous sin of sexual gratification; hence god condemned me to hate my father even more and more. The glance of rancour in my eyes did not have the catholic compassion to ever forgive him.

As the bright light of dawn enlightened the pale egg shell coloured walls, I awoke with the sensation of fear and destruction, but there was utter silence. Rural Ireland silenced the problem as if it had never existed. It became a dark secret that nobody was ever to know. The profoundness of such silence was so deep that I began to believe that it had actually never happened. But it must have been a reality, I clearly remembered the deluge of tears in my mother's eyes and there was still the visible trace of that broken vase in a million pieces on the floor. In fear of hurting my mother I silenced all of my questions, but the sound of the babies crying was deeply embedded in my mind. I totally suppressed my emotional feelings for my father and in a state of confusion I didn't remember why. It was at that precise moment of my life that I developed obsessive compulsive disorders, which dominated, devoured and diseased me. In the profoundness of my sufferance pervasive patterns of preoccupation with cleanliness and orderliness controlled me to perform irrational tasks. Something had changed in me, something was seriously wrong in my life, but in the rituals which destroyed me I found an overwhelming sensation of security. To purify my thoughts and calm my anxiety I had an absurd obsession of washing my hands incessantly. It was a particularly strong compulsion, which intensified when my father touched me or when he stood too near, but in the silence of my forgotten thoughts I still didn't remember why I completely hated him. That persisted to haunt me for seven long years, but when I left my rural home for university I didn't feel the need to wash my hands incessantly anymore. In my battle to forget that

night I sought solace in other strange behaviours too, which became noticeable. My mother was highly concerned because an abundance of tears fell from my blue eyes when the preposterous alignment of a certain vase was not respected. I became completely panic stricken that if there was the smashing noise of the "replacement" vase breaking in a million pieces, that there would be an eruption of more chaos in my life. It was extremely strange to designate so much importance to a mere object, but I thoroughly believed that it was a necessity to ensure that my father didn't abandon our catholic home. Nobody had the right to even touch it. One day the vase definitively vanished in my mother's direct combat to make me normal again. I was totally devastated by the brutality of her cold act, but I survived and no consequences fell to punish me. She heard me sneaking downstairs a million times at night; if I didn't verify that the front door security chain was attached I was not able to sleep. The false pretext of needing a glass of water justified my nocturnal ritual, but in reality it was to ensure that my father's whore was unable to invade our home again. There was no catholic compassion in rural Ireland to understand my distress. My devout catholic mother prayed to the almighty god as she battled with the utmost brutality to eradicate my abnormalities. Much to her greatest dismay, I was unable to abandon what comforted me. Much to my greatest destruction, the catholic hypocrisy of silence was the detrimental silence that destroyed me in the prison of my rituals. I made inhuman efforts to ignore the impulsion of committing the repetitive actions of my obsessions, but in the fragility of my instability I was not very victorious. One day my love enraged mother definitively removed the security chain, but there were too many memories of that calamitous night omnipresent in my catholic home for me to forget for eternity.

My mother's strong religious convictions granted her the serenity to survive, but I was abandoned to survive in the sufferance of silence alone. The love of god strengthened her to believe that her marriage would rise from the ashes of betrayal. "Thou shalt not commit adultery" was the biblical means to justify her abandonment of marriage, but the catholic god of Ireland still did not give the Irish nation the freedom to divorce and the liberty of falling in love again. She had vowed to love and honour one man til death, she was ensnarled forever in the so called harmony of love and god imprisoned her in eternal sufferance and tears. She should have abandoned my father, but my mother feared the wrath of the almighty catholic god. The Catholic Church forced two foes to battle when their love no longer existed. Perhaps she really forgave my father because it seemed that she genuinely loved him? Perhaps she sacrificed her dream of freedom

to protect her children from the destruction of a broken home? Perhaps she was unable to survive without his affluence? He bought her love; money became her almighty god and silenced her tears as she prostituted her cold love to him. Her fingers glittered in gold and sparkled in diamonds, but such ephemeral pleasures did not liberate her to forget her emotional sufferance. She should have liberated me from the prison of his cold love, but she feared being slaughtered by Irish gossips. She should have faced the tongue wagging of idle rumours, but she lived in fear of their catholic judgements. Rural Ireland certainly would have criticised the defeat of her marriage, but rather than be crucified in shame she abandoned her true desires. She made inhuman efforts to conceal her husband's sins from the world, but all the Catholics in rural Ireland clearly knew about his incessant cheating and the glorious myth of his bastard children also burned on their lips.

In the immediate aftermath I developed a strong need to overly protect my mother. I discovered her crying day after day. I absorbed her tears of distress. I saw her fade away in the silence of his sin. It was a difficult world of emotional destruction for me to survive in. I thought that my love could save her if I loved her with all my strength, but the extent of her sufferance destroyed all of her human emotions. It was clear from that moment on that nothing was ever the same in her life again. My pompous holy mother concealed the profoundness of her suffering behind a sublime smile. The affair was silenced forever, but it slowly eroded her interior beauty away. She emasculated my father incessantly and because her love had been betrayed she never trusted him again. Her dreams had been destroyed, her human compassion had withered, something inside her had totally changed forever and she was never the same woman again. She became cold, caustic and emotionless in the solitude of her silenced sufferance. My father had contaminated her thoughts with the eternal taste of another woman's kiss. As a scorned woman there were no limits to her fury. Her frenetic convulsions and excessive rages intensified. Her incessant anger became her revenge on the only man that she had ever loved. I promised her that nothing would ever destroy her again. I battled to fulfil her dreams, but I was unable to abandon my desire to denude men. My mother silenced his corruption, but she punished her queer son for the sin of his homosexuality. She had the bravery to ignore the continuity of his adultery, the strength to silence his betrayal and the catholic compassion to forgive his sins, but she crucified me.

My pious mother portrayed the image of a good Catholic to the world, but as the body of Christ withered away on her tongue her venomous words gossiped about all of humanity. With a contorted smile glittering on her face she passionately indulged in the rampant rumours about the sufferance of a local woman. There was no real difference between the betrayal of Mother and that of poor Mrs. Jones, but rather than defend her from the brutality of Irish judgement and rather than empathise with her tears, my cold mother cast the holiness of her judgement too. Everybody now knew that Mr. Jones didn't honour the Seventh Commandment of god, but my holy mother was still untouchable in her so called perfect marriage. Everybody certainly knew that my father didn't honour the Seventh Commandment of god either, but in fear of liberating my mother's rage nobody dared to challenge her. How many Irish women did she destroy? As she stared down on them with her proud air of catholic superiority, they lowered their heads and evaded her cruel glances in shame. Was her desire to focus on tainting others in order to deter attention away from her own problems? There was no repentance, but that was the hypocritical Ireland that I belonged to. The Irish worshiped the almighty god with reverence, they listened to the sermons and offered the sign of peace in mass, but they silenced their own sins and viciously spoke about the immorality of others.

My mother prayed to god with passion, but was not enriched with the compassion of god. She gracefully recited benedictions, but as the holy water evaporated from her forehead, she sinned and punished me in abundance for my immorality. My catholic mother found great shame in having a queer son, so she rightfully silenced my homosexuality with brutality. I loved and cherished her with all my strength, but behind the closed doors of my catholic home I was imprisoned in the aggressive blows of an angry woman that almost destroyed me. That was the sufferance that nobody knew about me. That was the savagery that I wanted to silence forever. In fact, there was an abundance of things that nobody ever knew about me. I don't know how I survived in the solitude of her holy judgement. There was no catholic god to save me from my prison of tears. There was no Google to liberate me from the immense feeling of being so alone. I battled in the sufferance of being the only homosexual in Ireland. The powerful ripples of the Stonewall movement had not contaminated the catholic nation with the notions of queer freedom yet. The almighty Irish religion still crucified homosexual Catholics and society zealously alienated what didn't conform. There was no super hero to liberate me from her brutality. Those that could have saved me from her didn't want to see my tears. My mother prayed to god to hetero-sexualise

her "fucking queer" son and my body was sometimes bruised by the force of her rages. What didn't kill me destroyed me, what destroyed me made me strong and what made me strong certainly made me become a better human being.

I was not able to escape my crucifixions and the brutality of humanity destroyed me from an early age. I was a normal child playing in the green fields of Ireland, but I was victimised "an arse fucker, a bender, fag, faggot, fairy, nancy, poofster, queenie, queer and sissy", without understanding the real signification of what their barbs meant. My oppressors lashed out openly and their aggressive blows generated the contagious spread of rancour that almost killed me. I tasted the crude reality of life as my peers imitated disgusting words that had transcended from catholic homophobic generation to generation. I endured the acceleration of inhuman insults in utter silence and fear. I cried an ocean of tears trapped in the interminable sufferance of my immorality. Was it normal that there was an abundance of suicidal thoughts in my head? I should have been carefree in the frivolous liberty of childhood, but I had an immense desire to taste death. I was so completely alone in the silence of my despair that I wanted to walk into the shadows of the valley of death. I lived more and more in solitude, isolation and reclusion because I feared human judgement. I endured extreme mental torture and physical violence and in the changing colours of the seasons I no longer wanted to live. I didn't understand why the catholic god had abandoned me, but there was so much almighty brutality in holy Ireland against me. Religion preached about love, but perhaps destruction was the strongest of all human emotions after all? I believed that the dream of freedom flourished from acceptance, but there was no rebellion to liberate my reverie of homosexual tolerance.

I was savagely hunted and preyed on every day at school. I didn't know how to defend myself from the punches, but I knew how to run fast. When I was twelve Mr. Breatnach turned a blind eye as Riordan crucified me with inhuman derogatory remarks. He did not defend me from the cruel insults that I was certain he had heard. He abandoned me to suffer without catholic or human compassion. One day I revolted without discretion and the aggressiveness of my words insulted Riordan as "a fucking stupid four eyed bastard". I tasted the injustice of the world as Mr. Breatnach judged me for my sin. I retorted that he collaborated with the victimisation that destroyed me. I criticised that he never acted in my defence. The Irish educational system completely betrayed me and he severely punished me

for my insolence. He shunned the tears in my eyes as I denounced the pain of my infliction. He did not want to hear about the abundance of homophobic wars that I endured. He did not want to protect me from my aggressors. He did not want to liberate me from the profoundness of my deep suffering. In his righteous catholic opinion I was guilty of a crime against humanity and my vulgarity was a sin against god. I was forced to write a letter of apology to Riordan for my contemptuous arrogance and Mr. Breatneach contaminated me with the prayers of his catholic religion. I was dominated by god, by the catholic hypocrisy of Ireland and by the brutality of humanity, but in the silence of my thoughts I was free. I became more and more contaminated by hate in my battle against the injustices of life. I hated god, I hated my father, I hate Riordan, I even hated Mr. Breatneach and I profoundly despised O' Leary, who had kicked me so hard that blood ejaculated from my penis. I began to hate all the Catholics of Ireland that brutalised me in the punishment of my homosexuality. Why were my gay thoughts ungodly according to the holy judgement of the catholic religion? Why was homosexuality so vehemently opposed by the Catholics of Ireland? Was "thou shalt not be queer" mentioned in the Decalogue of Moses? Prohibitions against idolatry, blasphemy, murder, theft and adultery were clearly highlighted as being the laws to abide by to be a worthy follower of god. Nothing in the words of the loving god forbade that I was to denude men. It was the ignorance of Ireland that brutalised me vehemently in the punishment for the sodomy that I had not yet committed. Perhaps having gay erections wasn't immoral, after all the bible said that I was made in the image and likeness of god? Perhaps in the beginning god created the heavens, the earth and homosexuality and it was only mankind that had created the concept of homosexual sin?

Since the beginning of time I knew that I was different, but I didn't know that the correct term to classify my difference was gay. In order to survive I found the courage to ignore the distasteful words against homosexuals, but that was the beginning of my eternal solitude. I slowly began to isolate myself from the world. I found security alone in the silence of my gay thoughts. I survived in the strength of my dream of homosexual liberty and I did not give humanity the victory of destroying me forever. I was determined that bullycide would not defeat me. I promised myself that I would conquer my freedom and I swore that one day I would liberate my homosexuality without fear. I silenced my agony and my sufferance in silence knowing that it would be an infinite battle to be completely free, but all dreams come true if believed in. My dream was not to justify my

homosexuality forever, but to live my homosexuality in a world that integrated homosexuals in a heterosexual society without judgement. Why did I imprison my inner thoughts in the solitude of silence? Why was there no justice in the world of catholic hypocrisy? Was it normal at such a tender age that I prayed to god to grant me the serenity and the courage to commit suicide? There was no human pity or catholic compassion for the queer children of Ireland. Homosexuality was portrayed as a flaw in the conception of human nature. Prevalence of suicide among young Irish queers was significantly high because the judgement of catholic Ireland slaughtered homosexuals with an abundance of brutality. The greatest destruction in my life was caused neither by god nor my almighty oppressors, but by the catholic woman who had given me birth. Her heteronormative culture forced her to believe that I was straight, but rather than seduce women I fucked men. She had an ocean of love and a world of heterosexual dreams for me, but she didn't have the strength or the serenity to ever love a homosexual son. Like all queers I worshipped and cherished my mother, but indeed she was the greatest foe in my battle to survive.

Holy catholic judgements naturally resurrected and "birth to a monster" were the tearful words she liberated in the battle of my coming out. I implored her to wipe away my tears of despair and to find the forgiveness to grant me her eternal love, but I saw the glance of disgust corrupt her eyes with her perpetual rancour of homosexuality. I begged her to always love me, but I was contaminated by the bitter taste of her dying love. In the intensity of her fury my holy mother zealously declared that she should have aborted or miscarried me. Tears of woe fell from my blue eyes because she caustically disclosed that she would never have given birth to me if she had known that I was "a queer fucker". Why did the catholic god punish her with the shame of having a homosexual son? I had promised her that nothing would ever destroy her again, but the tragedy of being a homosexual made it become a promise that I was unable to respect. Her emotions faded away and her love for me withered; something inside her changed forever. My catholic mother crucified me for the first time that day. I begged her in error to love me, but I should I have implored her sufferance to mercifully disown her gay son instead. I certainly would have survived in an ocean of tears, but I would have been free from the prison of brutality that destroyed me for years. She brutalised, traumatised and victimised me with extreme catholic homophobic devotion. I longed for her to kiss away the pangs of my suffering, but I no longer recognised the violent and aggressive woman that she had become. Instead of loving me she now destroyed me and she prayed to her almighty god to hetero-

sexualise me. If only she had had the strength to warmly whisper that she loved me again. If I had the power to turn back time, would I return without hesitation to that forgotten moment of maternal love before her eternal disgust? Would I deny that I belonged to the gay culture so that she would love me forever? If only puberty hadn't betrayed me would the battle for my gay freedom have never begun? Her judgement of homosexual immorality certainly destroyed me, but it did make me stronger too; I have no regret that I suffered such brutality.

It was a small step for humanity when the first straight man walked on the moon in July 1969, but it was a giant step for homosexuality when the BBC broadcasted the first gay kiss in January 1989. I visualised the beauty of gay seduction in Colin Russell's passionate mouth to mouth osculation in Eastenders, only to realise that I wasn't the only man with a desire to kiss men. The unnaturalness of such a kiss shocked the majority of catholic viewers in Ireland, but it gracefully liberated me from the prison of my loneliness. It was a glorious kiss that freed me from the fear and the solitude of homosexuality. I had always thought that I was the only gay in the whole world, but suddenly I understood that there were millions of others. A gay culture had been concealed from me by the brutality of catholic Ireland and by the heterosexuality of god. There was a world of freedom outside the prison of rural Ireland waiting to contaminate me with homosexuality. There were other men corrupted by the same morally debased thoughts as mine. It was a significant step to integrate homosexuals into the straightness of society, but it was a traumatic scandal against the traditional family values that dominated catholic Ireland. Television battled to destroy the queer taboo, but in the liberation of homosexuality I tasted both hope and fear alike. Pious catholic housewives were completely repulsed by such unholy behaviour. The gay community was represented on mass audience mainstream television with such normality, but illiberal viewers denounced the immorality of the queer kiss. It caused widespread horror in rural Ireland and it thoroughly sickened my catholic mother. She literally galloped across the sitting room to aggressively unplug the television with disgust and fury in her eyes. She was completely outraged that the BBC had broadcasted ungodly images in our puritanical home. Her catholic prudery certainly didn't want me to have the liberty to define my homosexual identity. She sprinkled me with holy water to purify me, but it was too late. The "queer fucker's kiss" was deeply implanted in my mind. The BBC had contaminated me with a passion for the gay culture forever. She boycotted her favourite series in the immediate aftermath of her trauma, but her hunger for drama and

gossip forced her to abandon her decision two weeks later. The extremity and excessiveness of her homophobic reaction confirmed that she would never condone my sin.

I was forced to silence the profound desires of my inner thoughts in fear, but puberty began to betray me. My penis elongated, darkened and pubic hair surfaced. That was the real beginning of my gay struggle. Almighty erections imprisoned me in homosexuality more and more. The changes that converted my child-like dreams into the body of a man consumed me with a strong attraction towards men. Step by step I began to understand the real depth of my innate difference, but did my deep lust for men signify that I was to be gay forever? Was I contaminated to suffer eternally due to the most beautiful sin of my life, the sin of making love to men? Would my homosexuality have faded away if I had been catholic enough to ignore my gay feelings? I was liberated into the difficulty of homosexuality because I had directly seen and tasted the profoundness of her hate. I battled passionately to imprison my ungodly thoughts in perpetual silence. I didn't want to be "a queer fucker", but I wanted to taste the virility of masculine kisses so much. My erotic sensation to devour and consume men was stronger than me. I was unable to escape from the sin of my gay corruption. I struggled to purify my life in the constraints of a straight existence, but homosexuality defeated me more and more. I was totally aroused and profoundly infatuated by men. I admired men in the silence of my erections. I wanted to be kissed by men with force and passion. I wanted to know the sensation of a masculine touch on my denuded body. I wanted to taste the reality of all my ungodly dreams. I hungered ravenously to liberate the natural homosexual desires of my unspoken thoughts, but it was blatantly clear that I had to live in total silence. The world became a lonely place in my struggle to survive. I battled in confusion not to be gay, but there was no escape from its almighty contamination. My penis had changed and my homosexuality was no longer dormant. Adolescence forced my gay identity to betray me and puberty condemned me to taste the eternal glance of disgust in her eyes. She was unable to find the strength to cherish and love her queer child for eternity. The destructive blows of her homophobia intensified her rancour more and more. My holy mother only had the catholic compassion to crucify me again and again.

A wave of polemic media coverage now disclosed that a gay plague silently slaughtered queers in abundance. Certain pulpits further dehumanised homosexuality in the belief that it was the wrath of the almighty god having revenge on homosexual immorality and the contagion of such ignorance contaminated my mother with even a deeper fear of the gay culture. The propagation of misinformation stigmatised homosexuals as the mythical founders, and despite the widespread occurrence of the disease in non-homosexuals environments too, the gay community was affirmed to be the carrier of a human immunodeficiency virus. Heterosexuals strongly condemned the liberalism of gay promiscuity and romanticised that only homosexuals were concerned, but AIDS didn't have a homosexual boundary. It certainly did not discriminate in accordance to colour, creed or sexual orientation. I already knew that the kingdom of heaven didn't want queers fuckers, but I now learnt about the real hostility of god. My tears fell; I certainly didn't want to die of homosexuality. I wanted to silence my sin forever, but in the late 1990s my social sexual revolution began and I fell in love with men.

The Damnation of Holy Ireland

Living in rural catholic Ireland meant that the glorification of sex was blasphemy and taboo. It seemed that all the children of Ireland were the fruit of an Immaculate Conception. I had a fragmented and limited understanding of the riddle of sex. I knew that my mother had been penetrated and fertilised by my father, but it was difficult to imagine that such a shrew woman had been corrupted by the pleasure of an orgasm. She lowered her eyes when I aroused my curiosity. She silenced my audacity to understand the natural changes of puberty. She condemned me to learn about the complexity of sex alone. I clearly didn't understand the indiscreet noises that I systematically heard every Sunday morning. I didn't understand why I was forced to watch breakfast television alone. With my ear on the door I could hear strange noises in her bedroom, but I was unable to decipher the exactitude of their origin. I listened attentively to the sound of my mother moaning as if she was dying, but she was moaning in pleasure and not in pain. I was too naive in the innocence of catholic Ireland to understand that the gentle murmurs signified her climax. Did she not taste the contamination of his lovers' kisses on her lips when my father kissed her? Did she not recognise the embedded smell of his lovers' perfume when he penetrated her with his hard erection? Why did she silence his crimes of adultery, forgive his betrayal, absolve his sins and passionately fuck the man that cheated on her incessantly? There was no justice in the prison of his love. With catholic obedience she submissively accepted the tragedy of his adulterous sins. In the silence of her tears she granted him the liberty to fuck other women. Sometimes I knocked incessantly until they unlocked the bedroom door. I imposed my presence in the warm bed between them, unwittingly depriving my father of sex as I cuddled my mother with the favouritism of my love.

On one occasion I intruded on their passion to find my father fondling my mother's voluptuous breasts. My invasion enraged him, but I wasn't responsible for his imprudence of forgetting to lock the door. It wasn't the first time that I had seen her denuded body, but the hypocritical excessiveness of my father's reaction portrayed nudity as being a dirty crime. My father prudishly lowered his eyes when I requested him to unriddle the mystery of heterosexual sex. I knew that the catholic god of Ireland silenced the immorality of the gay religion, so I certainly did not question about the glorification of homosexual sex. He became utterly furious that I had the insolence to be aroused by the natural curiosity of human nature. In rural catholic Ireland it was strictly forbidden to contaminate children with even the basic notions of sexuality. Straight teenagers had to struggle to understand the general aspects of sexual intercourse alone and for the queers of Ireland the struggle was a million times more difficult. His penis controlled all his thoughts, but his catholic devotion concealed the corruption of all his ungodly crimes. My father prayed to god with profound faith, he bowed his head and accepted the body of Christ with utter reverence and he devoured a series of women in the violation of the Seventh Commandment. His bastard children were banished to silence, but the silence of rural Ireland and the compassion of the catholic god were unable to silence the forbidden fruit of his adultery forever. My father was a sinner, but his sins were forgiven in the Sacrament of Penance and Reconciliation with god. He was a devout Catholic, who prayed with awe before the altar, but he also preyed on his whores in the silence of his sins. In the changing colours of the seasons I was to learn what no man should about his father.

My catholic mother was not very prude in regards to nudity. She did not flaunt her intimacy to the world, but I was familiar with all aspects of her femininity. It was completely normal for my gay eyes to behold her denuded in the bath tub and to observe the sensuality in her actions as she delicately washed her feminine body. Before the eruption of my puberty she had even permitted me to bathe in the warm water with her. There were no underlying sexual thoughts in such liberty. It was simply the profoundness and the innocence of our bond, but she had never exerted the same freedom with my straight brother. She must have known that I was gay because it was transparent in my gentleness and in the obviousness that I did not derive any erotic pleasure from her denuded beauty. My penis elongated, darkened, pubic hair surfaced and homosexuality dominated my thoughts. The Tree of Knowledge of good and evil made me become aware of my nakedness and from that moment on she bathed alone. There was

love in the mother and gay son relationship that we cultivated, but there was hate in his sporadic outburst as my father demonstrated his jealous disposition. The strong emotion of the green eyed monster frequently contaminated him with rage and resentment against me, but she never denied me of her affection. Was the overly close maternal relationship the root cause of the disease of male homosexuality? Having a close relationship with my mother didn't make me queer, but being queer did make me closer to my mother. Being gay made me more sensitive in my emotions, more compassionate in my human feelings and it enhanced the close bond that only a devout gay man can have with his mother. I thoroughly hated my father, I flourished in the profoundness of her unique love, but neither factor made me gay.

I still remember the tenderness of her smile that symbolised the profoundness of her love, but that was before my homosexuality caused immense destruction. The catholic religion strengthened her passion to crucify me. Her holy judgement and her devotion to god destroyed me with a glance of disdain. She hated me with tears of shame falling from her blue eyes. I tasted her dying love for me in the beautification of her disgust. As her affection for me faded and withered away I battled to survive in the woe of my deep sufferance alone. The catholic definition of holiness was to love thy neighbour and to hate all queers, hence in accordance to the wrath of god as a homosexual I had to be banished. I was cursed by her almighty god to suffer an Irish eviction. The brutality of her religion forced her to forsake the precious son that she had always loved so dearly. That was my eternal punishment for being gay. The days of silence became weeks, months and years in the solitude of my exile. She waited for me to repent for the sin of homosexuality, but I did not have a glorious resurrection like Jesus Christ. Such sufferance was predetermined on the road of my homosexual brutality. It was predestined by her catholic god that I was no longer worthy enough to be loved by her. For years she silenced her desire to abandon me, but she didn't have the serenity to silence her profound hate forever. She did not have the catholic compassion to forgive my immorality, so she caustically proclaimed to the world that I was dead. I loved and cherished her with all my strength, but I no longer existed in her life. I never returned home to become the prodigal son in repentance and my kisses never embraced her again. Was the crucifixion of catholic queers the real reason that I became forsaken? Was it in error that the catholic god punished homosexuals for the immorality of gay love? Perhaps she was to suffer in the eternal damnation of regret of

her sin? Her brutality punished me for my homosexuality for so many years, but the greatest punishment of all was still to come.

In the lust of an erotic dream I passionately kissed a man. In the profoundness of that dream I became aroused with an erection. In the beauty of that dream I ejaculated into the liberation of homosexuality for the first time. My homoerotic thoughts had betrayed me in the profoundness of my sleep and I began to fall into the adventures of homosexuality forever. I thought that death was seducing me, but in the sensation of that death I found a feeling of immense pleasure that I had never tasted before. There was immense confusion in the nocturnal emission that had suddenly awoken me from my deep sleep. I was totally unable to identify what the sticky fluid was. I didn't understand that my body was producing testosterone. I didn't understand that I had had a wet dream. I didn't know that I had been baptised to be gay by my first discharge of semen. With tears in my eyes I believed I was dying. In total fear I alerted my shrewd father, but he abandoned me in the difficult struggle to understand the riddle alone. He lowered his eyes in a sensation of shame and he coldly informed me to simply change my pyjamas. The next morning my catholic mother changed the bed sheets without attributing a word to my passage into the corruption of manhood. What was the strange mystery that had invaded me? The cloudy liquid was too viscous in texture and too insufficient in quantity to have been urine, but I had absolutely no understanding of the natural changes that my body manifested. I thought I was dying, but there had been no sufferance in that glorious death. I was intrigued to understand the erotic sublime feeling, but there was so much shame in the natural development of my body that I didn't ask any questions. I knew that sexual curiosity in catholic Ireland enraged my father, so I didn't dare to provoke his anger. The rich values of the almighty god vehemently silenced the glorification of sex and all the catholic sinners of Ireland believed that Mary was a virgin. Perhaps Jesus was an asexual, who had never tasted the pleasure of an ejaculation or the emotions of a wet dream, but I was human and unable to forget the divine sensation that had corrupted me.

In the silence of my thoughts I wanted to be contaminated by the glory of homosexuality. I closed my eyes harder and harder in need of the corrupt taste of male kisses on my lips. In the freedom of my fantasy the profound touches of virile men denuded me. They began to fondle my penis and in lust I pushed my erection up and down with indiscreet but gentle

movements on my bed. My homosexual desires aroused me more and more. I pushed harder and harder wanting to be devoured by such a forbidden sensation of pleasure. The rapidity of my heart beat intensified, my breathing got heavier and I suddenly began to moan in the gratification of my first masturbation. My hard penis stiffened, an inner force erupted in climax and with a spurt I reaped the fruit of homosexuality. I didn't feel guilty of a catholic sin, but I certainly silenced my ejaculation in rigorous fear of the catholic judgement of Ireland. Did I revolt to become a sinner or was the liberation of my sexual desires normal? Did I have to justify the corruption of my gay thoughts to god or on my journey of self discovery did I have the right of freedom to govern my own body? It became instinctive that I began to understand the complexity of sexuality, how I was created, the inevitable changes of my body, the mechanisms of ejaculation and all the different aspects which categorised me as homosexual. In baptism I was enriched with the love of god, but my homosexual liberation had begun and I was now contaminated with the eternal sin of homosexuality. I revolted against the righteous values of the Catholic Church, my homosexuality was liberated from silence forever and the ingenuity of masturbation became my ardent religion. The wrath of the almighty god and the brutality of catholic Irish judgement were unable to force me to abandon the gay culture. The corruption of homosexuality devoured me more and more and without a catholic thought I freed all of my queer desires. In the silence of my thoughts I created naked heroes that kissed and denuded me in my erotic dreams. Each time my muscles contracted, my heart beat harder, my body tightened up and I moaned involuntary as my sperm stained my underwear again and again.

My indiscreet method was to wash away the sperm that had stained my multi-coloured underpants in the bathroom sink, but it was more and more difficult to justify to my holy mother why my underwear was always wet in the laundry basket. I now began to master the art of clean masturbation and baptised my body with sperm instead. There was a sudden increased in my daily consumption of tissues, but more importantly my secret was silenced again. My mother was an avid reader of the highly sensationalised scandal gossip magazines, which corrupted her with rumours rather than educate her. She did not know that the photos of the seductive men on the glossy pages aroused me or that they fuelled my erections with passion during my masturbation. In the freedom of my thoughts I was conquered by their beauty. Their virile kisses completely devoured me and sometimes afterwards a trace of ink blackened my lips. Not only was it important not to forget to flush away my sperm, but also to remember to glance in the

mirror too. I was beginning to accept that I was gay and I now understood what type of men attracted me. The pop singers and film stars that I fucked in my mind certainly shaped my choice of future lovers. I particularly cultivated a profound appreciation of men in leather. I had always associated leather with the enhancement of masculine beauty since the beginning of time. I admired leather-jacketed catholic men at mass in Saint Joseph's Church rather than praying with reverence to god. During the Sacrament of Confirmation I had an erection because I was aroused me by the black leather jacket that I wore. A few years later it was several sizes too small, but it enslaved my naked body in a sensation of virility during my masturbation. Men in leather were almighty looking gods created to corrupt me, but did gays and leather go hand in hand in a fetish sub culture of the homosexual world? The divine touch, the seductive noise and the masculine associated smell of leather became my eternal erotic stimulus. I was condemned to the damnation of loving homosexual men and to the virile taste of leather forever.

The catholic god dominated Ireland with the pretence of virtue and righteousness, but the clergy concealed the perversion of religious crimes in extreme silence. The monstrosity of paedophile acts surfaced to betray god's compassion. The servants of god that read sermons from the pulpit and forgave Irish sinners in the Sacrament of Confession were not so righteous after all. The holy hands that distributed the body of Christ from the chalice and baptised to liberate the Irish from the tragedy of original sin molested catholic boys in the silence of god. There was no truth that the blood of the covenant was poured for the forgiveness and the remission of sins, because the holy men that raised the Eucharist to praise god on the Sabbath Day raped the innocence of Ireland. The catholic religion savagely abused Irish altar boys without a sentiment of remorse. God didn't want to hear the screams of terror that echoed from the sacristy as they were denuded. God didn't want to see the tears in their eyes as they were fondled by priests. God's love was so destructive that such sin was silenced for eternity in the tears, sufferance and shame of many Irish men. The sexual abusers that pompously reined the altar were not punished for their crimes in catholic Ireland. Irish sinners knelt before the tabernacle in repentance for their human failures, but the men that preached the sacred laws of god committed the worst crimes against humanity in Ireland. The catholic culture of secrecy and self-preservation enabled paedophiles to remain active within the clergy, but there was no punishment for that sin.

Religion was an endless mundane monologue. The priest denounced the beauty of homosexuality at mass to feed the Irish with the enthusiasm to crucify, forsake and stone me in my hour of need. The catholic world openly condemned homosexuality. The servant of god on the pulpit believed in the erroneous myths that dehumanise homosexuals. I listened to the relentless sermons in the silent knowledge that I was different. Apparently, I was the creation of the perversion of Satan and not the creation of the love of god. Did the catholic god really banish queers or was religious homophobia derived from the man made laws of holy Catholics? Statistically ten percent of the sinners that prayed to the almighty god were gay. Catholic homosexuals believed in the love of god, but the church didn't have the compassion to accept such gays. Homosexuals had the same reverence and the same devotion to god as heterosexuals, but queers knew that the wrath of god exiled them from the kingdom of heaven. Gays and lesbians lived with the utmost conviction to the catholic religion, but god ostracised them in punishment for the sin of forbidden love. I wasn't made in the image of the catholic god because I had the compassion to love homosexuals. I wasn't made in the likeness of any god because I accepted the differences that enriched the world with the diversity of the entire human race. The more I was forced to believe in god the more I hated religion and the more catholic hypocrisy I tasted the more I hated god.

Was the root cause of homophobia the rancour of god, the passion of the heterosexual sermons, the brutality of the holy bible or was it simply the destructive nature of humanity? The propaganda of the catholic religion contaminated Ireland to be repulsed by the catholic worshippers that practised gay sodomy. I was crucified along the tearful road of life because the Catholic Church condemned homosexuality. The judgement of god did not punish promiscuous heterosexuals for their sexual immorality, but the destructiveness of religious intolerance had the audacity to brutalise me more and more. Why did the almighty god judge homosexuality and not have the righteousness to equally punish heterosexual sinners for their promiscuity? Straights liberated their ungodly rampant desires in defiance of catholic laws without any consequence, but the beauty of love in the gay culture was criminalised in accordance to the rich political and social values of the Irish catholic god. It was impossible to liberate my coming out in rural Ireland. I suffered immensely in the solitude and silence of my homosexual thoughts. I wanted my homosexual freedom, but rural catholic Ireland denied me of the liberty to be gay. I lost the carefree sensation of youth because queers were banished from the mythical kingdom of heaven.

The Promise Of Silence

My homosexuality was silenced in the prison of my sinful thoughts because I feared the judgement of humanity. I wanted to taste the virile kisses of masculine men, to deflower my naked body in the passion of gay love, but I faded away in the silence of tears instead. I silenced my difference because the holiness of Ireland gave me no choice. Silence was an error that betrayed me. Silence was the sufferance that became my eternal regret.

The Irish were so afraid of the wrath of god, that they regularly regurgitated their sins in the Sacrament of Confession and prayed in repentance to survive in god's love, but behind the mask of each pious Catholic was the silence of their unholy deeds. There was no love in my mother's judgement of queers, but no wrong doing in her discrimination because it was the fundamental basis of catholic propagandism. Queers were banished from the kingdom of heaven in punishment for their despicable and sordid acts, so if god preached that homosexuality was a vile disease, it was completely natural for her to practice homophobia. She debased "queer fuckers"; such individuals were disgusting vermin in her eyes, but homosexuality was my profound religion. I strongly believed in the freedom of thought, the liberty to love men, but I pertained to the restraints of her catholic bible. Rather than be crucified forever by the holy sermons I now abandoned the promise of eternal life, the myth of a divine almighty god and the intolerance that had profoundly contaminated me since birth. I no longer belonged to the Irish religion and I certainly didn't genuflect in reverence before the catholic altar ever again. I now had a homosexual soul and I practiced immorality. I was no longer a cannibal consuming the body of Christ on the Sabbath Day and to my father's greatest dismay and rage I became a devout Atheist. Heterosexuality also rebelled; the righteousness of the catholic god was discarded by a new generation, who overtly manifested their sexual beliefs. It was a social revolution to govern sexuality with freedom. Religion was not the eternal prison of Irish fragility. God did not have absolute power to tyrannise Ireland for eternity. The suicide of religion was felt in the depopulation of the Church and promiscuity became the damnation of Catholic Ireland.

The Proliferation of Ungodly Desires

I became his prey and Kevin Kelly became my deepest foe in my battle to survive 1990. My oppressor's aggressiveness destroyed me in his inhuman war of pure homophobia. He imprisoned me in the vulgarity of homosexuality and persecuted me with disgusting words that had enriched catholic generation to generation. The Ireland that I belonged to was a shrewd righteous society of total intolerance. There was certainly no catholic compassion for homosexuals and it seemed that everyone despised and disdained gays. I tasted the repugnance, the aversion and the abhorrence for queers and the cruelty of the world destroyed me more and more. I cried an ocean of tears in the interminable sufferance of being "an arse fucker, a bender, fag, faggot, fairy, nancy, poofster, queenie, queer and sissy". It was so difficult for an emotional fourteen year old to survive the cold brutality of such insults. Perhaps Kevin had an absurd fear of homosexual contamination or perhaps he asserted his virility in order to conceal his own underlying homosexuality? He liberated so much rancour against me that I wanted to die. I was on the edge of despair, completely lost in the deep solitude of my desire for death. My passion to be seduced by the eternity of death reflected my need to abandon the abundance of my deep sufferance. I didn't want to taste the catholic judgement of queers for eternity, but was I condemned to flourish in a prison of silence forever? I tried to disregard my homosexual lust, but my head turned in the street in total attraction to men. I endeavoured to be part of the straight social structure that prevailed in the Irish catholic culture, but my sexual desires were certainly homoerotic. I desired to be normal, but homosexuality was profoundly ingrained in me and the corruption of naked men contaminated my thoughts again and again. I really didn't want to liberate my homosexuality, but I had no fucking choice.

The catholic world I grew up in was definitely not gay friendly. The almighty god granted the righteous sinners of Ireland the holy right to punish queers for the sin of homosexuality. I didn't really have friends in rural Ireland because other boys didn't want to be associated with me in fear of being taunted and such a profound solitude alienated me from the world. I didn't understand why straight boys were able to expose their dicks to other boys without being judged as being queer. O' Leary criminalised my homosexuality, the bastard destroyed me, but he zealously masturbated with Brian, David and Ross behind the garage wall. It was a weird heterosexual competition to see who could ejaculate the first. They liberated what seemed like queer desires without suffering in the social judgement of a homosexual crucifixion, but the injustice of catholic Ireland condemned me for a silenced sin that I had not committed yet. I cried alone in the sufferance of being called all the slanderous names generally used to crucify homosexuals. I was humiliated with a flow of unbearable demeaning words, " arse fucker, bender, fag, faggot, fairy, nancy, poofster, queenie, queer and sissy" and sometimes I was even punished by the means of physical blows. I was affronted with the tremendous suffering that no human should ever feel. I was cursed by a horrendously disgusting image of queers that society portrayed. I battled with immense difficulty to survive in the abundance of such almighty rancour. In despair the vigorous thought of suicide seduced me more and more. Perhaps my repentance would enable me to embrace god in the kingdom of heaven? I knew that suicide was forbidden; but god would surely find the compassion to forgive my mortal sin? I needed to walk into the shadows of the valley of death and silence my immorality forever. Death was a promise of freedom from the eternal sufferance that destroyed me, it was my liberation from the judgement of holy catholic Ireland and the only solution I knew that would silence her shame of having a queer son. Why was there so much injustice, solitude and sufferance in my youth? If I could turn back time would I have the strength and courage to confront the same wars again?

Why are gay teens three times more likely to commit suicide than their straight peers? Why did I feel so desperately alone that dying seemed like the only way out? Was it normal that I wanted to kill myself again and again? I simply wanted to close my eyes and fade away forever into the liberation of death, but I somehow had the strength to survive the brutality that had already perpetually destroyed so many homosexuals. I constantly felt unloved, rejected and alone. Nobody wanted to liberate a queer from the immorality of homosexuality or from the prison of solitude and silence. In the profoundness of such sufferance I didn't want to live that life

anymore. I simply wanted to die, but somehow I survived the catholic brutality that destroyed my youth. I believed that what didn't kill me made me stronger, what didn't destroy me made me into a better man and what didn't defeat me certainly enticed me to voyage into the liberation of my dreams, but not all homosexuals had the almighty force to battle with the same strength. How many Irish gays slaughtered themselves with tears of woe falling from their eyes? Was suicide the ultimate solution for queers in order to escape the sufferance inflicted by a homophobic catholic nation? Why was death so seductive in the profoundness of homosexual despair? In the darkest moments of my life I clung tightly to my reveries in desperation and it was my determination to conquer my dreams that probably saved me. I wanted to live long enough to display a victorious two fingered gesture of revenge to show all my oppressors that I had survived their blows. I believed that a beautiful phoenix would rise from the ashes of destruction. I battled to taste the liberation of my gay dreams; in doing so I certainly suffered, but life definitely got better in time. Death did not conquer me because I believed in homosexual freedom and the catholic judgement of Ireland did not destroy me forever either. In the changing colours of the seasons I abandoned the dark dusty closet of sufferance. I did not conceal, display or justify my homosexuality; I simply lived it. I snubbed the homophobic opinions of others. Those that believed in the myths that dehumanised homosexuals were deported from my life. If someone discriminated against queers they simply didn't deserve to know me anymore. I coldly abandoned each one of them without compassion or a second thought, so they could never crucify me again. I became a proud queer man and their intolerance didn't have any more importance. Tasting the liberty of homosexuality was my beautiful revenge on all the catholic fuckers that had once destroyed me.

Did she worship the catholic god of Ireland or had she abandoned the constraints of the tyrannical Irish religion? It was with human compassion that Yvonne Cashman comforted the tears in my blue eyes. I learnt from her that being different wasn't a sin, a disease or a felony against god or humanity. She believed that her catholic god had created me with love. She did not believe in the punishment of homosexuals and she certainly didn't judge me for being a queer. Being gay was completely normal in the liberty of her humble thoughts. She disclosed that there was no social shame in men loving men, but genuine beauty in the passion of homosexual love. Nobody in rural Ireland had ever defended homosexuality, so it surprised me that she battled with so much sincerity for homosexual freedom. No secondary school teacher ever intervened to

save me from homophobia. They surely heard the insults that demised my smile, they certainly saw the tears in my blue eyes every day, but they never asserted their power to defend me in my hours of need. Yvonne was a fifteen year old Irish warrior that heroically revolted, but why did life ripened adults choose to look in a difference direction away from my crucifixions? The pen was not mightier than the sword and it as with an abundance of violence that she punished Kevin Kelly for his insolent and impertinent behaviour. Without fear her hand collided with his face several times in the name of homosexual liberation. The force of each blow emasculated him publicly and I even found the serenity to grant Kevin the sentiment of my pity. He dared not look at me ever again; her brutality had silenced him forever. All the girls ostracised him after that, with the exception of besotted Fiona. She was too utterly seduced by his beauty to defend me and unlike Yvonne she was too catholic minded to become a martyr for the gay cause. I was liberated from the injustice of my sufferance, the profoundness of my despair and the detrimental words that had almost destroyed me. Yvonne believed in the resurrection of my dreams from the ashes of Kevin's destruction. In the desert of despair I found a vision of hope. I was not alone in my battle to survive intolerance anymore. Did the brutality of Irish rancour destroy me for the last time? Was I really liberated forever from the disparaging terms that dehumanised queers? Was homosexual liberty possible in a catholic heterosexual culture or was homosexual freedom just a dream that I strongly believed in?

Why do gay men connect on a deeper emotional level with women than their straight counterparts? In the male homosexual and female heterosexual relationship there were no underlying sexual desires to denude voluptuous breasts and penetrate vagina. In the total absence of such sexual tension there was the liberty and serenity to develop a balanced affinity with the opposite sex. I discovered sexuality in the profoundness of female discussions. I did not assume my difference, I did not come out to the world yet, but they naturally understood that I was homosexual. They integrated me without effort into their world of menstrual cycles, contraception and how they used oral sex as an efficient means to be a slut without falling into the trap of pregnancy. The girls implemented my advice on how to require victory in their seductions. It was a total contradiction that I had never even been kissed, but the world of sexuality belonged to me. I was aware that the daughters of Ireland were not so catholic in their thoughts, desires and actions. I knew who wasn't a virgin, Sarah's dark secret about the morning after pill and Angela's pleasure using a condom that I had stolen from my brother's bedroom. "Thou shalt

not steal" was immortalised in the holy bible, but he didn't challenge that I had violated the Eighth Commandment of god. Perhaps he didn't want to betray silence either; after all he practiced the sport of promiscuity too. Women always confided every detail of their sexual adventures in me because they knew that I didn't judge them. They clearly understood that the profoundness of their catholic sins was imprisoned in the tomb of my eternal silence. Women were created to destroy women in the war of rumours, gossip and back stabbing attacks. An inherent competitive entanglement complicated the social structure of communication between all females, but in the platonic values and the profound bond of homosexual men and heterosexual women, that competitiveness did not exist. Gay men didn't really bitch in the same way that certain women bitched about other women. Being gay made me more sensitive in my emotions, more compassionate in my human feelings and certainly enhanced the freedom of trust, which enabled females to confide all their secrets in me. The devotion to catholic hypocrisy in rural Ireland silenced the liberation of all ungodly desires. The vast majority of girls had become sinners, but they confessed their immorality to me rather than be condemned by Father O' Brien to recite penance. They did not regret that they had been deflowered because I absolved them of all their sins. Sexual intercourse had become a pleasure because I silenced their guilt and the righteousness and the wrath of the catholic god did not judge them. I granted them remission for their sexual lust and they sinned again and again in the silence of sexual gratification. Homosexuality enriched me with an insight of fashion and make-up too, but perhaps my greatest asset was that I was sensitive to their grief. I knew how to console the tears of their broken hearts, so they did not mourn for lost love for long. They lived in the dream of love, they dreamed in the passion of kisses and in the unholy liberty of promiscuity they seduced again and again. The girls never had the brutality to call me queer. My loyalty was compensated because they tenderly defended me from Kevin Kelly and others. Having a close relationship with women didn't make me queer, but being queer certainly did make me closer to women.

Summer 1990 was the abundance of World Cup in Ireland, with the entire nation singing "Ole Ole Ole Ole". It was a historical period in Irish football, the competitive winning streak of Jack Charlton's army gave Ireland the dream of victory and the whole of Ireland believed in that dream. Another major milestone was the liberation of forbidden desires, which contaminated my catholic generation with the need to discover the first steps of sexuality. The widespread hot spell aroused sexual curiosity

and the green fields of rural Ireland became the horny playground for adolescents. The majority of novice young lovers simply spent most of the days romantically hand in hand, but their savagery sometimes intensified with the passion of a French kiss. Perhaps it was even the beginning of promiscuity in the Irish culture, because it had already become common practice to recycle lovers. It was an undisputed fact that men and women did not have the same emotional values. Males were volatile in love with an earthly need to sexually conquer more and more, whereas females were governed by the fragility of their pure emotions. The infatuation of love was ephemeral for boys, but for girls sex was a major rite of passage into the eternity of womanhood. Catholic values were abandoned as enormous succulent breasts were exposed to male gratification for the first time. The greenhorns became more technically advanced and ventured to discover the different erogenous zones of the opposite sex. Ungodly girls indulged in fellation, which provided a taste of sexuality whilst preserving the catholic definition of virginity in rural Ireland. Oral sex was thoughtlessly done in complete unawareness of the transmission of sexually disease. The phallic penis was impure in the contamination of humans, but the main priority in catholic Ireland was not to fall pregnant. The catholic purity of Ireland did not give the liberty to have erections, so it was still difficult to procure a condom. The birth control pill was catholically permitted as an effective medical measure to control acne, but it did enable Irish virgins to become deflowered too. Irish men were from Mars and catholic women were definitely from Venus. In the fragility of feminine emotions women sought eternal love in procreation, but the volatility of masculine love caused tears because men did not make the error of falling in love. The barbaric notion of love for men was to conquer a maximum of vaginas in the promiscuous culture of a changing Ireland. For women sex was the culmination of pure emotions, after all love had been the precursor of sex since the beginning of time. Penetration was an intrusion into the intimacy of the denuded feminine body to ensure the genetic transcendence of humanity, but whereas women fell in love before sex, men fell in love through the act of sex. The sexual revolution changed Ireland. Promiscuity contaminated women with the need to use contraception. The gratification of sex became more important than the survival of the catholic race.

Of all the girls she was the most attractive, creative, generous and popular in rural Ireland. Fifteen year old Deidre McCarthy was overtly promiscuous all summer long. She had seduced, kissed, denuded, consumed and devoured the majority of local boys. It was near the end August 1990 that her flirtatious behaviour was directed towards me. I

understood that it was a golden opportunity for me to taste heterosexuality on my lips. I zealously kissed her with passion in a futile effort to be contaminated by heterosexuality, but there was no virility in her kiss to arouse me. Then, she fully unbuttoned to exhibit her voluptuous and succulent breasts. It was immediately blatant that I definitely didn't suffer from breast fetishism because there was no horny erection bulging in my pants. She implored me to touch her, it was clear that the technique of fondling breasts was far too complicated for me to master, so it was only the gentle wind that caressed her semi-naked body that warm night. She kissed me passionately again and again in a last effort to seduce me, but I wiped the feminine taste of her kisses from my lips. Judging by the look of disgust that glittered in her eyes my repulsion must have slightly enraged her. For some strange reason she impulsively enunciated that I was "a queer fucker". There was great injustice in her catholic judgement, but in her words there was certainly truth. I didn't have the courage to conform to the norms of society or the generosity to satisfy the dreams of others. I walked away from her denuded body and surrendered to the pink culture of homosexuality. Perhaps homosexuality was an ungodly desire, but it was clear that heterosexuality was not normal for me. I was condemned to love men in the prison of homosexuality forever. I belonged to the world of queers and it was in my perpetual abandonment of heterosexuality that I became eternally homosexual.

The almighty catholic god preached about the importance of sexual abstinence before marriage, but the majority of Irish teenagers had forgotten about such reverence. Deidre McCarthy's promiscuity proved highly problematic nine months later and to enhance the scandal she didn't know which sperm donor had fertilised her. Coming from an Irish home of high catholic principles and social morals an Immaculate Conception was credible, but Deidre knew that there was no compassion in Ireland for promiscuous whores. In the beginning there was no difficulty to camouflage the symptoms of her pregnancy from the world. She displayed no nauseous sensation of morning sickness and nobody needed to know that her menstruation cycle had abruptly stopped. She silenced the fruit that she nourished within whilst simulating the crisis conditions of her monthly periods, but it was impossible to deter attention away from her changing body forever. Despite all the radical measures taken to silence her sin, the visual aspects of her pregnancy started to betray her more and more. Like homosexuals sometimes heterosexuals were forced to have a "coming out" too, but homosexuality was certainly easier to dissimulate than pregnancy.

Her mother was a pompous catholic, greatly renowned for her caustic glare of superiority, the severity of her catholic judgement of others and her avid passion for Irish gossip. Holy catholic judgements naturally resurrected in her spontaneous reaction, "Abort the fucking bastard before the scandalmongers of Ireland destroy me". Mrs. McCarthy completely forgot that she had been judged with the same severe brutality many years before. Mr. McCarthy was a very respectable man, a devout follower of god, but he certainly loved Deidre more than god and he disclosed the truth that his wife had wanted to silence forever. There was an abundance of profound emotion liberated that day; with tears falling from her eyes Deidre learnt that her mother had tasted the sufferance of an illegal backstreet abortion in Ireland in 1964. Mrs. McCarthy liberated the truth from the years of silence that had destroyed her. She had the serene power to end the cycle of destruction and step into the light of freedom forever. Ireland was plagued with single mothers, so the immorality of another one on the long list wouldn't make a huge difference. Deidre was condemned by many as indecent to befriend, but I didn't have any catholic judgement of her. Holy Irish women belittled "the fucking whore and her bastard son". Some sniggered when his pram passed in the street, others pointed their index finger in her direction to disparage her and many cast a glance of disgust that degraded her further. That was holiness that the good Catholics of Ireland practiced on a social level. I thought that Deidre was strong, she never lowered her eyes and walked with her head proudly held up high, which gave me the impression that she did not let them demean her, but her tears fell in silence alone. The McCarthy family moved house a few months later and I never saw Deidre again.

The almighty god denied me of all homosexual knowledge. Catholic Ireland was completely hetero-sexualised and silenced the existence of an underground gay religion. The Irish community of queers was suppressed in the closet of eternal silence, so I didn't know that men could fall in love with men in the silenced promiscuity of the gay culture. Homosexuality in Ireland was still criminalised by the Irish god. Homosexuals were crucified by the righteous catholic influence that dominated Irish legislation. Irish catholic homosexuals denuded and fucked knowing that they were banished from the kingdom of heaven, but they were also liable for penal servitude. The main enemy for homosexuals in Ireland was the rigorous Catholic Church, which flourished in the hypocrisy of its own silenced sins. Homosexuality was a recognised Irish crime by god and politicians, but the discrimination of queers was tolerated by all and homophobia was even legal. The gay revolution in Ireland was nigh, catholic Ireland could

not silence queers forever, but it was certain that the road for homosexual freedom was going to be very long. Irish homosexuals battled for the equality of homosexual marriage in May 2015, but in June 1993 the homosexual battle was for the simple right for homosexuals to lawfully kiss. My insight into homosexuality was restricted to the social crucifixion of gays from the pulpit, the dehumanisation of "queer fuckers" in the core of my catholic home and the sufferance of being called "an arse fucker, a bender, fag, faggot, fairy, nancy, poofster, queenie, queer and sissy" at school. If all the holy Catholics in Ireland condemned the immorality of homosexuality, perhaps being queer was really a perpetual sin? If everyone lived in accord with the prevailing heterosexual values of holy Ireland, perhaps the myths about homosexuals were all true? I learnt by the sermons that homosexuality was profoundly wrong; perhaps I needed to abandon my immorality and silence it forever? In the Irish battle to silence homosexuals I tasted the tears of homosexual solitude and the immense sufferance of social isolation. I still believed that I was the only homosexual in Ireland, but the colours of the seasons were changing.

I knew almost everything about heterosexual sex thanks to the girls that I frequented, but the world of homosexuality was still a complete mystery. I didn't understand the methods of homosexual enticement and the subtle signs of homosexual seduction. I always believed that I was discreet when I looked at men. I thought that my silenced passion to kiss, touch and denude them was completely unnoticeable, but Barry had clearly identified that the admiration in my blue eyes was of homosexual desire. It wasn't the first time that I viewed his total nudity. It was completely normal, some men showered in their togs and others openly exhibited their manhood in the public showers of the local swimming pool. I began to question if Barry was gay like me? Indeed, he was a homosexual, but in the age of certain innocence I didn't recognise that a lustful desire glittered in his smile too. Step by step he befriended me into his world of seduction. My erections betrayed me more and more and sometimes he touched my hard penis under the water. It was difficult to judge if his hand had accidently or intentionally touched me as we swam, but I consented without feeling any sentiment of catholic shame. Sometimes he moved closer and closer to my lips, as if he really wanted to kiss me, but we were never alone to sin. I was highly attracted to Barry, infatuated to say the least. His dark brown eyes were wow, his naked body was so perfectly shaped and to top it off he had a gorgeous looking penis. Every Saturday when I saw him I was overwhelmed by a strong sensation of lust. I dreamed about the touch of his kiss upon my lips and I certainly wanted him to seduce me. I wanted

him to be the liberator of my homosexuality, but I still silenced my immorality. He was the man of my dreams I thought; perhaps I even wanted to taste the eternity of his love, but I didn't know what the real value of queer love was yet. My sexual revolution was beginning; but whereas I always dreamed of being deflowered with love, instead I tasted the brutality of the promiscuous gay culture for the first time.

The colourful leaves of autumn 1991 had just fallen; the long winter nights gnawed the short hours of daylight away and a cold rain fell in great abundance on that sinful day. I raced across the green fields of Ireland with a passionate desire to indulge in the rituals of Barry's discreet touches again. It was Mr. Moon on duty at the swimming pool when I arrived. He was a witty man with an intriguing surname and because he knew my father relatively well he never charged me the £1.50 fee to swim. In that way, I almost economised a million pounds, but rather than deposit my swimming money in the Allied Irish Bank, I always spent it on sweets in Walsh's shop immediately afterwards. There was absolute silence in the changing rooms; nobody else had had the bravery to battle the intense force of the Irish storm. I denuded from my white cotton underpants into my tight fitting togs; which enhanced the shape of my penis, but in doing so the cold surroundings caused me to shiver and goose pimples appeared. My hand mechanically touched the cast iron radiator, which barely emitted some warmth, so I opened the valve to full force to optimise the dissipation of heat. There was the sound of footsteps approaching on the tiles. I prayed in the silence of my thoughts for it to be Barry, but it was only Mr. Moon to inform me that there were no other clients. Furthermore, because I was a rather good swimmer, the life guard on duty had decided that there was no need for surveillance for my fifty minute swim. I was enraged in the concept that I would not see Barry for another week, but a few minutes later I recognised his glorious silhouette arriving.

His swimming togs clung to his well defined body to enhance his sex appeal. I eyed him from head to toe with lust and he flirtatiously smiled back at me. With his muscular arms and his divine body straight he majestically sprung into the air to assert the abundance of his virility. The water seemed to devour and swallow his beauty as he disappeared from my view, until he powerfully resurfaced a few seconds later. Then, he veered directly towards me and as the distance decreased his irresistible dark brown eyes seduced me again. I battled to silence the sensation of my arousal, but he already knew that he had conquered me. There was lust in

became engrained in me forever. Time seemed to last for an eternity in my head, but in reality his masturbation was a few short minutes. I heard the sound of his climax transpierce the silence and then a flow of sperm powerfully ejaculated from his penis onto the tiled shower wall. He then passionately kissed me for the last time before discarding me. The cast iron radiator now emitted an abundance of heat, but I felt so cold. I lowered my eyes to the floor in silence and mechanically clothed my naked body with great haste. I fled through the green fields of rural Ireland never to see him again. Barry belonged to my secret garden of silence forever. Perhaps I was to become as savage as him and flourish in the promiscuous paradise of the gay scene too?

Was it with savagery or with gay normality that I tasted homosexuality for the first time? I wanted to forget all about his seduction, but that night I closed my eyes fondly thinking about Barry. I hadn't abandoned the sensational taste of his virile kisses yet and while reliving his passion in my mind I caressed my penis. The velocity of my hand moving up and down increased as thoughts of his dark brown eyes and his denuded body aroused me. I certainly wanted to fucking cum thinking about him. An ocean of colourless viscous pre-seminal fluid lubricated the head of my cock to enhance the sensations of my pleasure. A cloud of thick sperm suddenly shot in my prone ejaculation and then an abundance of tears fell from my blue eyes. In my loving judgement I did not hate Barry, I still felt a sentiment of love for him, but I was certain that I didn't want to see him ever again. I found the serenity to understand his brutality; after all love was ephemeral in the seduction of all men. There was no apparent difference between queers and heterosexuals in the liberation of promiscuity. I now believed that all homosexual and heterosexual men fucked with hostility and not with love. Was homosexuality really about the emotionless consumption of men? In the changing colours of the seasons my voyage into the core of the gay culture began and I learnt that all the myths about homosexual sex were true.

The Fertilisation of Irish Fear

The daffodils in the garden surfaced, bloomed and danced in the freedom of the March winds. I dreamed of the same liberty to be gay. I wanted to abandon homosexual silence, flourish in the beauty of a coming out, resurrect from my sufferance and taste the liberation of homosexuality, but I knew that Irish women were so devout to the love of the almighty god, that some catholic mothers found the strength to coldly forsake their homosexual sons. But perhaps my pious mother would have the serenity to forgive my immorality and love me forever? Homosexuality was a very lonely place of intolerance. In the desolation of solitude I feared that the good Catholics of Ireland would crucify me, but I had to abandon the dark dusty closet of silence. I needed to liberate my homosexual dreams, but I didn't want to destroy her heterosexual dreams either. I knew that my mother didn't want "a fucking queer son", but I didn't want to be a homosexual in the imposturous life of a heterosexual forever. In despair I cried alone. In the barren desert of my tears I needed her perpetual love. I had a vision of hope that the profoundness of her affection was eternal, but it was indisputable that I was certainly wrong. She was unable to love the homosexual that I had become. My coming out was a cry of distress, I implored her to have compassion for me in my hour of need, but my holy mother loved her catholic god more than she loved her homosexual son.

I am totally unable to visualise the exactitude of that forgotten moment in early 1992 due to a huge lapse of time and the erosion of my memory. To survive the trauma of her utmost violence my mind independently deleted almost all the emotions of that day, but I do remember the insignificant details of the pale egg shell colour of the wall, the ruins of my ransacked bedroom in the aftermath of her aggressive reaction and the profound feeling that I wanted to die. I knew that there was no return to the dark dusty closet of silence ever again, but I never predicted that my coming out would be the source of so much destruction. For an ample time my mother

had chosen to ignore the telltale signs of my homosexuality. It was very clear since the beginning of time, but she had always blinded herself from the truth. She always wanted to believe in her dream that I was a catholic heterosexual, but I destroyed all of her dreams with the unwanted revelation of my homosexuality. Contempt consumed her emotions and I heard her wrathful judgement, "Birth to a fucking monster'. She pushed me physically and emotionally away with her blows of repulsion. My fragility was utterly disregarded, my tears were completely ignored and she didn't want to know about the abundance of my silenced suffering. I betrayed the silence of my gay thoughts to be punished in the abundance of her enmity. She mourned and lamented the death of her straight son. She besought me to repent for my immorality. She prayed imploring god to contaminate me with goodness, but my homosexuality was too innate for god to silence it forever. In the injustice of catholic judgement the almighty god banished me from the kingdom of heaven, in doing so I was also exiled from the eternity of my mother's love. There was no divine compassion for a queer in catholic Ireland. My mother's humble prayers wanted to save me from the eternal fires of hell. She begged god with tears in her eyes to hetero-sexualise me, but her sufferance was silenced. The almighty god was too assiduous reaping havoc and destruction worldwide, so her barren supplications did not baptise me into the religion of heterosexuality. Did my coming out liberate me or betray me? Her savage brutality became the most destructive force in my battle to survive. My homosexuality ravaged her life in eternal shame. She even wanted to intoxicate my body with hormones to make me straight, but Doctor David Davitt disclosed that Ireland did not condemn queers to that fate. In the silence of her glance towards me he also understood that I was no longer her son. In her cold catholic judgement I was "a queer fucker" and she certainly didn't have the serenity to forgive that sin. Love didn't glitter in her blue eyes ever again. My gay battle to survive her brutality had just begun. That was the fertilisation of Irish fear.

Was brutality a mother's reflex to battle her dying dreams? I really thought that in the changing colours of the seasons she would learn to love me again, but my dream of tasting the eternity of her love was an ephemeral dream. It was idiotic of me to think that she would find the strength to liberate me from the prison of my silence, solitude and sufferance. It was senseless of me to believe that she would have the bravery to say fuck off to all the homophobic opinions of the catholic world that she belonged to. In despair I learnt that not all reveries come true. There were no soft words to console my tears, no gentle hugs to liberate me from my suffering and

no maternal affection was really ever displayed for me again. After my coming out she closely scrutinised my life to eradicate my gayness with force, savagery and enragement. Her fury resurrected in an endless effort to hetero-sexualise me. I didn't know that the term for that was gay bashing, but it certainly minimised my camp behaviour. Was the objective of her brutality to make me strong in life or to completely destroy me? The demise of our relationship was so extremely painful that I wanted to die. What did she fear most, the wrath of her almighty god or the social shame of having a queer son? She slaughtered me because she didn't want her catholic reputation to be tainted. She silenced me, so that humanity would never know that she had mothered "a queer fucker". It was even made clear that she would have gone to England in 1975 to abort me, if she had known that my life was to turn out gay. She never forgave me for the liberation of my homosexuality, she never abandoned her rancour either and her physical violence towards me intensified as I aged. I endured so many years of animosity as she crucified me without any sign of remorse. My bruises disappeared, but the underlying scars became my perpetual sufferance. Sometimes love glittered in her beautiful blue eyes, for an episodic moment she had forgotten that I was gay, but then the binges of her brutality always resurfaced again. There was certainly no resurrection of maternal love after a homosexual coming out. The almighty god of Ireland had abandoned me to die in the prison of her rage. She crucified me more and more, but I always had the catholic compassion to forgive her. Homophobia was the strongest of her emotions, but I loved her no matter what. My catholic Irish home destroyed me, but I still loved my mother. More tears of sufferance needed to be liberated, before I found the serenity to hate her forever. Survival was a question of learning to advance in the ruins of destruction that my coming out to her had caused. Victory was in the beautification of accepting the injustice of her intolerance, while still believing in the dream of homosexual freedom.

Coming out to my holy mother was the beginning of my real sufferance. I implored her catholic compassion to forgive me; even though I believed that homosexuality wasn't really a sin. I besought her not to abandon me and she promised that she would love me again; but nobody in Ireland was to ever know that I was "a queer fucker". The solemn promise of silence was the hard condition she imposed and the profoundness of my need to be loved by her forced me to accept it. If I wanted the eternity of her love, I simply needed to silence my perversion, if not she would forsake me forever. In the harmony to silence her homosexual hate I silenced my passion to love denuded men. I humbly agreed to refrain from coming out

in rural catholic Ireland, but in doing so I liberated great desolation by tolerating the perpetual prison of silence. My detested adolescence was a long weary battle. When I should have been carefree I struggled to survive the catholic judgement of Irish homosexuals. The destructiveness of her blows to hetero-sexualise me increased in frequency and force. I didn't know how to stop the abundance of her violence. Nobody wanted to know about homosexual crucifixions and in fear of resurrecting her fury everyone certainly silenced the sufferance that glittered in my eyes. In the silence of my tears I was alone. The battle to liberate my dream of homosexual freedom became harder and harder to fight. I faded deeper and deeper into despair. A fascination to embrace death devoured me as regular thoughts of suicide corrupted my mind. In the profoundness of my sufferance I famished for the shadows of the valley of death to seduce and devour me. In my hour of need I wanted to die. Was it normal that I had a furtive thought for suicide at the tender age of sixteen? Was death the fate waiting in concealment to destroy me another day?

Father O'Brien almost succeeded in anointing each catholic home in rural Ireland with god's love in May 1992. I clearly remember being in Maggie Ryan's that day. She pepped through the net curtains when the door bell rang, the television blared in the background betraying her presence, but there was no welcome for the religious man. Unlike my holy mother, she didn't graciously serve him with coffee and double-sided chocolate biscuits. There was no eluding the holy judgement of Irish catholic women and their tongues crucified her in punishment for her irreverence. They judged that the poverty stricken woman didn't have a spare coin to place in the hand of a priest, but she simply didn't believe in the myth of the kingdom of heaven. She wasn't really a churchgoer, but her faith always resurrected for the Sacraments. Baptism had liberated her children from original sin, Communion had cannibalised them with the Body of Christ and Confirmation had enriched them with the love of the Holy Spirit. Listening to the sermons just wasn't her cup of tea, but in my humble opinion she didn't need to be a bible reader or a lover of god in order to socially prove that she was a good woman. She had known me since the beginning of time. Every Christmas she had a selection box with a Caramel, a Crunchie, a Dairy Milk, a Flake, a Fudge and chocolate Buttons just for me. At Easter there was several Cadbury Cream Eggs, she particularly knew that they were my favourite. John Hanlon came from a district that my mother referred to as the lowest stratum of underclass of urban Cork. I had heard that if in the same street as him it was best to lower one's eyes. I didn't really know him, however he certainly knew me;

"the queer fucker of rural Ireland". His fist was directed to my stomach, the impact of which made me fall to my knees gasping for breath. Maggie, who had seen everything in the distance, let her shopping bag fall to her feet. She abandoned the Brennans bread, the pint of milk, the quarter of corn beef and the alluring blue on white twenty pack of Rothmans that she had just bought in the local shop. As she neared, it surprised me to hear that she knew so many curses. Hanlon retorted "Fuck off you fucking blonde peroxide bitch", but Maggie revolted with even more fury than him. Before abandoning me in defeat he outed "the fucking queer" from the dark dusty closet of silence to her. An ocean of emotion devoured my blue eyes, but she lovingly wiped those tears of sufferance from my face. She had certainly seen my gayness surface throughout the years and now with my head close to her voluptuous bosom she liberated me from the silence of homosexuality. I learnt from her mouth that there was no immorality in being gay. She befriended me with another hug and I began to believe in Irish homosexual freedom. She solemnly promised that my mother didn't need to know, but 78 year old Maureen O' Toole had seen everything from the window of her catholic home.

In the coming days Maggie waved at me in the street and smiled with a discrete wink each time she saw me, but a few days later everything changed and she never looked in my direction ever again. Miss O' Toole read myths from her bible, listened to the pulpit sermons and prayed to her almighty god with reverence at mass, but as a good Irish Catholic she always put forth her holy judgement to crucify others too. The truth that she had seen with her righteous eyes was revealed to my mother, but she corrupted the innocence of Maggie's maternal affection and made it sound like a loving seduction. Peter had denied Jesus and I certainly denied Maggie three times with the same zeal, but in doing so my silence condemned her even more. The emotional tremble in my voice must have betrayed me, because my mother believed Maureen and graciously thanked her for having enlightened her. Maggie was in her front garden puffing on a fag. The dangling cigarette, which distended a cloud of light grey coloured smoke from her mouth, fell to the ground in total amazement. My mother had seen sin through the words of Maureen and revolted in revenge and enragement. "You fucking whore", she accused Maggie of sexually corrupting me and nothing could silence her fury once liberated. Maggie, with her finger pointed in my direction warned, "don't throw stones when you silence his sins". A catholic crowd of nosey women had gathered around and my mother's rage resurrected with even more savagery. Maggie certainly didn't want to out me from the dark dusty closet of

silence, but she liberated her revenge. "Your son is a fucking queer", she enriched everyone with the words that my mother had never wanted to hear. My mother threw another stone, "Your fucking husband is a fucking alcoholic". They all lowered their eyes in submissive silence. It was socially known that it was best to have my mother as a friend and not as a foe.

There was perpetual silence after that; the habiliments that my brother and I had grown out of were certainly not recycled to clothe Maggie's boys with hand-downs ever again. Almsgiving was forsaken and Maggie didn't prostrate before my holy mother any more. My school books, my clothes and everything that her hands had touched littered my bedroom floor. An ocean of tears contaminated my puffy swollen eyes with utter despair. The tingling sensation on my face was where the force of my mother's passionate rancour had impacted me again and again. To hetero-sexualise me she had almost killed me. That night there was another storm; she had abandoned silence to enlighten my father that I was 'a homosexual fucker". He mourned and lamented the death of his straight son. I implored him to liberate me from my sufferance, but his enragement resurrected and I reaped the fruit of his profound rage too. My father passionately listened to the holy sermons that resounded from the pulpit, so there was certainly no tolerance in catholic Ireland for queers. The bastard prayed to his almighty god to forgive me, but not living in abidance to the Seventh Commandment he fucked lover after lover. His penis seduced so many denuded factory women, but he silenced his promiscuity and dared to judge me for the immorality of homosexuality. He besought me to repent to the love of god and revert to heterosexuality, but I looked at him directly in his eyes in total refusal of both his desires. I knew that he hated homosexuals, but in revenge I wanted him to know that I was forever one of those queers that he hated so much. He clearly detested that I rebelled against him, but I accepted the barbaric savagery of another punishment in the name of homosexual liberation. His masculine blows were much stronger than the feminine ones that had befallen on me earlier that day. He crucified me with so much force that I thought that he wanted me to journey into the shadows of the valley of death. My bruises disappeared, but his brutality resurfaced to destroy me again and again.

The heteronormative culture of Ireland enriched my rancour for god. Thou shalt not be "a queer fucker" was not a Commandment, but my catholic parents portrayed the homosexual as a social outcast. Their catholic faith

contaminated me to think that the almighty god had corrupted all of Ireland to hate homosexuals. I was even led to believe that all the good Catholics of Ireland punished queers for their immorality and that if I had the stupidity to come out, I would be forsaken by everyone. Their brutality implanted such terror in me that my silence flourished. If the same disdain that glittered in her blue eyes, when she destroyed me, was to be reflected in the eyes of all Catholics, I didn't want that holy judgement to crucify me either. In the belief that they loved me, I had no reason to distrust their ruse, but perhaps the culture of such intolerance was a myth? I didn't want to silence my homosexuality, but my holy mother and father decided that nobody in Ireland was to ever know. I pledged in submission to the catholic god, which I did not believe in and they solemnly vowed in return to love me forever. The promise of silence was the liberation of even more solitude, sufferance and tears and silence was certainly a double edged sword that betrayed me. In the changing colours of the seasons I learnt that humanity had compassion for queers and that there was more sufferance in homosexual silence than in the sufferance of homosexual freedom.

Silence shielded my holy catholic mother and father from the shame of having a queer son, but it was a destructive force that destroyed me. It was an ocean of tears, a prison of social solitude, a world of perpetual sufferance and I wanted to die. I battled to survive as a closeted homosexual and closed my blue eyes when the abundance of brutality of their catholic judgement punished me. I dreamed of homosexual freedom, but my passion for life faded away and the shadows of the valley of death seduced me again and again. I wanted to die a heroic death hanging from the century aged sycamore tree at the end of the garden. I now believed that Irish catholic queers only found liberation from sufferance by embracing death. Another homosexual was defeated by the brutality of rural Ireland in November 1992. The official cause of his death was severe trauma to the upper cervical spine, but the words that had transcended from homophobic generation to generation, "arse fucker, bender, fag, faggot, fairy, nancy, poofster, queenie, queer and sissy", had destroyed his reveries and withered his passion for life away. Ireland had slaughter another catholic queer and his holy mother mourned and lamented in tears of grief by his graveside. Perhaps there had been a homosexual crucifixion silenced behind the closed doors of his catholic Irish home too? In his hour of need he had tied the noose around his neck, but was there justice in the death of a sixteen year homosexual? I cursed god in rage; queers were crucified on Earth and banished from the kingdom of heaven in despair. Was I to embrace the same fate or was my sufferance to strengthen me in time? I

didn't want to become another Morgan. I promised to liberate my revenge on the catholic world that had destroyed him.

There was no famine in our home when the clothing factory closed down; "Thou shalt not steal" was forsaken by my holy father, who savagely pillaged and enriched his catholic pockets. On the other hand, an abundance of tears devoured the factory women, but my holy mother believed that divine revenge was in such justice. Her almighty god had listened to her prayers for vengeance and those that he had seduced, kissed, denuded and fucked were now punished with the pungent taste of unemployment. My pious mother worshiped the gold and diamond rings that glittered on her ornate fingers. It repulsed me that she prostituted her ephemeral love to him in the prison of marriage, but I mirrored the same corruption. Silence was the creation of all my sufferance, but I needed to survive in silence if I wanted to conquer my dreams, after all they always reminded me that it was their generosity that housed, fed, clothed and educated me. I didn't want to be forsaken to the tears of a holy Irish eviction. I believed that there was less solitude in the brutality of her catholic judgement of queers than in the social solitude of being homeless. I wanted homosexual freedom, but I certainly didn't want to embrace poverty either. I clearly understood that money was the key to bestow the wings of liberty. In the changing colours of many seasons it was to become my two fingered gesture of revenge on the catholic world, but did I have the strength to survive long enough to buy my dream of homosexual freedom? There was no immediate road to liberate me from the catholic prison of rural Ireland. My financial dependency was the almighty force that still enhanced my silence. I needed to be patient in the dark dusty closet for many more years.

The Contamination of Silence

My mother was a creation of the love of god; she was baptised for the remission of original sin in 1948, in the Sacrament of Communion she was cannibalised in 1955 and during the years of her school-hood she was conditioned to be a good Catholic by the Sisters of Mercy; who apparently didn't abide by the grace of their name. In their perpetual vow of poverty, chastity and obedience to god, the Virgin Brides of Christ destroyed her in the prison of prayer and the passion of corporal punishment. She learnt the myth of the love of god and the morality of catholic judgement from them and turning the gilded pages of her holy bible enriched her to crucify queers. Their brutality slaughtered, her bruises disappeared, but the intolerance of god was ingrained in her forever and her sufferance hibernated in silence. The ripples of their blows resurrected when she slaughtered me, but god deemed me unworthy of catholic compassion and justified her rancour. Irish brutality was liberated from religious brutality; the tears of sufferance that destroyed me were certainly the fruit of god's judgement. The pulpit sermons enhanced her fear of the wrath of god, she venerated with reverence and refraining from giving alms to homosexuals she crucified me. She wanted a resurrection after death and believed that humanity needed to taste disaster, famine, poverty and war because suffering on earth granted eternal salvation. Ashes to ashes, dust to dust, I hated everything about the catholic religion and my faith was ephemeral in the belief that there was no heaven, purgatory or hell. I was condemned to homosexuality forever, but I still had no repentance.

The causes that created my mother's rancour were profoundly buried in the silence of her past. Much was deeply enrooted in the low socioeconomic status of her Irish childhood. She had belonged to a poor Ireland. She had never tasted hunger, but she had suffered immensely from a lack of enrichment in a catholic home of nine children. From an early age, she cooked, cleaned and slaved to rear her siblings, because her mother

suffered from bad health. She dominated them in terror of her almighty rages, she tyrannised them in fear of the severity of her aggressive punishments and her brutality silenced all desire to rebel against her. Step by step the hardships of life forced her to abandon her dreams and her emotions became cold in her silenced sufferance. She was contaminated by deep contempt for her mother and hated her profoundly in the eternal regret that she had never tasted the frivolous sensation of a normal childhood. It was oranges in her Christmas stocking year after year, that seemed like a real punished to me, but judging by her soft smile when she spoke, it was a happy memory that had resurfaced. With child-like eyes she dreamed of owning the bisque doll seen in the toy shop window of Oliver Plunkett Street, but in 1956, or the years after that, her reverie didn't come true. She resented that she hadn't felt maternal affection that day and the profusion of her hostility never ceased. She still refused to understand that food on the table was more important than her materialistic desire. She really believed that her mother hated her since the beginning of time, but I believed that it was at the age of eight that my mother learnt to detest poverty. At the age of fourteen there was no more brutality from the Sisters of Mercy to punish her, but in the fight against Irish starvation she was enslaved in the prison of factory work. She never reaped the liberty of her hard earned money. The vast majority was seized to feed her sisters and conquer their hunger in catholic Ireland. That injustice contaminated her with a passion never to taste poverty again and in the changing colours of the seasons money became her holy religion. She battled to rise from the rags and sufferance of poverty and after her social ascension gold and diamond rings glittered on her hands. It was her two fingered gesture of revenge on the world.

Her impeccable appearance totally opposed the shabbiness of their clothes. She was dressed far too glamorous to work in the dusty industrial environment of a sweatshop, but the mini skirt was emblematic of femininity and her social appearance always needed to look its best. My sexy looking mother sharply contrasted to the haggard faces of the other factory women too. Her blue eyes were a seductive colour, which allured the lust of many men, but being endowed with Double D cup breasts certainly enticed them more. Many a suitor tried to woo and conquer the eternity of her love, but it was clear in the coldness of her rejections that she didn't want to fall in love with impoverished men. My rigorous catholic mother was not ungodly in her thoughts or acts. She knew, that without an ornate gold ring on the digitus quartus manus of the left hand, that kissing was tolerated and that fondling, if practiced, needed to done

with utter discretion. Her holy judgement believed that Irish brides had to be virgins to marry. There was no promiscuity in Ireland; catholic women were only deflowered after the solemn vows of marriage were made before god. It was her attraction to an ordinary looking man, but certainly a charming man, which liberated the beginning of her eternal sufferance. My father's mission was to implement corrective maintenance action plans on all the industrial machines in the clothing factory and to increase the productivity of the workers that sometimes blundered. He was not really attractive, but for some strange reason no factory woman in Ireland had the power to resist him. My mother didn't know that he preyed on women, but she knew that he prayed to god, she had already seen him listening to the holy sermons at mass. In one glance she fell profoundly in love with him. It was love at first sight, but it was a catholic sin for Irish women to be overtly seductive. In the beginning her eyes turned away from her work station, just to regard him for another few seconds. In the weeks that followed the other sewing machine operators began to notice her real interest in him, but her attempts to allure were still too discreet for him to perceive. Cheryl O' Connelly enticed her to have more bunching thread, more breaking needles and more skipping stitches. Kathleen Collins half-laughingly suggested that if she really wanted to seduce him that she needed to denude her voluptuous breasts. My mother was a reputed perfectionist in everything she did, probably even the most professional and productive in the company, but surprisingly her performance indicators plummeted and the number of machine breakdowns at her work station skyrocketed. Being holy she had certainly listened to the catholic advice given by Cheryl. He leaned over her, patiently explaining the industrial procedures again and again. The fragrance of her perfume enchanted him, lust resurrected in his penis and my mother was ensnarled in his ephemeral love forever. I don't know when they kissed in passion for the first time, but perhaps it should never have happened? She believed in eternal love, he believed in the freedom of love and in the changing colours of the seasons the destruction of love contaminated all of her dreams.

Her reverie of love was entangled with her desire to never taste impoverishment again, so the attractive taste of his money certainly seduced more than his charm. She desired the dream of his eternal passion, she believed in the promise of his eternal love, but in silence he seduced his lovers again and again. It was clear that the innocence of her love was doomed from the beginning, but nobody had the bravery to liberate her from the error of falling in love with a promiscuous man. Their silence condemned her to battle in the prison of his love forever. Every sewing

machine operator in the factory knew that he was already unfaithful in love, but they silenced his seductions and catholic Ireland created my mother's perpetual sufferance. The holy Catholics did not have the compassion to save her; perhaps they feared the liberation of her wrath? She was renowned for the brutality in her fury and the rage of her catholic judgement; perhaps it was best to befriend her in silence rather than have her as a foe? The almighty god of Ireland also betrayed her; "to have and to hold, to love and to cherish, for better, for worse, for richer, certainly not for poorer, in sickness and in health, from this day forward till death do us part". She wanted freedom from the prison of poverty, his affluence liberated her materialistic desires, but the taste of other women on his lips was the silenced sacrifice of such luxury. My father wanted to conquer her beauty, to seduce the woman that all men desired with lust and in error my mother completely fell in love. She married in accordance to the Sacrament of Money in 1971. My father conquered his virgin bride and she was deflowered with a ring on her finger. His affluence became her revenge on the poor catholic world that she had always known, but the holy vows she had solemnly sworn now imprisoned her in eternal sufferance.

The honeymoon in Dublin denuded my mother for the first time before the eyes of a man. The lust in each kiss enriched her more and more in the prison of catholic love. The serenity of god's blessing enabled her virginity to be forsaken and she then tasted all the injustices of being a married catholic woman in holy Ireland. Under the political, social and religious laws of obedience she became a loyal desperate housewife. The savagery of catholic wedlock forbade pious Irish women to flourish in the prosperity of a career and the rigorous work ban belittled them to live in total financial dependency on men. The revenge of god on the treachery of Eve doomed women to the eternity of domestic slavery and motherhood. The strong interdependency between money and love enhanced the fragility of all Irish women. My mother needed to silence his sins to survive, he needed to survive in the silence of his sins and the corrupt balance between money and silence was the creation of all her sufferance. The gold and diamond rings that decorated her fingers in an ornate fashion silenced my father's infidelity because Irish wives were submissive in the emotional brutality of god and men. God's repression of Irish women enchained them in the kitchens and enslaved them in the bedrooms of Irish homes. Religion governed their fertility, birth control was illegal and indeed childbirth was seen as a good catholic deed. They mourned in the tearful abandonment of their dreams, reproduced in abundance and reared holy Irish children. There was no judgement to punish licentious catholic men; god graciously

forgave their virile promiscuity and silenced their violation of the Seventh Commandment. "Thou shalt rightfully commit adultery" was a common practice for many Irish husbands. My father was reputed for his utter reverence for god, but he seduced, kissed, denuded and fucked many factory women in total betrayal of the holy bible. His lovers knelt before the catholic altar in prayer, but they also genuflected in veneration before his penis. In the silence of sufferance my mother blinded herself from the truth and zealously ignored the telltale signs of his cheating for years. Her catholic dreams battled to survive in the emotional agony of his silenced adultery. She believed in the myth of his eternal love, even if that meant being contaminated by the unwanted taste of other women's kisses on his lips forever.

My pompous mother flaunted her affluence to the world in such a way as to always belittle those that hadn't risen from the ashes of poverty yet. Her victory was seen in the gold and diamond rings that decorated her fingers with ephemeral happiness. With an indiscreet movement she brought attention to her wrist, which forced impoverished women to revere her sparkling bracelets; such veneration certainly enhanced her feeling of self-importance. In the ritual of superficiality, her left hand stroked her lower neck in a singular semi-circular fashion from right to left, from shoulder to shoulder as if she longed to caress her voluptuous breasts. The objective of that specific gesture was to encourage indistinct women to extol the beauty of her matching necklace. With total smugness she slightly moved her head forward several times; giving the false impression that she was attentively observing something in the distance, but that was only to highlight that her ear lobes glittered in the sunlight with the same splendour of gold and diamonds. Everything perfectly coordinated; after all the harmony of jewellery was of great importance in the judgement of the almighty god. It was the virtuous act of alms giving that enriched my mother with the grace of god. She was charitable, but rather than be subtle, she sang in self-praise that she assisted poor Maggie Ryan to cloth her six catholic children. The boys were always dressed in the perfect condition hand-downs that my brother and I had grown out of. Was her recycling of clothes part of a movement to put forth environmental protection against mass consumption or was such generosity to others a social need to demonstrate to the world that she was a good Catholic? Everybody in the district knew that the habiliments that I wore that summer were destined for Maggie's twin sons the next summer. I never understood if she had absolutely no dignity or no choice, but Maggie pathetically prostrated before my holy mother in sincere thanks. Life was an ongoing battle to nourish her children, Maggie

had nothing, but her husband had the money to get pissed in the local pub every night. Of all the women in Ireland my mother seemed to be the most pretentious and superficial, but those that knew her sister Ellen strongly differed in opinion. She was certainly the most venomous creature created by god and definitely the greatest ostentatious bitch that catholic Ireland had ever known. She never praised anyone without adding a captious remark and nobody could elude the holiness of her catholic judgement. She forced women to lower their heads in shame, tears fell from the eyes of some, but Ellen never repented for her destructive criticisms. She zealously slaughtered with such toxicity that she outshined all the gossips in Ireland and her natural talent to belittle everyone even surpassed my mother's crucifixions. Nobody could evade the caustic glare of her superiority, but the beauty of revenge resurrected from silence and the sinners that were judged by Ellen had vengeance in their judgement too. Ellen was renowned for the mass sufferance that her holy opinions caused, but her husband was overly reputed for his betrayal of the Seventh Commandment. He kissed her naked body, he fondled her breasts and he penetrated her with the virginal lubrication fluid of his lovers still on his penis. There were so many similarities between my mother and Ellen; the latter flaunted the ephemeral happiness of gold and diamonds too. Both tearfully tasted an abundance of sufferance, but rather than revert to poverty they silenced the treachery of love. In the changing colours of the seasons I tasted the venom of Ellen. Many years later her revenge on silence resurrected, she destroyed me with her sufferance and I learnt things about my father that I never needed to know.

I grew up hating my father and not understanding why my mother surrendered to the succulent taste of the fucked factory women on his lips. I wiped away the despair that fell from her beautiful blue eyes when I found her in tears. I promised her that nothing would ever destroy her again, but the tragedy of being a homosexual made it become a promise that I was unable to respect. I belonged to her world of deep sufferance, but I didn't know any different. In early 1993 I retorted that the social judgement of catholic Ireland shouldn't impel my mother to live in the prison of love with a licentious man. I encouraged her to abandon him, but I certainly didn't have the freedom to judge my holy father and with enragement she silenced my insolence. I didn't understand why she defended him so much. He destroyed her, but her brutality silenced me. Perhaps she really loved him or being a homosexual I didn't need to judge the promiscuity of a heterosexual man? My mother feared the wrath of god and believed in the sacrament of eternal love "from this day forward till

death do us part". God enticed her never to forsake her marriage, but perhaps the gold and diamonds that she venerated seduced her to abide in silence too? I mourned that she did not have the strength to survive in poverty again. It would have been hard, but her mother certainly would have sheltered her with the profoundness of her "cold love". She battled to silence his treachery from the world, but she should have battled for her freedom instead. She didn't want to face the hard judgement of Irish gossip, so she never liberated her silenced desire to abandon him. She did not give the catholic women of Ireland the pleasure of defaming her, but she could have survived the solitude of their destructive tongue wagging, if she had really wanted. I certainly suffered because she did not have the bravery to forsake him.

An ocean of tears devoured her dark brown eyes, her voice trembled with profound emotion and all the Irish brutality that had destroyed her resurrected as she liberated her sufferance for the first time. Isabelle disclosed to me what nobody was ever to know about her and abandoned the destructive prison of silence in total trust. As she voiced her tears I realised that the profound catholic silence of Ireland was deeper than I had ever imagined. There was the pungent smell of impregnated tobacco on his hand as he covered her mouth to silence her tears. He enticed her to fondle his denuded penis and his erections penetrated her with force. With her eyes firmly closed her catholic father raped her again and again, but he venerated the almighty god and prayed with reverence afterwards. She knew what the look that glittered in his dark blue eyes meant each time the door of her bedroom opened. She didn't recall what age she had been when his passion started, but she knew that at the age of twelve blood trickled from her vagina during his penetration and the churchgoer abandoned her after that. Perhaps he feared that his sperm would impregnate her or had he just found another toy to replace her? The cycle of menstruation was her liberation, but his touches were too deeply ingrained in her to ever forget. She hated him, but she still loved him. To purify her body she inflicted self-brutality and indulged in regular self mutilation. She justified that the sensations it provided appeased her inner sufferance. The longest scar on her arm, which immortalised the profoundness of her suffering, was approximately fifteen centimetres in length. She had used a carving knife from the kitchen to silence her sufferance that day. Cutting herself seemed really strange to me; I thought that she wanted to die, but she retorted that suicide definitely wasn't her cup of tea. She didn't believe in the holy bible or the righteous sermons, but she certainly believed that catholic men were never judged by the almighty god and that the desolation of god's silence

punished her forever. I believed that the silence of catholic Ireland had created her eternal sufferance. It was certain that the brutality that had destroyed her had created her too.

I knew everything about her life; that she kissed older men rather than the boys of her own age, that her love was always ephemeral and that her promiscuity was her revenge on the catholic world of intolerance. I even knew the names of all the men that she had fucked. I knew all about her immorality, but she didn't know mine. My homosexuality didn't come out of the dark dusty closet to her, even though she was my best friend. I silenced my mother's brutality because I didn't want her to be judged either. I certainly didn't disclose that my father seduced, kissed and denuded the factory women, because I feared her judgement of catholic men. I am totally unable to visualise the exactitude of that moment in 1993 due to a huge lapse of time and the erosion of my memory. I don't remember why Isabelle was alone with him, but upon my return she was on my bed in hysterical tears. I didn't know that my father's phallic penis desired to consume her, but it was the liberation of his lust that caused the destructive end of my platonic friendship with her. With catholic indignation my father denied his seduction. My holy mother condemned Isabelle as "a fucking whore"; the holiness of her catholic judgement wanted to silence the truth again. Isabelle's father directed a potent punch on her face to silence her; perhaps in doing so he was also silencing his own guilt? With immense brutality he punished her for her lie, but with insolence she still showed no repentance. She begged and implored him to believe her, but in the aggressive force of his final blow she became totally submissive. His barbaric rage silenced her forever, the desolation of catholic silence destroyed her again and her tears fell in the sufferance that nobody believed her. The corruption of Irish sinners condemned her to the prison of eternal silence. The catholic culture of secrecy and self-preservation certainly silenced the sins of all holy men. There was no sincerity in her apology to my parents, but the almighty god granted them the grace to forgive her. Did my friendly father really want to denude her or was his kiss on her lips an erotic flashback of her destructive past? Did his erect penis really want to fuck her or did she want to punish all the catholic men in rural Ireland for the deep sufferance ingrained in her? If the righteousness of Ireland completely liberated my father from all blame, why did my inner thoughts believe her? I clearly knew that my father wasn't innocent, but my silence profoundly betrayed her too. I silenced his corruption because I didn't want to destroy my mother in tears of sufferance. From that moment on, Isabelle either turned her head away or

lowered her dark brown eyes to the ground when she saw me. I tasted her revenge in the injustice of being punished for my father's savagery.

There was no heterosexual freedom in the catholic social politics which governed the Irish Free State. William Thomas Cosgrave believed in the myths of the bible and his creation of the divorce ban in 1925 certainly reflected his reverence for the almighty catholic god. All Irish citizens, Pagans, Protestants and Catholics alike, were subjected to catholic laws and the dissolution of Irish marriage was forbidden for all. Éamon de Valera believed in the preservation of Irish purity and that the institution of marriage was central to Irish identity. He upgraded the legislative prohibition to constitutional in 1937 and the holy institute of marriage became totally untouchable. The catholic god and holy politicians had condemned the Irish to the prison of eternal love. Only a referendum was empowered to liberate Ireland from such catholic repression, but that liberty was not forthcoming in such a heavily catholic mindset. For seven decades Irish women were enchained in kitchens, enslaved in bedrooms and silenced by god, whilst Irish men practiced promiscuity. Taoiseach Garret FitzGerald had a new vision of Ireland in 1986. He believed that the place of god was in a church and not in politics. He wanted the freedom of divorce for Ireland, but 63.48% of voters feared the wrath of god. That was another victory for the Catholic Church, but the powerful ripples of American and British freedom slowly began to infiltrate more and more.

Contraception was totally outlawed in order to preserve the sanctity of catholic Ireland in 1935. The almighty god now governed Irish politics and the uteri of Irish women too. "An Irish solution to an Irish problem" reflected the Catholic teachings on sexual morality and also signified that Charlie Haughey wasn't willing to jeopardise his political career for a condom in 1978. Heterosexuals needed the liberty to find birth control next to Corn Flakes in the supermarket or next to any other typical everyday product, but the right to govern the fate of Irish fertility was certainly not seen by politicians as a popular vote-getter. Haughey's Health Bill was definitely a stepping stone forward to sexual liberty, but also reflected the strong position of the conservative catholic element that was engrained in Irish society. Contraception was made available, but with the restriction of having a medical prescription provision. Was Ireland too righteous in the acceptance of such moderation or was a more liberal law too difficult to provide in that catholic era? As the government debated on more changes, the Catholic Church leaders further warned that promiscuity encouraged

the moral decay of Ireland. Perhaps god believed that holy Irish women were just machines to create catholic babies, but many promiscuous Catholics did not have faith in the pulpit sermons anymore. Garret FitzGerald joined the crusade to overthrow the catholic political laws and the dream of Irish sexual liberty resurrected from silence again. Ireland had changed, utterly changed and the defeat of the catholic god was on February 20th 1985. The Dublin archbishop rightfully claimed that the legalisation of contraception marked the beginning of the "slippery slope of moral degradation" in Ireland. It was clear that if Irish heterosexuals had to battle with so much vigour for freedom that the insurrection for homosexual freedom was going to be an even longer and bloodier war.

The 1995 divorce referendum reflected the urgent need for Ireland to change with the times. Taoiseach John Gerard Burton was the heroic proponent of the revolutionary vision of Ireland. As a Catholic he certainly believed in the kingdom of heaven, but as a politician he sought a legal remedy to address the high marital breakdown rate that Ireland had silenced for years. Righteous judgement revolted that divorce was contrary to the catholic social structure and the traditional values that enriched Ireland. It was the empowerment of Satan to destroy the fabric of Irish society and certainly the means to open the floodgates to encourage the abandonment of holy marriage. God led another weary battle against the fragmentation of Irish families and the destruction of the Irish identity. Leaflets littered the streets with propaganda fuelled by the Catholic Church. The billboards displayed the notorious slogan 'Hello Divorce...Bye Bye Daddy". By early November the print of word Daddy had faded in colour; in some streets it looked more like a homosexual pink rather than a lipstick red, but the catholic sermons were still enraged with as much passion as ever before. A no vote resounded from the pulpits, it seduced some, but there was another population of forgotten Catholics that no longer feared the wrath of god. They had once believed in a solemn promise to love forever, but the Sacrament of Marriage had become their eternal prison. They knew all about the sufferance of love and with enragement voiced their desire to seduce another. Even if divorce banished them from the kingdom of heaven, they wanted the liberty to fall in love again. Perhaps the cooling of religious zeal was the beginning of catholic apostasy and entailed a complete rejection of Ireland's strong catholic heritage?

It was the first time that I ever voted; I wanted Ireland to change, but what I really needed was my revenge on the catholic god. My mother's tears were still profoundly engrained in me and the colours, shapes, sounds and sufferance of 1987 certainly resurrected in my yes ballot. I believed in the dream of homosexual freedom, but the dream of heterosexual freedom came first. My catholic mother had vowed before god, "to have and to hold, to love and to cherish, for better, for worse, for richer, for poorer, in sickness and in health, from this day forward till death do us part", but she didn't believe in the eternal sufferance of other women. The Ireland of her dreams was struggling to rise from the ashes of Cosgrave's Ireland of 1925. She still imbibed the sermons of god and turned the discoloured pages of her aged bible in prayer, but her vote was the resurrection of her silenced sufferance too. She believed that the Sacrament of Marriage didn't need to be a perpetual prison and it thoroughly enraged my catholic father that she voted yes. He practiced promiscuity, kissed, denuded and fucked in abundance, but in blind agreement with the sermons that divorce was a sin, he firmly voted no.

The Catholic Church was unarguably the strongest single influence on Ireland's cultural identity. Cork, Kerry, Limerick, Claire, Tipperary and Waterford, all the counties of my beloved Munster betrayed me. Connaught feared the judgement of god, Leinster believed in the wrath of the almighty god and Cavan, Monaghan and Donegal had a catholic minded vote too. It was the urban turnout of sinners in Dublin that won the battle for Irish freedom. If the population of Dublin hadn't outnumbered the population of rural Ireland, divorce would never have been possible. 50.28% was the narrowest margin of any national ballot in the history of the Irish Free State. There were tears of victory in my mother's blue eyes on November 24th 1995. I danced in celebration around the sitting room with her singing "Ole Ole Ole Ole". It was in the exact same jubilant way that she had proudly sung on December 3rd 1990, when Mary Robinson was inaugurated as the seventh President of Ireland. My mother had believed that "it was a two fingered gesture of revenge on those that thought that a woman's place was not in Irish politics" and now she believed that "the new liberty of heterosexuals was a certain revenge on god". Irish women had acquired the freedom to divorce, liberate their dreams and fall in love again, but she still loved my father forever. Heterosexuals had promiscuous liberty, god was forsaken from Irish politics and Ireland was no longer entrenched in barbaric catholic laws. The real battle for homosexual freedom could now begin.

The Promise Of Silence

The Crucifixion of Queers

On the sixth biblical day god made man in his image and likeness to govern all the creatures on earth, but on the sixth day of my life I discovered catholic brutality as the force of a hurley collided repetitively with my fragile head. I had intruded his life to devour all of his mother's attention and it was apparent to everyone that she adored me more than her first born son. It was normal to a degree that the green eyed monster had passionately contaminated my brother, but the intensity of his resent never faded in the passing of time. There was absolutely no complicity with him, despite the fact that only four years separated us in age. I always wanted a profound life lasting bond to develop, but he displayed his rancour in every opportunity to emotionally hurt me. We were reared in the same catholic home of prayer to god, but despite originating from the same flesh and blood we were so completely different. The entanglement of love that had created him in 1972 had enriched him with an abundance of intolerance and led him to believe that homosexuality was a social repugnance. The Irish aversion of homosexuality that had transcended from catholic generation to generation suppressed his liberty of thought, but it was his choice to end the cycle of brutality and step into the light of tolerance if he really wanted. He abandoned our catholic home to work in a factory in Tipperary in the dramatic decade of socio-economic change in Ireland. He was immediately enriched by the pub culture that pervaded in the rural town of Thurles. He learnt that real Irish men downed pints of Guinness every night and he binged in the money fuelled hedonism of his new independence in 1991. On the Sabbath day my catholic brother needed his hangovers to dissipate, so rather than pray with reverence in mass, he certainly prayed to god to silence the humming sound of the cars on the main road outside that resounded in his head. In the catholic culture sexual relations were only sanctified in the prison of marriage, but the heterosexuals of Ireland cheery picked from the bible and sermons. My holy brother was the first to cast a stone on the immorality of homosexual promiscuity, but where were his catholic principles when he denuded and

fucked the women of Thurles? In the catho-macho social attitude of Ireland god had no judgement of his unholy lifestyle, but I was banished from the kingdom of heaven. Was there fraternal love before my homosexuality destroyed everything? I believe that the hate he cultivated for me was engrained in him since the beginning of time, but was my coming out to enrage him further?

For some strange reason my brother was rather insistent in his demand that I went to Thurles to visit him for some "brotherly quality time". The idea didn't enchant me with a high level of enthusiasm, but considering that he willing paid for my Iarnród Éireann train ticket made me reconsider my initial hesitation. My first impression was immense solitude; night had already fallen and I found myself completely alone on the disserted railway platform. A few minutes later there weren't any more passengers waiting under the dim street lights and no more cars on the road outside the station either. It was typical that he was always late; for me punctuality was a value that displayed human respect, but for him tardiness was normality. Perhaps he believed that his time was more important than that of others? I didn't know his address, which further enhanced my fear that he had completely forgotten me. Thirty long minutes slowly passed, but then I sighed in relief as the familiar beep sound of his car horn announced his arrival. He had always been overly susceptible to criticism of all kind and life experience had taught me that there was a high potential risk of provoking his brutality if he felt aggressed by the rigour of my judgement. I knew that he never forgave those that crucified him, so I displayed no verbal or emotional reaction to his lateness. I silenced my thoughts and forced a smile hoping that no facial expressions would disclose my irritation. I wanted nothing to jeopardise the balance of peace from the beginning. It was more pragmatic that I made absolutely no reproach or sarcastic comment, after all I didn't want to suffer a three day war. Physical contact wasn't an Irish practice and heterosexual men didn't show any emotion in public, so the kiss that he gently placed on my right cheek greatly surprised me. Perhaps at that moment I should have questioned which cheek Judas Iscariot had kissed before his treachery betrayed Jesus Christ? The few pints that he had savoured before he met me justified his lateness, but perhaps that also explained his elation too? There seemed to be sincerity in his repentance as if he didn't hate me anymore, but was the generosity of his emotions perpetual or ephemeral?

I discovered Liberty Square during the ritual of his pub crawl life in late 1992, needless to say that I didn't see much among in the smoke filled ambiance of the pubs that alcoholised him more and more. A glossy appearance glittered in his constricted blue eyes and drink after drink my brother became totally euphoric, which made me question if the freedom he tasted in Thurles had created too much liberty? Was he pissed to celebrate my arrival or had he created a certain dependency in the binge drinking culture of Ireland night after night? I didn't judge him, but the crisp wrinkles that appeared on my forehead certainly did. His speech was slurred, but due to my age I was sober enough to remember everything. He looked so blissful; he had fallen deeply in love with Molly. He disclosed with a smile that he now wanted the eternal vows of love before god in the Sacrament of Marriage. Drunken tears of happiness fell from his blue eyes as he showed me the dainty iridescent diamond engagement ring, but in fear of him losing it, it was placed safely in my pocket for the night. I definitely approved of his choice. I had developed a profound closeness to her and I even thought that Molly deserved a generous dowry or a bribe of some kind for accepting my brother in the prison of marriage. He was a relatively beautiful looking man, but it was clear that his egocentric personality was going to destroy all the beauty that she had within. It was predetermined for her to suffer an ocean of fallen tears by loving him, but she foolishly believed in her dream and in the sincerity of his eternal love.

He implored me to support him in the war against his mother's venomous disapproval. Nobody could ever elude the holiness of her judgement or the caustic glare of her superiority. In her condescending righteous opinion, blonde peroxide hair, with a fag daggling from the mouth and the cheap looking rings that decorated each finger enhanced his girlfriend's innate vulgarity. Furthermore, her accent symbolised the lowest stratum of underclass of a certain urban Dublin area. Rather than step into the light of tolerance, my mother severely judged her as belonging to an inappropriate social background and she never accredited Molly for her real merit. The years of so much disaccord in my mother's hateful relationship with my paternal grandmother had been completely forgotten. Rather than remember with empathy that she had been judged on the basis of her own impoverished origins in Churchfield, the same social judgement was made again. The destructive force of history was repeated and the toxicity of her words cast the same sufferance on Molly that my mother had already directly tasted in 1970. Deep enrooted opinions never changed and Molly was crucified with the same brutality for years, but there was never repentance in catholic Ireland. My holy mother had always stated that my

grandmother was "a fucking bitch" in her social judgement, but if she overtly displayed the same pretentious attitude in her social judgement of Molly, did that signify that my mother qualified as "a fucking bitch" too? Many rightfully thought so, but they silenced their thoughts, perhaps it was best to have my mother as a close friend rather than an enemy? Rural Ireland was a two faced culture of insincerity, many artificial smiles congratulated Molly and revered in total admiration of the luxury engagement ring, but behind her back they all agreed with my mother that she was of rather unsuitable kind to wed my brother. I hated catholic Ireland and the brutality of their judgement and I certainly did not abandon my brother in his hour of need. I wiped away the delicate tears that had fallen in sufferance from his eyes, but would he love or hate me if I had the courage to come out? I wanted to liberate my sufferance too.

The next day I disclosed the brutality that governed my catholic home in the belief that he would liberate me from my sufferance, but his deep embedded repugnance surfaced to destroy me. In his catholic social judgement promiscuous homosexuals were not worthy of the kingdom of heaven, but if his morality was based on the sermons why did he practice promiscuity too? He believed in the myths of the bible and not in the freedom of homosexuality, but where in the Holy Scriptures was it written "thou shalt not be a queer"? Aversion glittered in the coldness of his eyes; I was "a fucking queer fucking bastard". It was the same glance of rancour that I had already seen a million times in the eyes of his devout catholic mother and almost the same words that resounded, except that I was not just "a fucking queer" but "a fucking bastard" too. He didn't step into the light of tolerance; homosexuality was a sin against god, humanity and Ireland. I implored him to love me, but he crucified me in my tragic hour of need. I beseeched him to battle for my freedom, but my homosexuality was an abhorrence that needed to be silenced forever. He believed that homosexuality was a social contamination and not a natural creation of god. According to his theory, I had been overly nurtured in an ocean of maternal love, which had enticed me to become homosexual. He justified that the depravation of paternal affection was another major deciding factor that had seduced me to become a queer. That common belief was shared by many virile heterosexuals, but if my brother was reared in the same catholic home, did that mean that he had the potential to be homosexual too? My debate enraged him further and there was nothing I could say to appease his hostility after that. He didn't pray to god for my repentance, but he believed that he had the almighty power to hetero-sexualise me. He knew of a factory worker in Thurles, who provided unholy services to

catholic men for money and wanted to pay her to fuck me. The correct term was prostitution, not that I had any judgement of that, but even if it was a certainty that Tina could guide me on the road of heterosexuality I politely declined such generosity. He begged me to reconvert to heterosexuality naked in her bed, but the problem was that I was never heterosexual to begin with. He encouraged me to taste her virginal secretions, but I wanted to be baptised with a cloud of viscous sperm instead. I fueled his rage by demanding if Tina had a cute gay brother for rent that I could fuck instead. To his mind it was a fashionable trend at my age to rebel against the norms of society, but the time had come for me to revert to catholic heterosexuality again. His sermon became more and more aggressive and in the abundance of his intolerance my enragement began to manifest itself. If catholic fucking was for reproduction, why did he use a condom every time he fucked? What if homosexuality was engrained in his sperm too? What crucifixion was to befall if he fertilised gay children? He savagely silenced my irreverence towards him and my insolence was punished by his brutality, but I retorted that another potent punch in my lifetime didn't destroy. If I didn't fuck her that day from that cold moment on I no longer had a brother to share the smiles and tears of life with. He graciously gave me one hour alone in silence to decide and slammed the bedroom door behind him.

A few minutes later the rigour of my judgement informed him that if intolerance was so deeply embedded in his holy thoughts that there was no productivity in further discussion. I then learnt that his vision of me had changed forever. Humanity always had a tendency to focus on who I fucked rather than who I was and his narcissism clearly identified that I wanted to seduce him. The myth was so deeply engrained in him that my own brother really thought that I wanted to incestuously fuck him. That level of social ignorance repulsed me so much that I almost regurgitated on the carpeted floor. I retorted that being homosexual didn't mean that I was a gay missionary, queers didn't even flirt with straight men and it was certain that his heterosexuality wasn't of great physical attractiveness to me. Of course, my reproach encountered a flow of fuck words before he overtly demonstrated his virility by deciding that my departure was immediate. The aggressive way that he dumped my clothes and toiletries into my backpack a few seconds later displayed that he had absolutely no control over his emotions. In the critical moments of my life I survived in the belief that what didn't kill me made me stronger in my battle for homosexual freedom. There was a certain consistency in my coldness, a kind of emotional dysfunction that made me become totally indifferent to

sufferance. No tears fell from my blue eyes because I believed that flowers didn't bloom from tears. No barren enragement surfaced either; I honoured that homosexual dignity was a more powerful weapon than fighting with insults. The so called "brotherly quality time" in Thurles came to an abrupt end and he deported the dirty homosexual that I had become to rural Ireland without further debate. I believed that such brutality qualified as the ostracisation of a queer, but it enriched me with strength on my homosexual journey. It was a short distance from Liberty Square to the train station. I wanted to walk there alone, but he did insist on driving me there in total silence. On the railway platform he displayed no remorse or regret. The train arrived and he still hadn't shown any sign of repentance. I sarcastically placed a kiss on his right cheek; perhaps I believed that in my hour of need that he needed more compassion than me? It certainly didn't impress him much, but in a public place where he knew many people he was unable to display his repulsion. At that precise moment I understood which cheek Judas Iscariot had kissed before his treachery betrayed Jesus Christ.

A strong Corkonian accent announced each stop as the Iarnród Éireann train thrust its way through the green Irish landscape. "Limerick Junction, Charleville and Mallow", each town brought me a mile closer to the destruction of rural catholic Ireland again. I pondered on whether I had affection or rancour for my brother. Perhaps in the changing colours of the seasons his tolerance would flourish and my forgiveness would rise from the ashes of his destruction? Perhaps I was a dreamer, but I didn't want to believe that homosexuality was his eternal hate? He beheld the immorality of homosexuality with abhorrence far greater than what I had ever imagined. In his wrath we became total strangers and in his animosity of queers he destroyed me more and more. The moment the train emerged from the tunnel into Cork Kent Station I saw the abundance of her fury. Not a single word needed to be spoken for me to understand that my brother had betrayed me. During the ten minute car journey home my mother eyed me with wrath through the rear view mirror in silence. I judged by the glance of disgust that raged in her blue eyes that he had denounced my coming out. The front door opened and she sprinkled me with holy water from the font, "You certainly need the almighty god to escort you on the queer journey of your life". She must have practiced that mind game for hours because it echoed too rehearsed to have been spontaneous. I didn't want to listen to more verbal diarrhea or enrage her, so in silence I absconded in the direction of my bedroom. The staircase creaked behind me as she followed me up the fourteen carpeted steps, but I

still didn't understand what storm reposed underneath the surface of her smug appearance. Indeed my asshole brother had phoned her and I discovered a ransacked room. My clothes, my school books and everything that her hands had touched littered the floor. The Whitney Houston posters on the pale egg shell coloured wall had been clawed to pieces and my goldfish hadn't survived either. With a cold smile of revenge she ordained me to clean up the mess that she had created. I began to hate my holy catholic mother. I was punished that day for being "a queer fucker", for the insolence of coming out and for my betrayal of the promise of silence. I now believed that the almighty god had abandoned the homosexuals of Ireland forever. There was certainly no stepping into the light of tolerance for my catholic family. Irish queers needed a movement, but I wasn't a warrior for the liberation of Irish homosexuals. I wanted the liberty to be a homosexual without silencing or justifying that I fucked men, but catholic Ireland didn't grant me that dream of freedom yet.

Irish homosexuals were governed by catholic heterosexuals in the forbiddance of homosexuality. An anti-homosexual political structure enriched the catholic fabric of Irish society with god's morality and the legal sanction of penal servitude silenced queers. Homosexuals needed a warrior to battle for change, a hero to overthrow the almighty catholic god from Irish politics and a visionary to right the wrongs that discriminated against the gay community. David Norris was the founding father of Irish homosexual freedom. He abandoned the silence of the dark dusty closet to become a gay militant in 1971 and his long political struggle to raise Ireland from the ashes of homosexual repression began. In June 1993 Ireland decriminalised homosexuality and he became the liberator of Irish queers. Promiscuous homosexuals now had the legal right to fall in love, but I still belonged to the intolerance of rural catholic Ireland. Cooney encircled me with his gang and to crucify "a queer fucker" they slaughtered me with an abundance of physical blows. In their righteous war against homosexuals their potent punches floored me and their forceful kicks defeated me again and again. In the days of summer that followed reading in my bedroom alone and sunbathing in the wall enclosed garden of my home became my prison; I didn't want to risk another gay bashing, but was it possible to avoid Cooney forever? The heterosexual and the pink cultures were supposed to live in harmony hand in hand; June 1993 Senator David Norris had liberated me, but July 1993 Cooney destroyed my dream of homosexual freedom again.

The hours of natural sunlight noticeably began to decrease toward the end of August; that represented the beginning of my countdown to return to public school in September, but also the countdown to more brutality. I had heard that Bruce College was a selective establishment that maintained the highest standard of private education in Ireland. I wanted to enrich my passion for learning there and I certainly needed to be liberated from Cooney before he completely destroyed me. Wanting a resurrection from despair I implored my loving mother to hear my tears. I even begged in prayer to the almighty catholic god that I didn't believe in. The interview with Principal Sean Logan had some pinpointed questions to assess my reflection on effort, my commitment to persistency, my determination to reach high set objectives and the consistency of my studious track record was also scrutinised in great detail. After what seemed like an eternity he directed his beautiful dark eyes towards me. My candidature was apt for acceptance and monthly payments over the academic year were a feasible solution that could easily be envisaged. My father's oil stained jeans had enhanced his factory appearance and certainly fuelled such a reflection. He muttered under his breath that a book should not be judged by its cover. A short-lived facial twitch-like movement clearly indicated that Mr. Logan had heard. He smiled at me; he had definitely seen me raise my eyes to heaven. My holy father didn't possess a wallet and the mountain of bank notes that directly erupted from his pocket certainly surprised Mr. Logan. He stated that such payments were normally a cheque transaction, but my smug father simply placed £2,500 in cash onto the designer office desk in front of him. After doing so, he laughingly retorted that cheques didn't exist in rural Ireland. Lynda, the receptionist, counted the notes a second time; that money was embedded with the smell of corruption. I knew that my holy father had forsaken the Eighth Commandment of god and savagely pillaged the clothing factory, but I justified that it liberated me. I never saw Mark Cooney ever again.

Bruce College included supervised study, which consolidated knowledge in a studious environment totally adapted to the optimisation of learning. I zealously availed of that service every Monday to Friday evening, every Saturday and Sunday morning and during the Christmas, mid-term and Easter holidays with rigour too. Devouring books was a double effective measure of liberation. It certainly liberated me from the sufferance and the brutality of my mother's catholic judgement and it fuelled my dream of liberty from the prison of rural catholic Ireland too. Nobody understood why I studied so much, Clare, the study supervisor even passionately encouraged me to find a balance and practice other activities too, but I

believed that the Leaving Certificate Examination was the key to my homosexual freedom. Absolutely nothing had the power to deter me from my reverie of perpetual freedom. It was a civilised and cultivated world of tolerance with no catholic teaching there to enrich me with the myths of god. A sharp glance from a highly qualified teacher sufficed to rectify any rare disciplinary behavioral problems that surfaced in class and Principal Sean Logan enforced that a strict anti-bullying policy was upheld at all times. I still didn't have a coming out, but I flourished in the liberty that nobody had the right to call me "a queer fucker" and from the barren desert of despair I found the strength to believe in homosexual freedom again. I tasted the changing attitude of Ireland for the first time, but on the other extremity my mother's wrath did not pacify. The force of her brutality still hetero-sexualised me and her catholic judgement still ensnarled me in the promise of silence. Each blow continued to enrich me with the passion to conquer my homosexual dreams. I believed that there was silence before eternal freedom, ephemeral sufferance before liberty and a gay crucifixion before a homosexual resurrection.

Catholic Ireland was becoming more and more gay, but I still belonged to homosexual silence. I wanted liberation from the profound sufferance and solitude of silence, but I didn't want to taste the brutality of a catholic judgement. My holy mother still led me to believe that society hated 'queer fuckers', but after all I had heard about David Norris on RTÉ News, I began to question if her words really mirrored sincerity? A profound desire to come out corrupted my thoughts with a dream of freedom; perhaps Irish Catholics didn't believe in the myth or the wrath of god anymore and a social tolerance for homosexuals had contaminated catholic Ireland? In my search for the truth I found the bravery to disclose my homosexuality. I really thought that a glance of repulsion would glitter in her eyes, that a wrinkle of distaste would mark her forehead with aversion and that her body would stiffen in total repugnance. I anticipated that a gasp of horror would erupt from her mouth and that she would forsake me, but Rachelle Mc Sweeney didn't judge me for being "a queer fucker". Instead of crucifying me she hugged me with true sincerity and an ocean of emotion fell from my blue eyes. In the liberty of her thoughts homosexuality was not a felony against god, humanity or Ireland. There was to be no shame in loving, kissing, denuding and fucking men. I learnt there was no immorality in homosexuality and that catholic Ireland had compassion for queers. There was no cold judgement to destroy me and certainly no reversion to the dark dusty closet of silence ever again. Then, she silenced my liberty and retorted that her holy catholic mother must never know.

Was homosexual liberty really possible in a heterosexual catholic culture? Was coming out to the world a real liberation or the discovery of a different prison of judgement?

9

The Insurrection of Freedom

Was my sufferance perpetual? I abandoned the catholic judgement of my rural Irish prison in September 1994 and my dream of homosexual freedom was liberated in University College Dublin. I discovered the LGBT society by chance during Freshers Week, when I overheard some guys jeering queers. Previous to their snickering laugh I hadn't paid any particular attention to the attractive multi-coloured rainbow flag floating above the stand. I still didn't know that each colour represented the pride of the gay civilisation. The sermons had contaminated me to believe in the immorality of homosexuality, my holy catholic mother had nourished me to think that all "queer fuckers" were social outcasts, but the truth was uncurtained in the liberty of Dublin. Everything that I had known before Dublin was an absolute lie. I learnt that ten per cent of Irish Catholics were homosexual. I wasn't the only queer in Ireland and I didn't have to battle in the silence, solitude and sufferance of homosexuality alone. I had the right to be homosexual and for the first time in my life I had the sensation that I was able to breathe. I paid the two pound fee to become a member of the gay society, without realisation that the membership card in my wallet was to empower me to change my life forever. From that moment on LGBT became a huge stepping stone in my homosexual liberation. It provided a safe, respectful and friendly environment for lesbians, gays, bisexuals and transgenders along their journey of self-discovery. It encompassed the important steps of accepting one's own homosexuality and it certainly opened the door of promiscuity for me. I had survived the brutality of rural catholic Ireland and Dublin now granted me the liberty to be a queer.

The LGBT society initiated my outing to frequent Dublin's prime gay venue. "The George" had been a prominent institution in gay Irish history since January 1st 1985. It was a haven for homosexuals to socialise in without fear of prejudice, which had liberated gays long before the 1993

legalisation of homosexuality in Ireland. The doors of the gay club flung open as if longing to devour me forever. Profound terror consumed me in anticipation of the horrors that I expected to see. It was a world that I thoroughly feared because I was still a profound believer in the catholic myths of the queer scene, but without hesitation I zealously surrendered to the corruption of the gay culture. There were no screaming drag queens under the flashing disco lights, no hard core ass penetrations on the dance floor and there was nothing significantly different from any other ordinary club that I had frequented, except that the punters were pink. The catholic world had deliberately lied about the mannerisms of homosexuals. Gay men did not conform to the negative insinuation of homosexual effeminacy that was portrayed by rural Ireland and they battled in the disassociation of such flamboyancy. The queer stereotypes that condemned homosexuals were only barbaric straight minded generalisations of the gay community. Men were men, women with women, with gay couples instead of straight ones. Homosexuals were normal individuals of different profession, social class, colour and religion. The queer sons and queer daughters of catholic Ireland that danced before my eyes were ordinary human beings and I suddenly realised that the gay gene had contaminated all of holy Ireland. The liberation of my homosexuality was an amazing sensation, but there was so much about the gay world that I didn't understand yet. Step by step the gay paradise, where men fucked men without any sentiment of emotion, corrupted me. I became totally promiscuous in the smoke filled ambiance of gay clubs. I passionately kissed, romantically seduced, ravenously denuded and voraciously consumed men. I became a devoted follower of the gay religion and indeed I learnt that there was so much destruction under the pseudo appearance of homosexual love. My dream was to cultivate the eternity of love, but in despair I embraced the sufferance of love.

Social discrimination of homosexuals had led my mother to believe in the distorted grotesqueness and immorality of homosexuality. Reading the discoloured gilded pages of her aged bible and listening to the pulpit sermons had contaminated her further. In the savagery of her barbaric fury she sullied me because homosexuality was certainly a disgusting thing. Under the holy appearance of prayer was the wrath of her catholic judgement, which surfaced to destroy me again and again. It wasn't very catholic to crucify me in my hour of need, but that was the Irish sin that she always practiced. Rather than love me she loved the almighty catholic god. Far from the belief of Fraud that homosexuality was a normal outcome of natural development; my holy mother believed that it was a

dysfunction in the evolution of civilisation. I was educated that homosexuals were "queer fuckers" undeserving of god's love and rightfully banished from the kingdom of heaven. That certainly did not entice me to repent, but her threat that Irish society would forsake me if I fucked men definitely created my prison of silence. Nobody in rural Ireland was to ever know that her son was "a fucking queer" and that was enforced by her brutality. She didn't silence me in order to defend me from others' judgement, but in fear that Irish gossips would avenge her. My holy mother had the power to end the cycle of destruction and step into the light of tolerance forever, but she refused to lower her head in submission to Irish shame. She desired the eternal silence of my homosexuality, but step by step in the battle for my gay freedom I betrayed my solemn promise of silence. Rural Ireland was a hostile world of crucifixions, desolation, sufferance and tears, but Dublin was my almighty saviour.

My holy mother belonged to a relatively intolerant and highly catholic minded society. She believed in all the biblical myths of god and in the immorality of homosexuality too. Her faith in the pulpit sermons contaminated her with the banishment of homosexuals from the kingdom of heaven and her catholic prayers implored me to repent. The effeminate flamboyant stereotyping of gay men on television certainly did not enlighten her preconceived judgement of homosexuals either. In the standardised conception of homosexuality, queers were effeminated, dykes were masculinised and the broadcasted mockery of homosexuals enforced her intolerance even further. Actors accentuated gay femininity, actresses enhanced lesbian masculinity and the telecasting of the camp and butch tags that stigmatised homosexuality fuelled her brutality and enriched my sufferance more and more. The heterosexual categorisation of homosexuals portrayed "queer fuckers" to be morally degenerate and social judgement subjected homosexuals to be renowned for their promiscuous liberalism, but there was much more to the gay culture than fucking men. The catholic politics that had governed Ireland for years had cultivated her profound hate of homosexuality too. David Norris had liberated me, but she still battled to hetero-sexualise me. A sensation of true happiness liberated me under the flashing disco lights of the urban gay clubs in Dublin, but the glance of disgust that glittered in her cold blue eyes was perpetual.

Since the beginning of time everyone in rural catholic Ireland knew that I was gay. In the changing colours of the seasons they had seen my immorality surface more and more and the tears in my eyes had certainly

been silenced too. In my hour of need a discreet whisper of acceptance in my ear would have sufficed or they could have overtly waved the multi-coloured flag of gay pride in tolerance, but they condemned me to the dark dusty closet of silence instead. Their silence deluded me into believing that there was no acceptance of queers in holy Ireland. In the brutality of their silence they condemned me to the solitude of homosexuality. In the solitude of their silence I was led to believe that they judged homosexuals as "queer fuckers". Catholic Ireland was my prison, silence was my slavery and the abundance of my sufferance seemed perpetual as they pussyfooted before my holy mother in fear of her almighty wrath. Was there a difference between tolerance and real acceptance? In the silence of tolerance they always loved me, but they had lowered their eyes in total submission to my mother. In acceptance they should have battled like heroic warriors to defend my homosexuality, but they never liberated me from the brutality of her catholic judgement. Those that had the power to change my life had chosen not to grant me my dream of homosexual freedom. When I should have had a frivolous youth I wanted to be seduced by the shadows of the valley of death and in despair my homosexual blood nearly stained their hands. I was forsaken to the sufferance of silence and there was no social rebellion among my entourage to encourage my coming out. Where was the catholic compassion of god when she slaughtered me for falling in love with men? Did the catholic barbarity of Ireland readily want to punish me for fucking homosexuals? Everyone silenced that my holy mother crucified me for being "a queer fucker" and their silence enhanced my sufferance further. There was the injustice of her catholic social judgement, the injustice of her brutality to hetero-sexualise me, the injustice of her wrath to silence me, but the injustice that betrayed me the most was their silence. My solemn promise of silence defended me from the glance of abhorrence in the holy eyes of certain heterosexuals, it certainly saved me from the hostile aversion of some, but the same silence was a prison that destroyed me until my coming out in September 2010. Regret then surfaced to become contagious among those that had retrenched behind years of silence. They implored me to absolve their sin of silence, but their tears of repentance came too late.

Was the abundance of her brutality perpetual or ephemeral? There was no emotional balance between the liberty of my homosexual seductions in Dublin and the intolerance of her cold catholic judgement in rural Ireland. My life seesawed from total freedom to total oppression each time that I returned to what was no longer a loving home. The taste of her dying love for her queer son enriched me with sufferance again, but the immorality of

the urban gay clubs of Dublin always liberated me a few days later. "The George" was the core of the gay culture and a sanctuary for the drags, dykes, queens, queers and the trans of Dublin. Under the flashing disco lights the vibrant homosexuals of catholic Ireland were liberated from Irish catholic judgement, but beneath the surface of each smile was the eternal battle of the gay struggle. In the slaughter of homosexuality all gays had known some form of an Irish crucifixion. The majority were overly familiar with the homophobic barbs that belittled homosexuals. Some men had tasted the distain of gay bashing; such queers were deeply ingrained with the psychological scars caused by a heterosexual society. All homosexuals shared the common aspects of homosexual silence, solitude, sufferance and tears and knew about the complications of being in the closet and the difficulty of coming out. Other "queer fuckers" no longer belonged to the catholic world, they were not just discriminated by the holy sermons of god, but coldly disowned and banished by their pious catholic families too; that sufferance was known as an Irish catholic queer eviction. There was immense mortification in the shame of homosexuality, holy Irish mothers were enriched with the biblical strength to forsake their queer born children, but such a sin was absolved in the Sacrament of Penance and Reconciliation with god. Another category of gay men were sadly not there to give witness. The judgement of Ireland had crucified them so much that they had walked into the valley of the shadows of death. "Happy those who are persecuted in the cause of right, theirs is the kingdom of heaven"; I wanted to believe in "The Sermon on the Mount", but the pulpit violently preached about the immorality of homosexuality. There was beauty in the gay culture of harmony and love, but I heard so much sufferance from the mouths of the many men that I denuded. I learnt all about the history of their homosexuality and I began to believe that there was eternal despair in the dream of homosexual freedom.

The pink culture enriched me with a vivid insight into the sufferance which embodied Irish gay history and I learnt just how destructive catholic Ireland really was. The 1982 spate in homophobic attacks in Fairview Park in Dublin had clearly demonstrated that catholic politicians urgently needed to decriminalise homosexuality and bring solace to the gay community. Homosexuals were repressed in the almighty god's battle to hetero-sexualise the "arse fuckers, benders, fags, faggots, fairies, nancies, poofsters, queenies and sissies" that corrupted the purity of the Irish identity. The holy hostility against homosexuality provoked widespread gay bashing and as the autumn leaves began to fall that year, Declan Flynn was slaughtered to death merely because he was "a fucking queer". It was

the brutality of Tony Maher, Robert Armstrong, Colm Donovan and Pat Kavanagh that coldly executed the 31 year old Dublin homosexual as part of the purification of Ireland, but they were never punished for their breech of the Sixth Commandment of god. "Thou shalt not kill", the sacred law of god was violated, but catholic Ireland didn't want to defend homosexuality. The High Court Judge Sean Gannon clearly must have believed that the prejudiced malevolence against queers was completely normal, because the culprits walked out of court on March 8th 1983 totally scot-free. The capital punishment of homosexuals was not legalised, but apparently the Irish homosexual holocaust was overtly tolerated. Would the sentence of murder have been dismissed for the lighter charge of suspended manslaughter if the executed son in question had been Gannon's son? Would his pious catholic opinion of queers have differed if his son had been crucified for the cleansing of Ireland? The ruling caused mass outrage, Declan Flynn became a homosexual martyr, the catalyst for Ireland's fledgling gay rights movement and his death shaped a new revolution in the battle for Irish homosexual freedom.

Homosexuals now abandoned the dark dusty closet of silence in revolt. The activists of the gay rights movement invaded the streets of Dublin in a stance against the discrimination that was inflicted on the gay community. It was a major stepping stone towards the liberty to love and the right for homosexual equality. It was a revolution against all the political, religious and social injustices that dehumanised queers. Declan Flynn was paid homage and immortalised in the first Irish pride parade on March 19th 1983. It was not a demonstration of heterophobia, but a pacifistic need for homosexuals to openly put an end to all homophobia. It was not an anti-catholic movement to undermine the catholic god, but the voicing of Irish gays to have legal promiscuity like their straight counterparts. Homosexuals were heterosexual friendly, but was it only a dream that the gay and straight civilisations could live harmoniously hand in hand? In the changing colours of the seasons the ripples of the gay parade contaminated all the secluded catholic streets of rural Ireland. The rainbow of homosexuals embodied total defiance against the catholic morality, social brutality and the heterosexual politics that ruled Ireland. The swarms of hedonistic partiers heavily politicalised and radicalised the gay movement. Gays needed to defeat the injustices deeply ingrained in the catholic social structure of Ireland. Gay pride was the political statement to liberate homosexuals and to normalise homosexuality. Heterosexual public opinion debated that the flamboyancy of gay parades communicated a negative homosexual image, but the stereotype flamboyance of the gay revolution

was definitely needed for the insurrection of homosexual freedom. Declan Flynn, the founding father of the Irish Stonewall, became an almost forgotten memory in the vibrant ambiance that governed gay pride, but I believed that he had died for my homosexual freedom.

The university library was a paradise of knowledge, but I was a dreamer. The flashing disco lights of urban clubs seduced me more than lectures and I only battled through the labyrinth of books to socialise with my friend Paul Fitzgerald. I certainly didn't want condescending pity to solace me, but I needed to abandon the savagery of homosexual sufferance that destroyed me. Was it total idiocy for me to forsake the promise of silence or was there tolerance for a queer in a heterosexual catholic culture? Paul defended my homosexuality from the slaughter that crucified me and his undying friendship was my strength to survive the tearful injustice of the many social judgements that followed. Elizabeth was a devout prudish Catholic, but she did not betray me like Judas Iscariot; her soft kiss on my cheek overtly displayed her true acceptance. There was no catholic judgement and no crucifixion of a queer; her reverence to her almighty catholic god was in total harmony with the cultivated tolerance for queers that she practiced. Aoife had a tendency to immediately introduce me as being a homosexual, which rather focused on who I fucked rather than who I really was. Being "smoked out of the closet" was contrary to what I believed in, but she decided the moment of many of my coming outs. It was in that way that James discovered that I was "a queer fucker". He prayed before everyone to Jesus Christ for my redemption. He wanted me to revert to god's love and implored me to repent for deliverance from the homosexual sin. Catholic compassion was preached in his holy bible, but without a sign of remorse his spiritual judgement condemned my immortality. Irish legislation had banished god from Irish politics and liberated homosexuals, but Ireland was still heavily influenced by the catholic religion. The sermons had contaminated James with perpetual intolerance, but society had also corrupted him to believe in the myths of homosexuality too. I learnt that to cultivate homosexual freedom enhanced a certain social aversion. Coming out was a double edged sword, some Catholics defended me, but others crucified me, some liberated me, but others prayed to Jesus Christ for my repentance and my eternal salvation.

As a devout fashionista the must have accessory for Julia was a homosexual friend. A half glass of vodka extinguished the thirst that burned her lips with a desire to get heavily pissed again and her slim body

danced to Blur in her lace balconette bra and knickers before me in her feminised looking studio. Her nudity was a banal factor in my life, but such was the totally liberty cultivated between a gay man and his socially rebellious straight fag hag. I always selected from her doorless wardrobe each garment that was to embellish her with beauty and enhance her sex appeal for the nights of seduction in the straight clubs of Dublin that we frequented together. With "Girls and Boys" in the background she directed her flirtatious eyes towards mine and adorned her denuded body. The words of our song resounded in the air, filling the ambiance with a pre-taste of what was to come. Before the twenty minute walk into Temple Bar and after having poured another Smirnoff into her glass, we systematically listened to "Love me for a reason". Boyzone was too teenager for me, but the poster of Keith Duffy, Mikey Graham, Ronan Keating, Shane Lynch and Stephen Gately on the wall confirmed that it was her religion. A last look in the mirror before locking the door, wow she looked so fab. Julia was my Barbie and with the fidelity and passion of Ken I discussed fashion, make-up, pop music and men. It was even common practice that as her toy she kissed me on the dance floor under the flashing disco lights. It was her way to disregard certain men that preyed on her. Sometimes she forced me to initiate conversation on her behalf with the cute guys that she wanted to conquer. Such was the platonic complicity cultivated with a queer and his heterosexual girlfriend in promiscuous Ireland. There was no entanglement of emotions and unlike heterosexual men I didn't want to fuck her. I simply cherished her with the sensitivity that straight men didn't possess. Catholic Ireland was revolting and I was beginning to believe that my journey into homosexual tolerance had begun, but intolerance soon destroyed me again. The tides of our friendship changed when Julia fell profoundly in love. His ice blue eyes were the most amazing blue eyes that I had ever seen, his blond pointed hair enhanced his beauty further and when he evoked his smile he certainly became totally irresistible. Julia was completely engrossed in his physical appearance, but Aaron really wasn't the type that I liked to seduce. In the beginning I imagined that the green eyed monster had corrupted him to hate me, but then I learnt that some heterosexual men actually believed that all homosexual men wanted to fuck them. It enraged me that that unfounded myth was deeply engrained in him. I had no desire to denude him, but Julia's faith in his love was stronger than her love for me and the roads of our lives went in different directions. It wasn't surprising that she implored me to befriend her a few months later; she was single again, but I didn't have the emotion of forgiveness.

The Promise Of Silence

I prudently silenced the homosexual freedom of Dublin from the judgement of rural Ireland, but a fruitful parental invasion of my wallet resulted in the disclosure of my secret. I saw the familiar glance of disdain in her eyes as the gay society membership card was vigorously ripped up and it fell to the carpeted floor in a million pieces. She knew I was gay, but each time my cold hearted mother over reacted as if it was my first coming out. Perhaps such infallible proof was the creation of her eternal despair? Perhaps for the first time ever she understood that her holy prayers to the almighty catholic god could never hetero-sexualise me? It was normal to severely punish me because her dreams were perpetually destroyed; she now had the tangibility in her hand that her catholic son was "a queer fucker". The intensity of her passion to eliminate my homosexuality was always accompanied by violent scenes, but the storm that erupted that day totally outshone the wrath of all her previous destruction. I passively absorbed each physical insult that she directed at me. I wanted to feel loved, but the impact of her aggressiveness landed on me again and again. With each blow she discarded me with disgust, repulsion and vulgarity, but I didn't defend myself from the woman that I loved. I had a deep sentiment that my father didn't love me either. He had the coldness to console her tears of rage and the passion to encourage her to slaughter me more and more. The semi-naked man on the crucifix on the pale egg shell coloured wall of my bedroom engrossed my attention as my catholic father's fist collided with my face. I silently implored the compassionate god of Ireland to have pity on me, but Jesus didn't intervene to save me either. I hated my father with the same extremity that I hated the smell of the oil and grease smeared machines in his workshop and with the same repulsion that my mother hated the pungent odour of his lover's perfume impregnated in his clothes. He, who betrayed Seventh Commandment, was sanctimonious enough to cast judgement on me, but in the silence of my thoughts I believed that he was the sinner not I.

The hands that my mother held in a tight embrace in prayer to her catholic god were the same hands that destroyed me without displaying a tinge of holy compassion. Her biblical reverence was forsaken for destruction and in profound rage she screamed that she should have miscarried or aborted me. On the surface was her holy appearance, but she was never clement in her judgement of queers and certainly never indulgent in my crucifixions. I was "a queer fucker" banished by the catholic sermons from the kingdom of heaven and condemned to the everlasting injustice of her brutality. I battled to explain that there was homosexual liberty in the tolerant culture of Dublin, but my freedom was totally dismissed and her hand collided

with my face to silence me again. I displayed no emotional reaction, no tears fell to moisten my cheeks; the years of her gay bashing had strengthened me to survive without expressing my emotional feelings. She knew that my love for her was dying in the resent that glittered in my eyes, but she portrayed absolutely no regret. She implored the almighty god to hetero-sexualise me, but I had no repentance. The brutality of her prayers was not efficacious in the destruction of my homosexuality and I certainly did not abandon my passion for denuded men. I justified that I was "made in the image and likeness of god", but she denied that her catholic saviour had created my homosexuality. I retorted that if her holy prayers were silenced by god, that it was the tangible proof that the bible was a myth. My blasphemy silenced her for a few seconds, but she erupted with even more fury after that. The duration of her homophobic binge seemed to last for an eternity in my head, but in reality it must have been only a few short minutes. Everything that her hands had touched now littered the carpeted bedroom floor. The debris and ruins had defeated her queer son again, but the semi-naked man on the crucifix was not longer suspended on the pale egg shell coloured wall. In the midst of her wrath she had even decapitated Jesus Christ. A million tears fell from her blue eyes in regret that the son of god was beheaded. Perhaps her tears to god should have been tears of sincerity to implore me for forgiveness instead? An insolent smile of revenge must have betrayed me, because there was one last potent punch to punish me for my irreverence to his catholic god. The brutality of rural catholic Ireland totally slaughtered my dream of homosexual freedom that day and in despair I didn't know if I had the force to survive in the ashes of sufferance again.

What emotional limit of sufferance was required to force gays to become statistics in the high rate of Irish homosexual suicide? That lonely day I pondered a long time about death. I ruminated on where to find a robust enough rope in order to tighten a noose around my neck. I knew there was one somewhere in my father's workshop; it was just a question of rooting around to find it. I hated the smell of the industrial machines, but strangely it didn't disturb me much that day. It seemed even pleasant because I knew that it was for the last time. Without a great need to search I found exactly what I was looking for and its length corresponded to what I needed. The rope was heavily stained with oil and grease, which soiled my hand, but that didn't matter either. Death seemed so attractive and so seductive that nothing mattered anymore. In the barren desert of despair I needed to put an end to my sufferance and walk bravely into the valley of the shadows of death. I deliberated that my lifeless body was to be found hanging from the

century aged sycamore tree at the end of the garden. What were the last thoughts of homosexuals before suicide? Mine were mechanical as if I had become totally immune to all human feelings. I was even curious to know if suicide really provoked angel lust. If hanging dead with an erection was the only way to abandon the shame, silence, solitude and sufferance of homosexuality I definitely wanted to die. The rope was in my hand and I stood directly under the tree ready to embrace death. I had promised Morgan to liberate my revenge on the catholic world that had destroyed him, but now I wanted to suffer the same homosexual death as him. I implored him to forgive me and an ocean of tears fell from my eyes. Then, I heard the gleeful sound of seven year old Nicola and her nine year old sister Karen playing in their garden next door. My grip suddenly loosened, the rope fell from my right hand and it landed on the ground next to my bare feet. My near tragedy was the fruit of the injustice of catholic judgement. Death had almost seduced me before the almighty liberation of my homosexual freedom, but my dream resurrected from the ashes of my sufferance just in time. How many "queer fuckers" had Ireland slaughtered and perpetually silenced? How many "arse fuckers" had been crucified by the intolerance of the catholic god? Were their names engraved on the tombstones of cold cemeteries in Ireland forever in vain?

In the weeks that followed I totally succumbed to despair and my faith in all my dreams completely faded and withered away. In the months that followed I didn't have the emotional strength or the physical energy to battle anymore. There were some days when I didn't even leave the bed. It was the abundance of years of sufferance which had led to the sensation of depression that now enriched me and in my hour of need all the good Catholics of Ireland still had the serenity to silence my tears. Even before her mouth opened, my mother's eyes had created an eternal judgement. The middle aged woman certainly didn't glitter in gold and diamonds and as she neared my catholic mother remarked that her shabby looking appearance mirrored severe poverty. The stranger took possession of the empty seat opposite me and I saw that she had a lovely friendly smile. The train to Dublin hadn't even entered the 1,355 yard tunnel out of Cork Kent Station yet, but my mother did her utmost to ignore her. Judging by the singsong drawl of her accent Eileen was certainly a Norrie; my judgemental mother referred to that as the lowest stratum of underclass of urban Cork, but she had clearly forgotten that she was born and reared in Cork North-side too. "Miss Daly saved you from the contamination of such a common accent", I just prayed that the background noise of the train had silenced that comment from the ears of Eileen and from everyone else. In

the beginning of the three hour journey my mother yawned and closed her eyes to give the impression that she needed to sleep, then she turned her head away longing to be distracted by the green fields that flashed by, but poor Eileen really didn't notice such arrogance and continued to narrate her life. It didn't seem to bother her much that my mother wasn't an active listener. Perhaps the legend of Blarney Castle was not a myth? Perhaps she had kissed the famous stone to be endowed with the gift of the gab? On the Dublin platform Eileen waved goodbye, but I saw my mother turn her head away again. Father O' Brien outstretched his hands in acceptance of her almsgiving, she genuflected with reverence before the altar at weekly mass, but she forgot to abide by the compassion of god that was preached by the pulpit sermons. I believed that there was more to being a good Catholic than turning the discoloured gilded pages of her holy bible in prayer.

"I'm not getting on the same fucking bus as her" coldly declared my mother and she stormed off with the intention to walk from Houston Station to Grafton Street. She must have seen Eileen standing in line in the distant queue, but she certainly hadn't calculated that at a moderate pace it was at least a 35 minute walking distance. As we neared Christ Church Cathedral she hailed a taxi, but with the rush hour traffic jams she moaned that it had cost her a small fortune. She was now liberated on the streets of Dublin and a glorious day of shopping began. She completely forgot that I was 'a queer fucker". Her homosexual son knew all about the harmony of colour coordination of clothes and mastered the art of matching handbags and shoes, but she liked that. She looked so blissful each time that a shop assistant handed her another garment or accessory filled bag, but I knew that the serenity of such happiness in her eyes was ephemeral. That night we shared a double bed in the luxury of "The Gresham", that was another thing that she never did with my heterosexual brother. I wanted her to taste the horizon of tolerance of the gay culture under the flashing disco lights in "The George", but a glance of horror in her blue eyes immediately silenced that. I retorted that there was homosexual liberty in Dublin, but everyone in the lobby saw her hand collide with my face and her brutality had the victory to silence me again. I was devoured by a sensation of stress the next morning, but my mother was confident that my exam results would outshine everyone else's. The 30 minute trip on the number ten bus to Belfield seemed to last an eternity and on arriving at UCD I saw some students crying. According to my cold hearted mother they needed to control their emotions. Others smiled as we neared the notice board, perhaps it surprised them to see a guy of my age accompanied by his

mother. Her blue eyes passionately roamed the list, her finger stopped under student number 94343373 and she read it again in total disbelief. 1st Class Honours in Greek and Roman Civilisation and amazingly I didn't speak a word of German, but I had a 2nd Class Honours Grade 2 in that. Her enragement then resurrected; I had certainly spent too much time in the urban gay clubs of Dublin and I absolutely didn't master the language of Molière.

Professor Pascale McGowen was in the French Department that day. With a Parisian accent vibrating in her voice she disclosed that I knew nothing about the subjunctive grammatical mood. I accepted such criticism with grace, but the judgement that followed was politically incorrect. "A dreamer can always dream, but an Irish dreamer like you, will only dream in the language of William Shakespeare forever". I desired to dream in the language of Molière too, but she totally fueled that reverie with despair. It enraged me; I now wanted to have homosexual revenge on the catholic god of Ireland and certainly vengeance on that condescending bitch too. From Belfield to Heuston Station my mother didn't even look at me. From Dublin to Cork Kent Station she didn't utter a single word and to punish me further she cultivated such silence until the next morning. Before my eyes on the breakfast table was a plate with two rashers, two sausages, slices of black and white puddings, generous servings of scrambled egg, an abundance of baked beans and fried mushrooms too. She poured me a strong cup of Lyons tea and even buttered my toast. Perhaps such a delicious Full Irish Breakfast and her delicate attentions towards me reflected her regret of her previous coldness? After I had literally licked my plate clean, she informed me that she had pondered much and slept little that night. She then enlightened me that it would be an honour for my father to train me to work with him. I retorted that I hated him and that the oil and grease smeared machines in his workshop totally repulsed me. Two roads diverged to determine the ultimate direction of my life. The first was a road of brutality; it wanted to imprison me forever in rural catholic Ireland and in the profound intolerance that glittered in my mother's cold blue eyes. The other was a road of revenge that punished her by liberating my homosexuality perpetually. I had danced under the flashing disco lights and tasted the promiscuity of the gay culture in Dublin; it was certain that I didn't want to live in the prison of her catholic home ever again. From that moment onwards I needed to battle heroically for my dream of freedom.

I didn't believe in religion, but I prayed to god and I even splashed out to light a fifty pence candle in Saint Joseph's Church in total desperation. In the belief that the catholic god deemed me unworthy of the kingdom of heaven, I was probably condemned to the burning fires of rural Ireland instead. If homosexuals were silenced by the almighty god, I certainly needed to find a more miraculous solution than catholic prayer. I don't remember if there was an abundance of sunshine in summer 1995, but sunbathing in my garden didn't matter much to me that year. All the waking hours of each day focused on being victorious in the September repeat exams and with zeal my bedroom became a prison for two long months. I cultivated my garden of knowledge with French theatre, literature and cultural civilisation. From the light of dawn to the stars of dusk I absorbed Balzac, Baudelaire, Flaubert, Molière, Rimbaud, Stendhal and Voltaire. I memorised all the complexity of French grammar by rote and I particularly rebelled to master the famous subjunctive. I enriched my vocabulary to develop my language communication skills and did all that was humanly possible to optimise my chance of success. Victory was not just a question of the direction of my career, but more significantly it determined the road of my homosexual freedom too. As the colourful leaves of autumn began to arrive on the trees, I survived what seemed to be an insurmountable mountain. During each of the five two hour written exams I reproduced all that I had learnt and I even felt rather confident afterwards. By misfortune my oral exam was with Professor Pascale McGowen; the sternness of her emotionless face penetrated the office with a cold ambiance when she saw me enter. I politely shook hands with her before sitting down, perhaps it would have been more of a French touch if I had kissed her, after all she had grown up in that distinctive cheek kissing culture. It seemed to surprise her that I regurgitated the subjunctive grammatical mood without difficulty, but it was profoundly engraved in my memory.

Two weeks later the train emerged from the Cork Kent Station tunnel and on hearing the singsong drawl of a familiar sounding voice in the background I turned my head in its direction. Eileen smiled at me and on seeing that I was alone waved me over to the empty seat next to her. It surprised me that she spoke kindly of my mother, who certainly hadn't been very sympathetic towards her. Eileen wasn't a churchgoer, but in my humble judgement she was more of a good Catholic than my holy mother. "Your mam waz beautiful lookin wit al er jewellery". I retorted that she loved other women to extol her beauty and genuflect before it. There was no reaction or reply, which led me to believe that Eileen didn't really

understand the art of sarcasm. It was true that I had one of those faces that encouraged strangers to confide overtly in me. I learnt that her husband, "that fuckin' bastard" as she rightfully related to him, had blackened and blued her face a million times. He had destroyed her for twenty long years, but one day she just packed a suitcase and abandoned the abundance of his blows. She now tasted poverty and not his affluence, but in poverty she tasted freedom too. "Men're fuckin scumbags, I'll never touch another one in me life boy", but all I wanted to do was denude another promiscuous man. Listening to her problems certainly made me forget about all my problems and I almost laughed and cried at the same time too. The hefty price of the train ticket was a battle for her to find, she certainly struggled in the prison of a hand to mouth existence, but come hell or high water she never missed the three hour journey to Cork each month. She couldn't do more than that, but her siblings in Farrenree had only a few kilometers to drive to the retirement home, which reassured her that 'me mams grand". The Iarnród Éireann food and beverage trolley arrived, "£2.50 for a fuckin cup of hot water and a fuckin tea bag, you'd need to be shittin money in this country to survive". I removed the neatly folded twenty pound note that my father had given me for lunch and I bought her a cup of tea and a pack of two custard cream biscuits. "You must be fuckin loaded boy", she was the natural spontaneous type of woman that voiced the first thing that came into her head. By the time we arrived I knew everything about her personal problems. On the other hand, I had disclosed nothing about my life. I certainly didn't come out of the dark dusty closet on a rural train in catholic Ireland. It was nice that she hugged me and patted my back on the platform in Dublin Heuston Station. She sincerely thanked me again for "the cuppa" and with a final wave goodbye she disappeared forever into the horizon. My finger abruptly stopped under student number 94343373 on the notice board in UCD. I verified with a pen that the alignment of the number that I had just read really corresponded to the positive result parallel. An abundance of tears fell from my eyes; I had the sensation that I could breathe again for the first time in months.

My mother and father continued to hetero-sexualise me during my short visits from Dublin to their holy home, so I went there less and less. It was certain that they didn't want to know that I was a flamboyant homosexual, so I silenced that I seduced, kissed, denuded and fucked men. I was silenced in the dark dusty closet in rural Ireland, but rather than liberate their brutality I didn't rebel. Silence deluded them into believing in my repentance to the almighty catholic god and their dream of my hetero-sexualisation bedazzled them more and more, but when my mother was

enraged I became her "fucking queer son" again. I did not parade my homosexuality in rural catholic Ireland because their generosity housed, fed, clothed and educated me. Their money certainly silenced me too, but it also enabled me to afford to socialise in the urban gay clubs of Dublin. Perhaps my prostitution to silence betrayed all the homosexuals that battled for queer freedom, but I certainly wasn't going to abandon my dreams to become an Irish gay militant. I believed that to live in the solitude of silence before my homosexual freedom was like trifling with a pen in an ephemeral fashion. I needed to taste more sufferance before my voyage into the horizon of eternal tolerance began.

10

The Beautification of Passion

In the distance of the smoke filled night club our eyes met. I beheld him as he danced in harmony to Abba and the flashing disco lights enhanced his beauty as he danced closer and closer in my direction. He was totally straight looking in his virile appearance, which enticed the attraction that glittered in my blue eyes further. His unbroken glance intensified his sensual look, seduction enlightened his face with lust and I was completely besotted by his charming smile. I wanted him to corrupt me with homosexuality and judging by his flaunting with me on the dance floor he certainly wanted to liberate his erection too. In the silence of my thoughts I desired to be deflowered in his bed that night, but I didn't know much about the prevailing manners of allurement. For homosexuals eye contact was the key to seduce and conquer men. I also learnt that queers had the liberty to consume lovers in abundance and that emotional feelings were not needed to practice the art of casual sex. Men were flirtatious products in the pink market of ephemeral love, but did I really want to belong to the immortality of such a sinful culture? He gulped his pint as if he was dying of thirst and his empty glass seemed to lament as if in desperate need of some more Irishness. I discerned a presence behind me; I wanted it to be him, but perhaps I was the prey of another man? Indeed it was him; the mirror behind the bar reflected his virility. In response to a sign I made, Bridie the lovely barman poured me a Guinness; not that I appreciated the taste of the legendary drink of real Irish men, but because I wanted to seduce a Guinness drinker. I handed him the creamy headed pint, which had just settled. It was at that precise moment that I was able to distinguish the dark brown colour of his eyes, which in the obscurity of the dim lit club seemed to be almost black. Looking into the desire in those glorious eyes I knew that I was going to be promiscuous for the first time.

I am unable to recollect any details of his life. Perhaps the loud music deafened me to his words or was I too besotted by the erection that shaped his jeans to attentively listen? Perhaps I simply didn't care about the things that had created him; after all did I really have to know what his favourite colour was in order to fuck him? In the gay world the only factor that we needed to have in common for a transient sexual adventure was passion. It didn't matter if I didn't fall in love with him because our lives had only crossed for the duration of a one night stand. There was no righteous god in the homosexual culture and certainly no forbearance to denude an abundance of men. Every queer in "The George" had the freedom to be licentious without holy judgement of their ejaculations. In recreational promiscuity the homosexuals of catholic Ireland fucked a web of interchangeable lovers. In the volatility of homosexual love ephemeral lovers were discarded with the used condoms. Homosexuals were certainly renowned for fucking a multitude of different sexual partners, but was such behaviour more prevalent among gays or was it also inherent among heterosexuals? Did the ripples of homosexual promiscuity contaminate the catholic heterosexuals of holy Ireland in the same fashion? Some heterosexuals believed that homosexuality destroyed the catholic values that had enriched Ireland for centuries, but others revolted against the rigors of religion and practiced the same licentiousness as queers. Indeed both homosexuality and heterosexuality reflected the trends of a consumption society. The catholic social structure believed in the eternal silence of immorality, but the pink culture believed in its liberty. The intolerance of the pulpit sermons condemned homosexuals, but those Catholics that ardently judged certainly tasted promiscuity too. "He, who is without sin among you, let him be the first to throw a stone" Jesus Christ had more compassion than the many holy heterosexuals that had forgotten to live by the words of the bible.

I thought that his beautiful face was to be engraved in me forever, but ageing in the changing colours of many seasons must have betrayed me. Due to the natural erosion of my memory I have completely forgotten all his physical traits or was it because on the road of my homosexuality I liberated my erections with too many promiscuous men? It was a short walk to his apartment to a district that I didn't know. The streets of Dublin were enchanted by the behaviours that typified any Irish city on a normal Saturday night. There was the familiar sight of binge drinkers regurgitating and the beautiful taste of romance in the air between lovers that had just met. Some heterosexuals feared not finding a taxi after the pub closing rush, others devoured a greasy burger to sober up and it was totally banal

in holy Ireland to see pissed catholic guys urinate in the middle of the pavement. There was a sensation of total security walking among the neon lights of O' Connelly Street, but was there a queer basher lurking around South Great George's Street desiring to cleanse Ireland of homosexual immorality? That was my fear, not the violent mugger two minutes away in Exchequer Street that had made breaking news on the front page of "The Irish Times". The passion of his kisses aroused me, but my eyes were more attracted to the disarray of unironed clothes, which abundantly decorated a Voltaire lounge chair in a corner. His jeans fell to the carpeted floor to enhance the slovenly state of his bedroom further, but I hesitated to denude before him. He lowered the blinds to conceal our intimacy and the four heavily stained coffee mugs on the window still disappeared from my view. Richard unbuttoned my shirt and then his flabbergasted smile discovered my white cotton underpants. Perhaps I should have worn something sexier, but I hadn't really planned on getting naked that night. Lying on his bed I touched his penis and moved it up and down in a slow erotic movement. My tongue, lips and mouth stimulated it for a few minutes more. "Spit or swallow"? I didn't care where the fucking sperm landed, but tasting that cloudy viscous liquid certainly wasn't my cup of tea. He moaned in pleasure and baptised his body instead. A few seconds later I ejaculated on him too; I now belonged to the promiscuous practices of the gay culture.

Some cold water revived my face the next morning, judging by the pale appearance that the stained mirror in his bathroom reflected I had certainly fucked too much. A squirt of gel moistened my fingers, which then ran through my blond hair and I generously sprayed his cheap deodorant to reduce the pungent smell of smoke that the night club had impregnated in my clothes. In the light of a new day I noticed that the general disorder in his flat was everywhere. The clothes that littered the floor were not only the clothes that had denuded him during our passion and what seemed to be a historical layer of dust decorated the furniture in each room that I visited. Richard, with his eyes half-closed, sipped on a coffee and lit a cigarette. A cloud distended above his head as he savoured his Marlboro with pleasure. We had kissed, denuded and fucked with a feigning passion, but in promiscuity no sentiment of love flourished. I believed that a last kiss wasn't really even needed, but he did kiss me adieu. Then, the roads of our lives diverged and I abandoned him forever. I walked at a brisk pace longing to devour an Irish breakfast alone in an unpretentious café that I liked in Talbot Street. I admired the architecture of the Four Courts, which towered over Inns Quay. I revered the Ha'penny Bridge, which ornately

decorated the river Liffey. I saluted the statue of Daniel O' Connell, pondering was it visible to everyone that I had changed? I now believed in the voyage of promiscuity and dancing every night under the flashing disco lights of the urban gay clubs in Dublin with gay hedonists further enriched me with the techniques of homosexual seduction. I passionately denuded an abundance of interchangeable lovers, but was fucking so many men a real liberation or was there too much freedom in the liberty of the homosexual culture? There was beauty in falling in love, brutality in the liberation of ephemeral love, despair in the dream of eternal love and the promiscuity of homosexuality certainly nourished me with the sufferance of love too.

The homosexual dream for all queers was to live in white-picket fenced suburban homes of perpetual love, but the homosexual culture practiced promiscuity. What was forbidden by the catholic god enticed, what was silenced by heterosexual society allured and homosexuals learnt to flourish from flower to flower. It was practical to consume an abundance of denuded lovers and the liberty of promiscuity certain seduced and enriched me. I loved Patrick for the duration of two beautiful seasons. Spring flowers bloomed in my eyes and summer sunshine glittered in my smile when he kissed me, but before the changing colours of autumn arrived I was alone again. I was besotted by my desire to be in love, but indeed infatuation had deluded my emotions into believing in his perpetual love. I wanted to love him forever, but the eternity of that love was an ephemeral dream. Ripples of the American social culture had popularised the recreational aspect of drugs in Ireland. The Dublin accented dealers in Merchant's Arch allured hedonists to party into the ensnarement of consumption. Ecstasy and cocaine ravaged under the flashing disco lights of the gay clubs that I frequented, but the mechanics of such euphoria definitely revolted me with a sensation of abhorrence. I certainly wasn't catholic anymore, but I did have a holy judgement. In the beginning Patrick silenced what I didn't see, but a certain bloodshot constricted look in his eyes every weekend aroused my suspicions. He deluded me into believing that he was overly tired from his work, but as our love flourished the telltale signs of his faith in drugs began to surface more. His hyper-active bouts of energy turned into a type of lethargy mixed with an overbearing sensation of paranoia, but it was only after another Saturday night nosebleed on the dance floor that I understood that he had snorted in the toilets again. Under the flashing disco lights I disclosed that I couldn't love a man that practiced the immorality of a pleasure that I didn't believe in. He retorted that I needed to love him the way he was, but the kisses that

I wanted to last forever suddenly faded away. I didn't want to survive in the perpetual solitude of homosexuality, but perhaps the brutality of my mother's holy judgement was right? Homosexuality was forbidden by the almighty catholic god, perhaps "queer fuckers" didn't have the liberty to love for eternity? In the coldness of my repulsion I abandoned Patrick, but falling out of love with him was a more difficult technique to master than I had ever imagined. I mourned in despair as I tasted the sufferance of love for the first time. He implored me with tears in his eyes a few days later. I still profoundly loved him, perhaps there was something to salvage if he changed as promised? "Fuck off", it was with such vulgarity that I silenced my emotions. I preferred to forsake him and in revenge I liberated my journey into promiscuity again.

In the homosexual culture there was the sublime leather sub-culture that Alexander passionately belonged to. I was contaminated by that virile beauty from the very first moment that I saw him. He was the most masculine creature that I had I ever seen under the flashing disco lights; even if his porno star style mustache enhanced a certain touch of gayness to his appearance. He bestowed an affable smile that sensualised his seduction, but the leather that clothed his muscular body most certainly enhanced my physical attraction to him further. The mere thought of kissing such a gorgeous man completely aroused me and the lust that glittered in my eyes reflected in his blue eyes too. We kissed erotically on the dance floor; I had never kissed a man with so much passion before. The erection that bulged in my pants completely betrayed me and he understood that I wanted to fuck him. Alexander believed that all desires needed to be brought to full fruition and I believed in such enrichment too, so my homosexual journey into promiscuity continued in his home in Howth Road that night. Judging by the opulent appearance of everything he certainly had affluence and the intellectual books that heavily decorated his bookcases reflected that he had a vast culture of literature too. He was a true connoisseur of whiskey, who disclosed that the tulip shaped design of the Waterford crystal glass, concentrated the charismatic fragrance to the nose and optimised the tasting experience to deliver the full-bodied aroma sensations to the palate. I had absorbed Balzac, Baudelaire, Flaubert, Molière, Rimbaud, Stendhal and Voltaire, but I was a philistine concerning the Irish whiskey culture. He retorted that we both needed a stiff drink before the liberation of our immorality and even though I never consumed such spirits I was completely seduced by his passionate discourse. I cultivated my taste buds with the spicy sensation of Jameson 12 without a second thought that it was probably going to elate me very quickly. A few

short minutes later I even willingly savoured a second double whiskey and the euphoric effect of alcohol was almost instantaneous after that.

In homosexuality there was tolerance of all immorality. Alexander enticed me to liberate my silenced fantasy and have a deep insight into his passions. The thought of being clothed from head to foot in his black leathers completely allured me and I zealously denuded except for my socks. His skimpy studded leather G string imprisoned my penis and enhanced the shape of my erection. Then, he buttoned up a leather shirt on me with a lustful smile glittering in his eyes. One of his numerous leather pants masculinised me further and the strong smell of a military style leather jacket incrusted my body with a deep feeling of sensuality. High length motorbike boots, a leather police cap and sleek leather gloves beautified me with even more virility again. I felt so fucking horny in his leather that I almost immediately ejaculated. The cigar connoisseur opened his humidor, each differently sized cigar was named, Belicos, Churchill, Corona, Magnum, Rousto and Toro, but the only cigar I had ever heard of was "Happiness is a cigar called Hamlet". He laughed when I explained that such a television advert had introduced me to Bach. With a couple of long firm puffs a Havana cigar glowed uniformly and a cloud of smoke distended above his head. Alexander wasn't pretentious in appearance, a little snobbish on the surface perhaps, but he assumed in full that he belonged to an affluent world of certain luxury. The prestigious product, from the James Fox Dublin Store, was directed with encouragement towards my mouth. I had never smoked a cigar before, but the alluring temptation of such masculinity lured me into total corruption. The virile feeling of his leather glove caressing my lips with such enticement utterly subdued my little resistance. I smoked a few puffs partially to satisfy his high level of zeal, but mostly to yield to my sudden need to liberate my forbidden desires in full. Perhaps my alcoholised state was the major factor which made me long for the same gratification as him, but I found a certain pleasure in it too. Another match was struck, with a couple of short firm puffs a Havana glowed uniformly and a cloud of smoke distended above my head too. I deeply inhaled to particularly like the immediate calming effect, despite the sensation that it was extremely pungent in taste. The virility of Alexander corrupted me with a sensation of freedom that I had never felt before. I was seduced by the masculinity of the cigars, the euphoria of alcohol and the sensuality of leather on leather as we fucked. In the definition of fantasy there was a certain mystery not to unriddle, but was the real enactment of silenced thoughts more satisfying than the intangibility of erotic dreams? There was definitely a strong enriching

potent stimulus in the entangled web of non-conventional sex. I now thoroughly believed in the importance of the non-judgemental liberation of all silenced sexual desires and I had the confirmation that all fantasies needed to be fulfilled to fruition.

We fucked in abundance in the weeks that followed. It was meant to be just an ephemeral journey of sexual pleasure, but needless to say, while feigning the emotion of love, affection certainly began to flourish. It was a reputed common practice that homosexuals consumed poppers to increase arousal during the fucking process. The undesired side effects were headaches, nausea, dizziness and for some men an erectile dysfunction, but physiologically it clearly assisted gay men by completely relaxing the sphincter muscle during penetration. I had already lucidly identified a direct dependency on poppers and intimacy in the homosexual culture, so it didn't surprise me much that Alexander was relatively dependant on the instantaneous aphrodisiac sensations evoked by the nitrate based liquid. The sudden surge of blood to the brain accelerated his heart beat, decreased his inhibitions and greatly contributed to his immense pleasure during anal sex. There was a strong disaccord between my righteous beliefs and my lenience concerning his indulgence in poppers. He had totally fallen into its corruption, but despite my intolerance I strangely condoned his compulsion. For a certain population of the gay community it had even become impossible to fuck without it and Alexander sometimes gave me the impression that I was having sex with a bottle of poppers and not with a man. He justified that it intensified all the physical and emotional sensations of sex, which gave credence to the claim that poppers enhanced homoeroticism. I had the perspicacity to understand that it was truly very efficient in making him more aroused. It was a harmonious balance, I accepted when he desired or needed it and he respected that I never consumed it. Alexander betrayed me and disclosed "I profoundly love you". It was typical practice for queers to be deluded by love, but that was the common emotion of homosexual infatuation and not the sincerity of love. He was contaminated by a sensational sentiment of love and desired to conquer my cold emotions with the same zeal, but there was sufferance in that dream. Everything about him seduced me, I denuded him with lust and fucked him with passion, but for some reason there was no liberation of my eternal affection. I certainly felt an abundance of physical attraction, but I wanted to taste the liberty of promiscuity that governed the homosexual culture. I sincerely wanted to be a promiscuous homosexual again. I certainly dreamed of a white-picket fenced suburban queer home of perpetual love too, but in the belief that Alexander wasn't the man that I

wanted in my dream the road of our lives diverged in different directions. I returned to the emotional destitute of one night stands again, but in the changing colours of the seasons my true love for him resurrected.

All the colourful people I encountered under the flashing disco lights had tasted the brutality of catholic Ireland to some degree. The promiscuous men that I kissed had all known some form of an Irish homosexual crucifixion. Indeed it was common practice to silence queers in the dark dusty closet of silence and my lovers knew about that social solitude too. There was so much desolation in homosexuality, "arse fucker, bender, fag, faggot, fairy, nancy, poofster, queenie, queer and sissy", such barbaric barbs had transcended from catholic generation to generation to enrich the homosexual culture with tears. What holy catholic heterosexuals believed was immoral, catholic homosexuals believed was love and there was certainly more to the gay culture than fucking men. I heard so much sufferance from the mouths of the many lovers that I denuded, but they also gave me the strength to survive. Their personal experience testified that I would rise from the ashes of destruction, but if I wanted to be liberated from the prison of silence I needed to accept the inevitability that there was immense sufferance too. They believed in the resurrection of the homosexual dream of freedom. They made me a solemn promise that my life would get better in the changing colours of the seasons and in the desert of despair I found a vision of hope. The homosexual rebellion began, but righteous Catholics heavily criticised the political movement for homosexual rights. Indeed gays needed to battle against the righteous god of Ireland for their freedom. If I had seduced and fucked so many interchangeable lovers, it certainly wasn't to return to the love of her almighty god in repentance afterwards, but my mother still didn't believe in the homosexual liberation. The holy sermons banished queers from the kingdom of heaven and she destroyed me more and more. Her catholic judgement crucified me, but did the social tolerance of brutality make homosexual sufferance more acceptable? Turning the discoloured gilded pages of her aged bible completely deluded her into believing that all Irish Catholics needed to practice homosexual rancour. Homosexuality was forbidden; the catholic god of Ireland was the enemy that slaughtered gays and her love for religion justified my punishments. Perhaps tolerance would flourish if heterosexuals had a real voyage into homosexual sufferance? Perhaps the destruction of the catholic faith was needed to make Ireland more liberal in thought? In the social revolution for homosexual freedom Ireland changed, but did equality surface in a tide of political correctness or did heterosexuals really become civilised?

There was great vulnerability in the moment of every coming out, a foreboding feeling of crucifixion and the incertitude of whether humanity was going to slaughter me with disdain or not. Disclosing my homosexuality liberated me, but equally exposed me to a perpetual socio-cultural brutality towards queers. Sometimes there was intolerance, sometimes there was clemency, but there was mostly the glance of catholic judgement to destroy me. Homosexual prejudice was deeply ingrained in the Irish heterosexual culture. It seemed more normal for the good Catholics of Ireland to display hate rather than social acceptance of queers, but wasn't the bible supposed to be renowned for the teachings of goodwill and compassion? Some felt impelled to be overly polite, but as they lowered their eyes to the ground their abhorrence became visible. Their condescending tolerance was decorated with an abundance of insincerity, which systematically led to their treachery. It was clear in the awkwardness of their political correctness that my homosexuality was problematic, but they respectfully didn't practice the act of queer bashing overtly. For them an important value of life was courtesy, they certainly didn't believe in homosexual rights, but they thought that even queers deserved humane treatment. It was a kind of mutual agreement that such straights never slaughtered gays and in the balance of such peace they didn't befriend them either. In a quest for open-mindedness other heterosexuals made inhuman effort to create platonic friendships with queers, but their silenced homophobia always surfaced too. Total transparency was better that befriending a foe; it was easier to accept frank opinions rather than suffer later in betrayal. Others, like my catholic mother, were so holy and feared gays so much that it was even forbidden to utter the word homosexual in their presence. I thought that such behaviour was highly ignorant because everyone knew that heterosexuals were immune to verbally transmitted homosexual contamination. The gay disease was only contagious if a queer sneezed on a straight. They referred to the gay community indirectly without using any precise term that related to homosexuality. It was common practice for them to categorise gays as "those kind of people", which dehumanised me more than if someone had directly called me "an arse fucker, a bender, fag, faggot, fairy, nancy, poofster, queenie, queer and sissy" or even worse. I believed that sufferance was actually less acute when homophobia was blunt and direct. Other straights were more genuine in their disparagement of homosexuals. In their forthrightness I immediately knew that I was "a fucking queer", but perhaps I respected them more for that?

I began to understand how to detect false tolerance in the immediate seconds after my coming out. A close analytical regard of all emotional reflexes revealed the real judgement that dwelled deeply under the surface of appearance. It wasn't difficult to determine that non-acceptance was apparent behind a sharp smile, but it required deeper observation skills to clearly identify the more discreet indicators of hostility. Many heterosexuals politely repressed their antipathy, but they were unable to conceal the natural repulsion that glittered in their eyes. I distinguished the minuscule wrinkle of distaste that marked their foreheads in disapproval of my immorality. I pinpointed that nervous twitch as their body stiffened in repugnance. I identified in a second the subtle gasp of horror that betrayed their silenced aversion. A subtle touch of indignation suddenly dominated their voices to signify that their opinion of me had changed forever. Was it possible to affirm that such natural signs were never there before my coming out; perhaps I unjustly suspected some straights of being homophobic when they were not? Perhaps homosexuality had enhanced my paranoia or was I really becoming heterophobic? Had experiences in life enriched me to correctly master the art of heterosexual body language interpretation? The atrocity of being judged was part of the brutality of belonging to the gay culture, but did humanity need to condemn me because I passionately ejaculated with men? In the puritanical civilisation of Ireland queers were oppressed in the prison of righteous and moral catholic judgement, but heterosexuals did not justify their promiscuity. In the social discrimination against gays I became a survivor. In the tenacity of judgement queers became warriors for homosexual liberty. Destruction was certainly the strongest of human emotions, but Ireland was also changing in the battle for homosexual equality.

Was there solace for homosexuals in Ireland? I liberated my homosexuality to be devoured by the wrathful savagery of god's judgement and holy Catholics crucified me for years. They certainly did not enrich me to revert to the grace of god's love, but nourished me to hate their religion more and more instead. I didn't abandon the homosexual culture in repentance for my immorality and seek their absolution. I didn't believe in the almighty catholic god that governed Ireland, so I certainly didn't need to justify why I promiscuously fucked men. I sincerely believed that homosexuality enhanced my ethical principles with more goodness than the pulpit sermons. I didn't need to be churchgoer in order to practice the compassion that was preached by Jesus Christ. There was sincerely more virtue in the homosexual culture than in the heterosexual bible. The gay revolution was not a movement to undermine the morality of the Catholic Church or a

precursor in the creation of heterophobia, but the dream that all heterosexuals and homosexuals could live hand in hand in eternal freedom, peace and harmony. There was so much rancour in the catholic eyes that judged me, but the more I tasted homophobia the more I became immune to sufferance. The over-righteousness of some destroyed me, but there was earthly kindness in the clemency of others. In the balance of justice homosexuality was not condemned with abhorrence by all Irish Catholics. In the beauty of certain judgements I was even seen as the creation of god. Some heterosexuals prayed with reverence and befriended queers waving their straight ally flag in the belief that there was nothing intrinsically immoral about homosexuality. They had the same profound faith in the almighty catholic god as my oppressors, but in the liberty of their thoughts being gay was not a felony against god, humanity or Ireland. Some heterosexuals crucified me with so much disdain, but others made me believe in the goodness of humanity again. When I walked in the shadow of the valley of tears their tolerance enriched my faith in freedom and I abandoned my despair. There was brutality in some judgements, but there was less sufferance in coming out than living in the prison of perpetual silence. Perhaps my militant dream of homosexual freedom and tolerance in catholic Ireland was to come true after all?

A handful of heterosexual drinking establishments in Ireland practiced the art of political correctness and were reputed as being gay friendly. The rainbow coloured flag sticker in the corner of their pub windows indicated tolerance of homosexuality, but in my gay militant judgement that was a doubled edged sword in the battle for real homosexual freedom. It enriched catholic Ireland with the normalisation of homosexuality on a certain social level, but it also underlined that homosexuals were alienated and segregated in a heterosexual world. I knew that the colour of queer money was the same colour as heterosexual money, but many still believed that it was pink. Heterosexual men didn't particularly want to frequent cohorts of arse fuckers in their virile local pub every night, even if a queer with a cocktail enhanced the trendy image of a changing Ireland. Everyone knew that homosexuals were effeminate creatures that danced in tutus to Madonna under flashing disco lights in high heels and that queers knew nothing about the technical rules of Gaelic football, hurling or rugby. Their interest in snooker was the balls, in soccer it was the changing rooms and in golf was it the driver, fairway, hybrid, iron, wedge or putter that they used with anal lube for fucking? It wasn't a legend that drag queens had a dream to pub crawl every heterosexual pub in catholic Ireland; all homosexuals wanted that freedom. Queers just wanted to get pissed like

ordinary men, but the latter believed that homosexuals wanted to ensnarl pissed heterosexuals in order to seduce and fuck them. Ripples of tolerance began to contaminate heterosexual pubs and enriched heterosexuals to understand that queers did not have pink handbags and promiscuous homosexuals were not gay missionaries. Homosexuals were not just queers, lesbians were not just dykes, they had the same professions, social classes, colours and religions as heterosexuals and they drank pints of Guinness in abundance too. Irish queers knew about Irish history from Michael Collins to David Norris and they knew all about the history of Irish sport from Roy Keane to Donal Óg Cusack too. I wasn't a sports philistine either. My eyes had directly seen Sean Kelly in the Tour of Ireland on Saint Patrick's Hill in 1987. I had admired Packie Bonner singing "The Boy's in Green" for the Euro 88 on "The Late Late Show" and I had also witnessed the Irish Celtic Warrior Steve Collins slaughter Chris Eubank in Millsteet in 1995. The gay friendly culture was a stepping stone towards homosexual freedom, but it was a liberation and discrimination at the same time. The homosexual bars that I frequented were certainly not heterophobic, but whereas heterosexuals tolerated queers, homosexuals accepted straights and the gay movement did not rebel against such injustice with the creation of a straight friendly concept.

The Resurrection of Tears

The seed of voyage was deeply engrained in Irish history. Ireland had been forsaken in despair by the survivors of the 1845 - 1849 famine. Shadows had walked into the horizon of dreams in Queenstown and coffin ships had faded away into the ocean distance. Whereas they had fled poverty, starvation and death, I merely desired freedom from the catholic brutality that destroyed me. The almighty god enticed me to relinquish my love for Ireland and the seed of voyage seduced me to seek harmony far from Irish brutality too. I was passionately enslaved in a dream of homosexual freedom and in my need to forsake social intolerance I tasted my vision of liberty. I kissed my mother and abandoned the catholic Ireland that Saint Patrick had created. She knew that I hated being sprinkled with holy water, but just before the door of my rural home closed behind me, she polluted me with her faith again. I retorted that I wasn't in need of a golden shower, but judging by her silence she didn't understand that pissing was an erotic sport practiced by some and my irreverence to her catholic god certainly did not enrage her. She mourned in tears, her prayers implored Jesus Christ to protect me on the glorious journey of my life and an ocean of emotion fell from my father's cold eyes too. I believed that if sufferance had crucified me for so many years that it was too late to cry in repentance. She placed a handful of hard boiled sweets in my jacket pocket for the flight, perhaps her love for me had resurrected after all? The language of Molière seduced my ears and I now lived all of my dreams in the liberty, equality and fraternity of France. In the months that followed her silenced affection for me was eternalised in each hand written letter that my mother wrote. Tears devoured me as I read the affection that she liberated. I wanted to believe that she had changed, but in the changing colours of the seasons I learnt that certain dreams never came true. I treasured those love embellished letters, but in 2010 I boxed them away in my basement far away from thought. In 2012 I re-read each one in tears knowing that it for the last time. It was not the flames of rage that consumed her words into ashes, but the flames of my eternal freedom. I didn't need to visualise the

tangible sufferance of the past; it was ingrained in me in silence forever. Ashes to ashes, dust to dust, I consciously ignited a match and I created the burnt ruins of my forgotten dreams.

Dublin had denuded me, but in Paris glory holes enhanced the hedonism of homosexual promiscuity and I learnt all about the erotic methods of the homosexual subcultures. In the dark rooms of the basement night clubs that I frequented men savagely fucked men. The odour of sperm seemed to be impregnated in the walls and an abundance of poppers distended in the smoke filled air. I wasn't catholic, but I did believe that even the most tolerant of humans had a judgement of some kind or other and I certainly didn't practice all the immorality that I saw. Each Parisian district specialised in liberty, brothels aligned the pavement of Rue Saint Denis, strippers danced and denuded in eroticism behind the neon facades of Pigalle, sex shops ornately decorated Montmartre and homosexuals flourished in Le Marais. It was a consumption society with a laissez-faire attitude, but underneath the surface of such liberty there was a certain degree of silenced intolerance. It certainly wasn't as straight forward as I had thought. Tolerance encircled prostitutes in Rue Saint Denis, strippers in Pigalle, hard core worshippers in Montmartre and queers in Le Marais, but outside those sexual ghettos it was a completely different story. I simply didn't have a deep enough insight into the social structure of France to understand that tolerance wasn't everywhere. The catholic heterosexual judgement of the gay culture was strongly enrooted in a secular society too, but I hadn't tasted such brutality yet.

If I had seen a wedding ring of his left hand I would never have kissed him, but he systematically removed it each time that he consumed men. His digitus quartus was always naked when he liberated his homosexual desires with me too, but this time something glittering attracted my eye. He had forgotten to denude his finger, which forced him to enrich me with the truth. Society and god had ensnarled him in the prison of heterosexual love, but my judgement retorted that he had the freedom to abandon the facade of heterosexuality and step into the light of homosexuality if he really wanted. My lover justified that he had the compassion not to destroy all of her dreams with tears. His holy catholic wife kissed him with passion, but did she ever recognise the taste of his lovers' sperm on his lips? He sincerely loved her, but in the profound belief that there was no sufferance in silence either. I believed that he betrayed her, but Xavier rebelled that he feigned his affection when he fucked promiscuous men.

Why was the guise of heterosexuality still a perpetual prison for a homosexual man in 1996? Heteronormativity was encrusted in society, so he lived as a catholic closeted queer in the Sacrament of Marriage. Wasn't homosexuality banished from the kingdom of heaven? He feared that the heterosexual judgement of society would punish his immorality more than the almighty catholic god; after all there was forgiveness for repentance in the bible. Then, he beseeched me to become his eternal lover and my forgotten sufferance suddenly resurrected as I penetrated him with rage. I still remembered how I had wiped away my mother's tears and perhaps my brutality wanted to punish him for his betrayal of the holy Seventh Commandment of god? As I savagely fucked him everything about 1987 resurfaced. All the colours, shapes and sounds that I forgotten awoke to destroy me again. I relived the smashing noise of the vase that had fallen to the floor and the ocean of tears that had contaminated her beautiful blue eyes. I never wanted to know whether it was my father's sperm that had created them or not, but for first time in my life I questioned were they the forbidden fruit of his adventure? I re-battled to find the serenity to banish those fucking bastards from my thoughts, but they were deeply engrained in my history. I had the sensation of a time dilation, but my lover's moans of pleasure enticed me to revert to 1996. I condemned my Irish sufferance to the prison of silence again, but was the catholic silence of Ireland eternal? It was the last time that I was naked in the euphoria of his ephemeral love. After ejaculation I looked at the silver diamond cross pendant that decorated his naked body and it inspired me never to fuck a Catholic closeted homosexual ever again. I abandoned Xavier forever; from that moment on I just wanted to denude homosexual Atheists.

There was profound loneliness in the consumption of interchangeable lovers, but one night stands certainly distracted me from the sensation of such sufferance. My lovers liberated me from the desolation of solitude, but in their kisses I tasted despair because in the light of dawn I was alone again. I lusted to love and to be loved infinite times more than absolute infinite, but a profound feeling that I was never to fall into the passion of eternal love devoured me more and more. I wanted to share the smiles and tears of life in a durable relationship with fidelity, but the changing colours of the seasons withered my reverie away. Homosexuals wanted to live in white-picket fenced suburban homes of perpetual love, but I feared that that was another ephemeral dream. Perhaps homosexual love was a myth or did the almighty catholic god punish homosexuals to suffer an eternity of promiscuity? Perhaps the fate for licentious queers was to taste the brutality of love forever? An abundance of colours softly danced in the

wind to seduce my eyes. Jovial children played with carefree smiles among the fallen leaves of autumn and innocently skipped among the mass pollution of used condoms that littered the ground. In the obscurity of the night the sound of their gleeful laughter faded away and the hunt for homosexual sex enchanted the castle walls of Caen. Homosexuals lurked among the moonlit bushes and trees longing to fuck other queers. It was a sordid world of erections, where anonymous men of gay distinction fucked in the undergrowth. The sound of their penetration conquered the nocturnal silence with harmonic moans of pleasure, but there was tolerance of that passion in the gay culture. It was certain that such homosexual liberty gave rise to the heterosexual social judgement of queers, but god and politicians had ensnarled too many closeted gays in the prison of heterosexuality. I wasn't catholic anymore, but I had a tendency to judge the desperation of those that sought the brutality of sex under the stars and not under the flashing disco lights 'of urban gay clubs. As a fellow homosexual I should have been more lenient and clement, after all the oppression of queers was the founding father of street sex. I believed that the men that fucked in the social network of such gay cruising practiced immorality, but in the history of homosexuality not all homosexuals had tasted the freedom of the gay movement. I had a catholic judgement because I didn't want to understand the real mechanism behind the art of such seduction. In fact, was there a real difference between the lewd conduct of their sexual liberation in public parks and the lustful methods of my consumption of men in gay bars? Queer cruising existed because the catholic bible, heterosexual judgement, political intolerance and social discrimination had created the crime of homosexuality and what was forbidden definitely enticed certain gay men. In the laissez-faire attitude of the gay world homosexuals were endowed with absolute freedom, but what was a haven for promiscuity was also an abundant paradise for sexually transmitted disease. The secluded areas were also a beacon for homophobes and homosexual crucifixion was a common practice, but the shadows of the night were the only liberation for some gay men. Homosexuals had revolted for the right to love, but beneath the surface of liberty in France there was certainly intolerance.

In Ireland I had socialised among a million friends, but in France befriending required a substantial period of time to develop. The Irish had an openness to converse with everyone, but in the city of Caen discussion with strangers was perceived with utmost suspicion. My small talk certainly attracted a glance of wariness from all, particularly on the public bus, where it even seemed forbidden to speak about the weather to a fellow passenger. It was strongly recommended to sit in total silence and the

distinctive cheek kissing culture also gave me the impression that I had just landed on Mars. There was a high level of social solitude in France, not speaking the language of Molière very well alienated me further, but the major contributing factor was the anti-social movement that seemed ingrained in the judgement of a jingoistic nation. What I initially judged as arrogance was my lack of insight into the complex web of social races that enriched the French culture. Colour, origin and religion enticed many Frogs to practise racial discrimination overtly and I began to believe that the revolutionary heritage of liberty, equality and fraternity was a just myth. Heterosexuals in general were cold, distant and distrustful of others, but the aloof homosexual world was composed of the most caustic creatures that I had ever encountered. I began to miss the harmony of the flashing disco lights of the urban gay clubs of Dublin. In time I learnt that socialising was not pub crawling, but conversing and dining in the intimacy of French homes instead, but in the beginning I felt a solitude that I had never known before. The coloured leaves of autumn had completely fallen, a glacial winter decorated the nakedness of the leafless trees with a layer of snow and in the waves of my new freedom I forgot my Irish sufferance.

Snow decorated the post-war streets of Caen, but I returned to another catastrophic Christmas in rural Ireland. My mother kissed me with immense tenderness, but in doing so she contaminated me with her ephemeral love again. In the euphoria of her emotions she deluded me into believing that she had changed. In that blissful instant I dreamed that she loved me forever, but a few hours later the ornate Christmas tree was dressed in full splendour and I became a "fucking homosexual" again. The harmonious peace and goodwill of Christmas certainly wasn't everlasting. With catholic generosity she gave Susanna a tin of Jacobs Afternoon Tea biscuits. With a friendly smile I stated that my favourite was the Jelly Star biscuit and that I couldn't imagine an Irish Christmas being traditional without it. My mother stiffened and struggled to silence her agitation in the company of our neighbour, but judging by the air of enragement that governed the glances that she directed towards me, I was led to understand that the resurrection of my Irish sufferance was to come. It was behind closed doors that she liberated her brutality to destroy me. Tears devoured her blue eyes, but I retorted with a laugh that there was no homosexual pun behind the name of the biscuit. "I know what fucking Jelly Stars are" and her hand rebelled to punish my insolence. She was enriched with a wrath that I recognised and my holy mother justified that I had physically betrayed the promise of silence. She was certain that Susanna had noticed

that my wrist had fallen limp like "a queer fucker". An effeminate gesture that she hated in queers had manifested itself in me during the conversation and she needed to hetero-sexualise me again. I now understood what had fuelled her fury and I even had the serenity to forgive her. I solaced her in my embrace, but she pushed me away in repulsion. There was certainly no sentiment of love for a homosexual son in catholic Ireland.

On Christmas Eve my catholic mother stood semi-naked in her bra and knickers in front of the homosexual that she had crucified a few days before. I admired her comeliness as she applied her make-up with delicate effeminacy. Foundation smoothed out all the imperfections of ageing and the natural flaws that had blemished her face with the imprint of the passing years. Blush created a discreet rosy colour to her cheekbones to enhance the radiance of her beauty. Eye-shadow complimented the profound colour of her blue eyes, a layer of eyeliner created depth and dimension and mascara rendered her eyes even more attractive again. Pale red lipstick made her more alluring looking and an abundance of lacquer stiffened her hair. Her outlandishly stylish clothes were so perfectly coordinated with a matching bag and shoes, all which were worn for the first time. The gold and diamond rings that decorated her fingers glittered more gloriously than the star of Bethlehem. Perhaps her affluence had allured her to forget that the Blessed Virgin Mary was clothed in rags of poverty and that Jesus was born in a stable and not in a palace? She venerated her reflection in the bedroom mirror with grace as if she wanted to immortalise her beauty and I extolled her sublime appearance too. She knew that heterosexual men of my age didn't share such close intimacy with their mothers, but at that precise moment it didn't enrage her that I was "a fucking queer". I cherished that ephemeral love, it enriched me to dream of homosexual acceptance, but her intolerance was certainly perpetual.

That night in mass she certainly prayed to her almighty god for my plenary indulgence. As she implored the lord's gracious compassion to hetero-sexualise me, I seduced a homosexual in the dim deserted streets of rural Ireland. He was approximately the same age as me; perhaps just a year or two younger, but he already mastered the techniques of homosexuality. As she sang hymns of praise, I lustfully kissed him. As she recited her faith in prayer, I denuded behind an Irish blue limestone wall in a field with him. As she venerated her catholic god, I revered the beauty of his naked body. As she passionately listened to the pulpit sermon, I touched his erection

under the stars. As she silently enriched the church collection plate with £20, I sucked his penis. As she genuflected before the altar and uttered Amen, my lover began to moan. As she tasted the body of Christ in the sacrament of Holy Communion, my mouth was enriched with the taste of his sperm. As Saint Joseph's church bells rang in the distance, I sighed in the pleasure of ejaculation. As he smiled I felt the coldness of my clothes, which had absorbed the wetness of the grass. The orange glow of the cigarette in his hand disappeared as he walked into the night and I realised that I didn't even know his name. Who was guilty of sin, me for kneeling in adoration before his moonlit penis after I had judged others for the immorality of queer cruising among the bushes in Caen or my mother for kneeling in reverence before her god after she had crucified me for fucking men?

The family tradition was to sing blissfully together and Christmas hymns resounded in the house the next morning; "Away in a Manger", "God Rest Ye Merry Gentlemen", "Hark the Herald Angels Sing", "Joy to the World", "O Come, All Ye Faithful" and "Silent Night". Molly had given birth to Naomi and it was certainly "The First Noel", which was sung with the most pleasure and passion by everyone. "Merry Christmas Goddaughter" was printed on the card that I had bought for my niece and inside it my hand written words promised to cherish her with my perpetual love. My brother coldly stated that I was "too fucking queer" to be her godfather and crumbled it in his hand. God condemned homosexuals to the burning fires of hell and my almighty brother condemned the fuchsia pink coloured card to burn in the flames of the coal lit fireplace. It was for certain that he didn't want my words to be immortalised in ink. I didn't think that his wrath against homosexuals was engrained with so much intolerance, but his brutality resurrected to destroy my dream. He didn't want me to contaminate her with homosexuality, but I retorted that his wrathful act would not preserve her from the profanity of lesbianism. My insolence fuelled his rage with even more rage. He punished me with physical force, but I didn't silence my enragement either. I felt my fist clench; was the brutality of rural Ireland engrained in me? In the Sermon on the Mount Jesus preached true righteousness, 'An eye for an eye and a tooth for a tooth, but if any one strikes you on the right cheek, turn to him the left cheek also". I didn't have faith in those biblical words and I didn't believe that the pen was far mightier than the sword either. I rebelled with utter violence; it was "a bruise for a bruise" and each mighty blow I received I returned. My holy mother and my catholic father certainly condemned me with the same hard judgement; otherwise the good

Catholics of Ireland would have defended me. Molly betrayed me too; in her passive acceptance of my brother's vengeance she tolerated his wrongdoing. It was just a typical homosexual Christmas in my catholic home with peace to all heterosexuals and rancour to all queers. A few hours later a delicious dinner was placed under my eyes, but I refused to eat and everyone else ate in total silence. I boycotted the mouth watering ham, which had boiled in the salty cabbage water, the potatoes that had roasted with the fresh herb and onion stuffed turkey, the marrow fat peas, which had first soaked overnight in bicarbonate soda water, the spiced beef that had been baptised with Knorr Savoury Gravy and even the Brussels sprouts, which was certainly my favourite veg. At the end of the meal my mother sincerely thanked me for spoiling her Christmas and then she crucified me with her brutality. Jerry Morey, my brother's old school friend, accepted to be her godfather and he solemnly vowed to eternally give Naomi catholic guidance on the road of her life. Ironically in the changing colours of the seasons it became a forsaken promise, but that night they raised a glass of honour with him. I refrained from being a hypocrite and stormed out of their catholic home. I hated the almighty god of Ireland and in revenge I pissed on the arch door of Saint Joseph's Church. There was so much sufferance in being an Irish homosexual, but in the resurrection of tears I became a survivor.

12

The Romanticisation of Dreams

I didn't really want to celebrate my birthday in a heterosexual ambiance, but twenty one candles did blaze on a chocolate cake in a straight pub in Rue Saint Jean. I certainly needed some homosexuality, but nobody wanted to go to the "Phil n' Bea" with me. Samantha screamed that she needed a heterosexual fuck. She nourished her heterosexuality under the flashing disco lights and practiced the same promiscuity as queers. She believed that there was no immorality in the liberation of ephemeral love and seduced, kissed, denuded and condom fucked in abundance. Samantha implored me to stay, but I whispered in her ear that I needed to find a homosexual to fuck. Deborah rightfully slurred that she was too pissed to walk the distance. Judgements of her binge drinking habits vulgarised her, but she retorted that it was the catholic culture of Irish women to drink pints of Guinness. Whereas the French prudishly consumed with strict moderation, it was socially incorrect that the Irish puked in the streets of Caen every night. Lauren turned her head away in silence, which clearly signified a no. She justified that Hollywood had glamorised smoking, which clearly explained the cloud of cigarette smoke, which always distended above her head. The delicious looking barman sang "Appy Bertday", but judging by the attention he paid to Lauren's voluptuous breasts he was certainly heterosexual. Alan retorted that there was too much Abba, too many flashing disco lights, too much cigarette smoke and far too many men in the gay club that I frequented. He always socialised by grumbling and his discontentment mood certainly made me laugh. Either he bemoaned that the music was too loud or the beer was too highly priced, but what enraged him the most was that a pint was never filled to the brim in France. Benjamin was extrovert and introvert at the same time, virile and emotional, endowed with the attributes of charm, intelligence and breath-taking beauty. I was highly attracted to his eyes too, but the sublime shape of his penis in his tight fitting jeans further enhanced my deep fascination of him. He was certainly the type of guy that I could have easily given my perpetual love to, but heterosexuality governed his

erections and I knew in silenced sufferance that he was a forbidden kiss. An impressive quantity of empty pint glasses littered our table. Benjamin winked that he needed his beauty sleep. He lived in a flat in proximity to the Winton Churchill Bridge; which was in the same direction as the "Phil n' Bea", There was no seduction in his beautiful heterosexual brown eyes as we walked into that cold night together.

The history of Caen deluded many into believing that the leaning facade of l'église Saint-Pierre was the visual sufferance of the 1944 bombardment, but I enlightened Benjamin that that was a myth. It fascinated him to learn that the foundations had naturally subsided in the late 1850's and he certainly admired that I wasn't a philistine. On the other hand, he had walked Rue Saint Pierre a million times, but had never been inspired to enter the church to be enriched by its history. I wasn't catholic, but the architecture of each church in Caen had allured me to learn so much. Whereas the other Erasmus students knew everything about the pub culture in Caen, I cultivated a passion for a city that had resurrected from the ruins of war. Rather than attend university lectures I preferred to frequent the monuments, rather than socialise in the language of Shakespeare 24/7 with the others I learnt the language of Molière in the streets alone, rather than get pissed on Guinness in the heterosexual Irish pub I danced under flashing disco lights in the wine drinking culture of homosexuality and rather than live in a clan of Irishness in the campus I house shared with François and Françis in a suburban heterosexual residential area near Jardin Les Plantes. I loved the sound of opening the bedroom shutters in the morning, the abundant fragrance of baguette that floated in the air and the taste of an espresso on a crowded café terrace. I needed to unravel all the legends and clichés of France and everything about its glorious culture seduced my eyes.

As we neared the "Phil n' Bea" he kissed me. I tasted so much passion as his luscious lips caressed and devoured mine, but Benjamin was forbidden. He kissed me with an abundance of ardour, but Benjamin was heterosexual. He implored me to liberate his silenced fantasy and we kissed again, but Benjamin was pissed. He certainly wanted me to seduce him and insisted that his flat was just a four minute walk away. I was so profoundly attracted to him, but it enraged him that I didn't want to denude him. He savagely rebelled that I was "a fucking queer". He abandoned me under the stars and the cold emotion of his hostile betrayal devoured my eyes with tears. I did not see him the following day or the next twelve days

after, not knowing was it me avoiding him or that it was Benjamin avoiding me. Perhaps it was normal as we had never frequented each other on a daily basis, but it was certainly unusual that our paths hadn't crossed somewhere in Caen. More snow had fallen, the first snowdrops had bloomed and his kisses still danced wildly in my profound thoughts. I recognised Benjamin in the distance, but I wanted to pretend that I hadn't, however his friendly wave to attract my attention forced me to acknowledge his presence. Everything was completely normal, which led me to believe that had forgotten his passion and his enragement too. He wanted a coffee, but a glance at my watch confirmed that Monoprix was closing in an hour. I needed to abandon him, after all my fridge needed yoghurts, fruit and some other important things. He besought me to meet him in Jardin Les Plantes at 4p.m the next day. Was there seduction silenced behind those dark brown eyes or did he want to crucify "a queer fucker"?

A light spray of Schwarzkopf enhanced the shiny aspect of my blond coloured hair and hardened to strengthen the gravity-defying spikes that I had created. White cotton underpants didn't enhance my sensuality, but I decided on comfort rather than beauty. My blue Jeans had a small hole near the knee, which I thought looked kind of trendy. A flowery pink shirt, the thirty franc price in the January sales had certainly attracted me more than the colour. The L sized flecked Aran jumper didn't flatter my physical appearance very much, but it was relatively cold outside. My grandmother claimed that she had knitted it for me, but she had forgotten to remove the label that always itched behind my neck. My reflection in the mirror confirmed that I really looked like a sack of potatoes and I certainly needed to look more attractive for Benjamin. I denuded and a tight fitting red briefs now enhanced the shape of my penis. The flowery pink shirt did marry well with my denims, so I didn't change either. The Irish Aran was abandoned for a charcoal coloured medium sized sweater, which enhanced the slimness of my body, but why did I need to look sexy to meet a heterosexual man? With my prompt urban walking pace it was exactly a thirteen minute journey and Benjamin was sitting on a wooden bench when I arrived. There was some initial small talk about the weather, but then there was a moment of deep silence. "You're not a queer fucker", Benjamin apologised with sincerity. Not wanting to resurrect his kiss I replied that I couldn't remember much about that heavily drunken night. Benjamin smiled in appreciation, but he had certainly seen me lower my eyes to the ground when I lied. He affectionately put his arm around my shoulder, but was that a platonic gesture or was there ephemeral passion

flourishing again? Was it heterosexuality that glittered in his beautiful brown eyes or was a homosexual seduction resurfacing? He moved his head in the direction of mine and a second later a kiss caressed my lips. There was so much lust in each succulent forbidden kiss that followed.

We admired Spring, Summer, Autumn and Winter together; the four erotic statues that decorated the Botanic garden were each named after a different season. We kissed with passion again and an elderly woman glared at us in total disapproval of our immorality. Benjamin wanted to rebel against her judgement, but I silenced him with another lustful kiss. She walked away into the distance verbally condemning our sin to her dog. He disclosed that he wanted to denude and fuck with me, but society had deluded him into believing that he needed to define himself as either a heterosexual or a closeted "queer fucker". I had passionately read some books about the theory of Alfred Kinsey, the creator of a heterosexual-homosexual spectrum in 1948, but Benjamin had never heard of it. I explained that the Kinsey Scale determined the level of heterosexuality as zero, bisexuality as three and homosexuality as six on a range from 0 to 6. That the not aforementioned ranges of 1 and 2 liberated heterosexuals to taste homosexuality without being homosexual and the range of 4 and 5 liberated homosexuals to taste heterosexuality without being heterosexual. I hadn't yet mentioned that the X range determined asexuality, but judging by the blank look on his face it was already far too technical. He battled the emotional challenge in his mind for a few seconds before liberating his thoughts; "In your spectrum a heterosexual can fuck with a homosexual and still be a heterosexual afterwards"? I confirmed that he had the freedom to govern his own sexuality; after all heterosexual fantasy into homosexual fruition had been a common practice in ancient civilisation before Christianity had converted everyone to social heteronormativity. A gay experience was not an entangled web that led to the road of homosexuality forever. Our lips touched in harmony again.

Benjamin wasn't a smoker, but he now savoured a Benson and Hedges and a cloud of smoke distended above his head. "Are you cultivating a James Dean look or what?" His cigarette glowed, he deeply inhaled another puff and justified that he sometimes needed a calming soothing pleasure. He directed his fag towards my lips and smoke distended above my head too. I really desired the same sensation, after all what was forbidden definitely enticed that day. A bell signalled that the gates of the botanic garden were closing. I had never homosexualised the lust of a heterosexual before and I

still hesitated a lot. I concluded that Benjamin's cupidity for a homosexual fuck was too much of an emotional challenge for me. Everyone knew what happened in the castle grounds at night; he retorted that he would fuck a homosexual there in the undergrowth instead. "Fuck off Benjamin", I was enraged by his insolence. There was no beauty in the homosexual culture by the castle walls; I didn't want Benjamin to taste the brutality of that promiscuity, but he disappeared into the distance. A few minutes later Boulevard Richemond and Boulevard Jean Moulin met and I turned to see his beautiful brown eyes behind me. We walked Allée de la Verte Vallée each smoking another Benson and Hedges. In the belief that all his forbidden desires needed to be liberated we arrived in Rue Robert Castel. I unbuttoned my pink flowery shirt and Benjamin denuded too. His underwear was stunning; a multi-coloured fluorescent striped boxer shorts seductively showed off his masculine physique and enhanced the overall beauty of his silhouette. I was glad that I hadn't worn my white cotton undies and strutted around my bedroom in my tight fitting red briefs. The passion that followed was forgotten in a promise of silence forever afterwards.

He kissed me passionately and I fondled his erection, but had he closed his eyes in the pleasure of my kiss or in the sufferance of a homosexual touch on his penis? All my promiscuous homosexual lovers fucked with brutality, but I didn't know how to succumb to the desires of a gentle heterosexual man. Benjamin smiled and crawled over me on the bed. His mouth caressed my naked penis and I simultaneously sucked and titillated his penis too. He certainly knew that such a position was called a 69. Water-based lubrication was generously applied on my erection and I delicately penetrated his anus. I jerked deeper and harder with gentle movements. "Fuck me, fuck me, fuck me" he was living the liberation of his silenced homosexual dream. Our bodies harmonised in orgasmic moans and in the sensation of euphoria I ejaculated. A sperm filled condom now littered the floor of my bedroom and he smoked another cigarette. I liked the sweet fragrance of his Hugo Boss on my naked body that night, but homosexuality was not engrained in him forever. He was not ensnarled to become a queer and his ephemeral voyage into the passion for homosexuality faded. From the bedroom window I watched him disappear into the horizon the next morning. A cloud of cigarette smoke then distended above my head, he had forgotten his Benson and Hedges. Benjamin became a forbidden kiss again, but there was no sufferance in our solemn promise of eternal silence. Our platonic friendship continued to flourish as if I had never fucked him.

I was enriched with so much aversion for catholic Ireland, but I flourished in Caen and resurrected from the ashes of my Irish sufferance again. I nourished my homosexuality and her heterosexual money became pink in the queer culture that I abundantly frequented. I certainly denuded her fingers of gold and diamonds that year, but I justified that my holy mother needed punishment for all the desolation that she had created in my life. Homosexual fucking was forbidden in her heterosexual bible, but I believed that fucking men was my revenge on her almighty catholic god. I lived under the flashing disco lights of homosexuality, but that freedom was not perpetual. The glorious days of Erasmus were fading away. The brutality of her catholic judgement was going to betray my liberty and destroy me again. Was it possible to have the emotional strength to love a man if the eternity of that love was never to be? Was it better to know the taste of ephemeral love rather than never have loved him? Hervé fell so profoundly in love with me, but the beauty of that love was doomed to become the brutality of love. I implored him not to love me with all his heart because my departure from Caen was nigh, but he was unable to restrain his emotions in the same caustic fashion as me. There was so much passion in his dream of eternal love that I wanted to love him forever too, but knowing that that forever was just a reverie I silenced my love for him. I had completely fallen in love with Hervé, but I never disclosed that an abundance of love had conquered me too. I sincerely loved him in a passionate way that I had never loved a man before, but he never knew just how much I really loved him. Ireland was to become my prison again and I didn't rebel and battle for the eternity of his love to last. I didn't want Hervé to feel the sufferance of love, but we were star crossed lovers contaminated with an adverse fate since our very first kiss.

Hervé dreamed of loving me forever in a typical half-timbered Norman house. For my blue eyes he wanted to cultivate a garden of blooming flowers and to immortalise my happiness he wanted to cherish me forever. He wanted to age gracefully with me in the beauty of that dream, but Ireland destroyed everything. Caen had resurrected from the ruins of destruction to become the haven that liberated my freedom. Hervé had seduced me to fall in love, but I now kissed him passionately for the last time. I wanted to love him for eternity, but the path of our lives separated on the platform of the train station in Caen. There was an abundance of emotion in his eyes, but my love did not flourish in the ocean of his tears. There was a certain consistency in my coldness, a kind of emotional dysfunction that made me become totally indifferent to his sufferance. I passionately kissed him knowing that I would probably never see the

beauty of his face ever again. I deluded him into believing that I didn't love him as much as he wanted, but in the silence of my thoughts I solemnly promised to love him forever. I really wanted to share that dream of everlasting love, but I had to liberate him so that he could fall in love again. I wanted Hervé to be happy, so I gave him the freedom to love another man. A deluge of tears devoured his eyes as the doors of the train closed. I abandoned him; the flowers in the garden of the half-timbered Norman house that he had imagined withered away and Ireland crucified me again. His sufferance was ephemeral, but the brutality of my sufferance in catholic Ireland was certainly perpetual. I thought that everything about Hervé was engrained in me forever, but the changing seasons ravaged my life with so much destruction that I even forgot the colour of his eyes.

My mother still prayed to the catholic god, but I had forgotten the sound of the gilded pages of her holy bible turning as god enriched her with the passion to crucify queers. It was a sensation that I hated, but she still sprinkled me with holy water from the font at the bottom of the stairs to contaminate me with god's love. She burnt so many candles in Saint Joseph's Church in the belief that her almighty god would liberate me from my immorality, but I still had no repentance. Her catholic faith had strengthened, but my faith in homosexuality had deepened in Caen. Her reverence to the sermons governed her intolerance and she certainly did not have the freedom to love me. Rural catholic Ireland became my prison, I was a "fucking queer" and my sufferance resurrected again. Well balanced delectable meals were served before my eyes, she perfectly ironed my clothes without the slightest crease, but she needed to crucify a homosexual and destroyed me. The freedom that had flourished in Caen was now forgotten. All of my dreams faded away and I tasted the brutality of my mother's enragement. She battled to hetero-sexualise me and the holy judgement of Ireland savagely slaughtered me again. There was so much passion in her love for god and so much hostility in her rancour for homosexuals; if I wanted to survive I needed to revert to the dark dusty closet of silence again. I knew that my silence created her serenity and appeased her enragement, so in despair I silenced my homosexuality again.

Ireland was less glamorous and had no beauty or attraction in my eyes anymore. In the reversed culture shock I certainly had difficulty to being Irish again. I suffered from post Erasmus syndrome and a feeling of depression devoured me. I missed the sound of an espresso on a crowded café terrace, the taste of baguettes that floated in the air and everything

about the glorious culture of France that had seduced me. When I closed my eyes the fragrance of Benjamin's Hugo Boss on my denuded body resurrected, but the pale egg shell coloured walls of my bedroom were my prison again. When I dreamed I felt the touch of Hervé's kiss caressing my lips with the eternity of passion, but when the light of dawn arrived I was alone in catholic Ireland again. Hervé did not abandon the emotion of perpetual love and letter after letter aroused my mother's curiosity. Fortunately, whereas the language of Shakespeare would have betrayed me, his deep feelings were immortalised in the language of Molière. In the darkest moments of despair his promise of eternal love gave me a vision of hope, but the reverie of the typical half-timbered Norman house was in ruins. I still loved him, but the destruction in my life impeded me from really loving him. Ireland crucified, slaughtered and destroyed me, but I didn't want Hervé to solace me. I was lured by the belief that no lover ever needed to know about the brutality of my Irish sufferance. I profoundly loved him, but to live his dreams he needed to forget me. I didn't want to delude him into believing in the eternity of my love, so I didn't lick stamps to the envelopes of all the letters that I wrote for him. There must have been so much sufferance in the silence that I created, but I didn't have the freedom to love him forever. There were tears in the following letter that he wrote, rage in the next and finally hate for me in the last. The blooming flowers in the garden of love that he imagined had certainly withered away and now there was eternal silence. He must have really believed that I didn't love him.

What if I write the next part of life differently and if I travel back in time to be on that train platform in Caen again? A deluge of tears devoured his eyes, but just before the doors of the train closed I decided to abandon my Irish sufferance. Rather than voyage into the horizon alone I descended the train and kissed Hervé with a passion that became eternal, but in doing so, that kiss changed everything. The beautiful faces of the people I know today disappeared from my memory and were replaced by faces that I never met. The smiles that I tasted became forgotten and my Irish homosexual eviction in 2010 never happened either. The seduction of 1999 was eroded from my mind and I never loved or met Philippe. But instead of liberating that eternal kiss with Hervé in 1997, his dream of love was forsaken without my regret. I needed the freedom to taste more brutality, to liberate more tears and to unravel more sufferance. I needed to battle for my homosexual freedom and became who I am in the destruction that followed.

The Promise Of Silence

It was near Saint Joseph's Church that I met him for the first time, but whereas I had completely forgotten him, he had lived in the despair of never seeing me again. We had kissed, denuded and ejaculated with passion in a field a few months earlier, but whereas I didn't know his name, he had dreamed of me since. He had frequently walked in the same street desiring to see me there again, but it was if I had never existed. The winter snow was shared with Benjamin, the flowers of spring with Hervé and the summer sun of June 1997 was with Dylan. The road of our lives now encountered in Merchant's Quay, but I was shirt shopping with my mother. I battled not to be betrayed by my flirtatious attraction to him, but homosexuality was engrained in me and I desired his kiss. He knew what the lust that glittered in my smile in the distance meant. It was certainly another journey into the ephemeral love of promiscuity that I wanted, but in her presence my seduction needed to be very discreet. A few minutes later the mirror reflected that Dylan had followed me into the Marks and Spencer's fitting room. He caressed my denuded body and there was so much pleasure in a forbidden kiss. I fondled his penis and he touched mine, but we definitely needed to practice our immortality elsewhere. It was agreed to meet in the farmer's field at 7p.m. That night the beauty of erections was revered, there was the liberation of sperm and that's how my next crucifixion started.

He was generously handsome and endowed with a certain beauty that seduced me, but I was really more attracted to his penis than anything else. Nothing in particular about him aroused me; we didn't have the same taste in music culture, he didn't pertain to the latest fashion and he had never seen the world outside of rural catholic Cork. On the other hand neither of us wanted to fall in love and I certainly believed that fucking was more efficient like that. There was no passion in his Irish eyes to seduce me forever, his kiss liberated me from solitude and sometimes when I denuded him I thought of Hervé. In the silence of my thoughts I still profoundly loved the latter, but was my fucking the manipulation of Dylan or the betrayal of Hervé? I forgot my sufferance tasting his ephemeral kisses and in the thirty days that followed Dylan enriched me with a profound passion. Living my homosexuality in silence was an emotional challenge and in doing what was forbidden enticed me to sin in places that I had never imagined. It was a balance of creativity and a calculation of risk, which varied from a kiss to a fuck depending on the location. We were cultivated lovers among the Greco-Roman sculptures in the Crawford Art Gallery in Emmet Place, savage and barbaric in the toilets of the Capitol Cinema in the Grand Parade and uncatholic when the gates of Saint

Joseph's Church closed at night. The brutality of homosexuality totally corrupted me, but the almighty catholic god did have revenge on my irreverence. I had exactly one hour to do what was really forbidden, but Maureen O' Toole had seen everything from the window of her catholic home. She saw my holy mother and father depart for vigil mass as usual, but a few seconds later Dylan arrived, homosexual lust was liberated and he planted a kiss on my lips. She didn't know that we denuded among the pale egg shell colored walls of my bedroom and that I fucked him with so much passion afterwards, but the little that she had seen was tangible enough to betray me. We planned to meet in a field the next day at 3p.m, Dylan happily walked away into the distance smoking a cigarette, but it was the last time that I ever saw him.

My holy father informed me that he had prayed for me at mass. He certainly didn't care that I was watching a television series and took the remote control from my hand to impose Sky Sports. "Fetch me my slippers", I didn't believe in such slavery, but it was far better not to rebel, after all I didn't want to enrage him. My mother complained that I had had a second shower that day and that the bathroom was a mess. She then made him a cup of tea and buttered a slice of toast for him. The vow of obedience was honoured in my catholic home and my father didn't even grunt a word of thanks. The next morning as I laid in bed I heard a voice downstairs, which I correctly identified as belonging to Maureen. Perhaps she needed my catholic father to help her do some DIY in her home again? My mother's brutality resurrected a few minutes later, "that fucking queer contaminated my catholic home". I immediately understood that Maureen O' Twoole had seen everything from behind the net curtains of her catholic home. Indeed, my enraged mother had learnt about the immorality of my homosexual kiss and there was so much sufferance in the intolerance of catholic Ireland that followed.

The door of my bedroom flung open and she savagely pulled my hair with so much force that my naked body landed on the carpeted floor. Kick after kick my holy father hetero-sexualised me. In rage she ransacked my bedroom, my books, clothes and all the love letters than Hervé had written became ruins. I implored her in tears to have pity, but in vengeance she destroyed my only photo of Hervé too and the beauty of his face faded from my memory forever. She wanted me to abandon my immorality and to repent to the love of her almighty catholic god, but I retorted that "I was a fucking queer forever". My father queer bashed me for my insolence, but

to enrage him further I didn't silence that "I seduced, kissed, denuded, sucked and arse fucked homosexual men". She spat in my face with so much venom and I felt an abundance of potent punches as his clenched fist destroyed me. The key turned in the door to imprison me in my bedroom for the day. Dylan must have waited for me for hours, but I don't really know. Perhaps he thought that I had abandoned him to fuck another homosexual instead or was a catholic headstone in Saint Catherine's Cemetery engraved with my name? Did he live in the despair of never seeing me again or did he forget me as if I had never existed? Her holy battle had silenced my homosexuality again, but in the ripples of my sufferance there was the creation of my resent. I wanted my two fingered gesture of rancour to destroy her. I really wanted to betray her in the revolt of a coming out, but I didn't subside to the barren sentiment of that vengeance. Two roads diverged, to walk into the perpetual shadows of the valley of death or seek revenge in the liberation of my homosexual freedom. The mirror reflected that my body was badly bruised in defeat and it certainly mirrored that I needed to battle for my dreams. I was now contaminated with the fascination of liberty, but did I have serenity to live alone and forsake rural catholic Ireland forever?

The Promise Of Silence

13

The Fascination of Liberty

Early the next morning, I abandoned rural catholic Ireland to conquer my dreams in the liberty of Dublin again. When they found the letter on the kitchen table it was certainly too late; I had already walked the thirty one minute distance to the train station and the exorbitant price of the Iarnród Éireann ticket had been paid. I stared at the green Irish fields with a vacant glance in my eyes as the train advanced faster and faster into my precipitated search for freedom. Mallow, Charleville, Limerick Junction, Thurles, Templemore and Portlaoise, each stop intensified my emotional journey into the unknown. Despite the fact that I had always been rigorously over-organised, nothing had been prepared in advance. I had a medium sized backpack, which for my naive survival alone, merely contained some favourite clothes and some Cadburys Chocolate. The majority of my luggage consisted of the problems that ravaged me, but most importantly I had a dream of freedom. I felt extreme solitude in the rushing crowd in Heuston Station as I descended from the train. Everybody knew in which direction they were going, except me. I walked mechanically in tears not knowing where to go. My wallet was a paucity of resources with not enough money to survive for more than a few hours alone. I began to question if I had I made the right choice. In great need, I phoned my brother imploring his compassion, but there was no love for a homosexual in the intolerance of his catholic judgement. I begged him to shelter me in his Malahide home for just one night, but my fucking homosexuality wasn't his problem. I retorted that I preferred poverty to enrich me forever rather than taste their brutality again. He told to reap the shit that I had harvested. Perhaps he really wanted my lifeless body to be found hanging from the century aged sycamore tree at the end of the garden? "Fuck off"; words that I only uttered when enraged dispersed from my mouth and his telephone handset was directed back to its cradle. It was common knowledge that Phoenix Park was the haven of male prostitution, but was the desolation of poverty to allure me into the web of loitering among the pavements too? Was there a real difference between the non-

amorous promiscuity that I practiced and the remuneration for non-emotional sexual services practiced by rent boys? A need for money and a sensation of extreme despair devoured me. I wasn't catholic anymore, but I certainly still had a choice to be righteous.

Was I condemned by the holy society of Ireland to become part of the hidden population of homeless Irish homosexuals? I had never thought that it would be me, but that night a wooden bench in the Garden of Remembrance homed me. The latter commemorated the bravery of heroes that had died for Irish freedom, but Ireland had forgotten to liberate Irish queers and I had nowhere to go. Stars littered the sky and the emotion of fear, insecurity, solitude and uncertainty devoured me. The sound of the traffic around Parnell Square East began to fade, the moonlight beautified the statue of the Children of Lir and I felt the coldness of the damp air caressed my body. There was so much despair in the fascination of liberty, but had I forsaken rural Ireland in error? No, the sufferance of each bruise that decorated me still enriched me with the brutality that I had fled. It was from a market stall in Moore Street that I bought some fruit from a strong accented Dubliner the next morning. I devoured it ravenously to calm my sharp hunger pains. I headed for the National Museum in Kildare Street next, not to be enlightened with the rich history and culture of Ireland, but to shelter from the Irish rain that had begun to fall. I had always been acutely sensitive to ensure a high standard of physical appearance, so I eagerly availed of the toilets there to freshen up. Some cold tap water tried in vain to remove the shade of tiredness that protruded from the puffy bags under my eyes. The squirt of hair gel that had generously ejaculated from the tube onto my hand was overly applied, giving my hair a visibly sticky appearance, which consequently darkened its blond colour. There was the reflection of a ruined man obtrusively gazing back at me in the water stained mirror as I brushed my teeth, but that haggard looking young man was me. Forbidden thoughts resurrected and the valley of death wanted to seduce me again. I was beginning to believe that the river Liffey was my only liberation into the kingdom of heaven.

I journeyed on foot to Howth Road; I really needed his help, but he certainly had the right to forsake me if he wanted. The old fuchsia in his garden bloomed in splendour and I observed that he had planted a purple coloured hydrangea under the sitting room window, which had an abundance of flowers too. I knocked on the door of his home and judging by his smile he hadn't forgotten me. "You look like fucking shit", in the

silence of my thoughts I wanted him to kiss me, but I wasn't his lover anymore. Alexander hugged me close to his virile body and solaced the tears that fell from my blue eyes. He must have been surprised that I had emotions; after all I had abandoned his love with so much coldness. In the belief that he needed to know everything I disclosed what had happened and all the sufferance that I had silenced for years. I explained that a kiss with Dylan had betrayed me and that a fucking bitch called Maureen O' Twoole had seen everything from her window. He smiled "you never knew how to keep your penis in your pants", but the deeper the insight I gave him the more he hated my holy mother. The brutality of rural catholic Ireland enraged him, but he hadn't seen me naked yet. I unbuttoned my shirt and revealed with just how much passion they had destroyed me. More rancour devoured him and he believed that no catholic values were ingrained in their righteous culture. It infuriated him that my fucker of a brother listened to the pulpit sermons, because in my hour of need he certainly didn't live in respect of what the bible preached. Beneath the surface of his jovial appearance was Alexander's silenced sufferance. He enlightened me with his forgotten past and I learnt that he had battled for his homosexual freedom too. His catholic home had practiced the same brutality and the coming out he had lived in 1982 was engrained in him forever. His mother was in heaven and he couldn't remember her much, but he liked to think that she would have had tolerance for her homosexual son. His father had reared him and his sister alone without displaying love, but Alexander used the word genitor instead of father when he spoke of him. "That fucking bastard wanted to hetero-sexualise me", in a flashback Alexander remembered the potent punches of his father's clenched fist. On his eighteenth birthday there was no candle flickering on a cake, his genitor queer bashed and banished him instead. Alexander believed in the resurrection of my dreams, he had risen from the ashes of such desolation and in the profusion of my despair he housed me for as long as I needed. He gave me a vision of hope and I found the strength to resurrect again.

I heard Alexander practice promiscuity with an abundance of interchangeable lovers. He kissed, denuded and fucked other men, but I didn't know that his love had re-flourished for me in silence. I desired to seduce him, but was my passion for him ephemeral again? I wanted him to conquer my eternal love, but I still believed that my love for Alexander wasn't perpetual. I certainly didn't want to journey into the brutality and sufferance of love again, so my love flourished for Alexander in silence too. My bruises had faded away and I now passionately worked in a prison of slavery in Burger Queen. The stench of fast-food became embedded in

my blond hair. The strong smell of urine and puke entrenched in the restrooms repulsed me as I cleaned the toilets. No disposable latex gloves were provided for such a task, which I particularly found highly unhygienic, but cleaning the shit and piss of Dublin symbolised my freedom. The Celtic Tiger had created the Irish system of exorbitant rent, but it was a world that I wanted to belong to. I visited an attic room that was undersized and minimally furnished with objects that seemed to belong to a completely different era. The mattress was heavily stained, the paint on the ceiling was peeling, but such was the luxury that I could afford. The landlord was a well dressed ruffian, who extorted all rent in cash without providing receipt of payment. For some strange reason he was incapable of providing me with a lease, but he accepted to lower the deposit to £150 and handed me the key. The Georgian house was in Mountjoy Square, which was an area reputed for its high criminality, elevated unemployment rate and also the drug related problems associated with certain downtown districts of central Dublin. The idea of me residing there didn't enchant Alexander very much, but it was in practical walking distance to Grafton Street where I worked. I now battled for the freedom of my dreams alone.

The bathroom was shared with three other tenants, who did not the conduct the same level of cleanliness as me, but they all had the same precarious lifestyle. The sufferance of the 1994 Rwandan Genocide was ingrained in one tenant forever. He found the dream of liberty in the entitlement welfare culture of Ireland. Asylum seekers didn't have the legal right to work, which fuelled the rise in racism and Gahiji was crucified by righteous Catholics for bleeding the Irish economy. In Irish history holy Ireland didn't want to be enriched with homosexual fuckers, but judging by the intolerance that was overtly practiced by white supremacy I was beginning to believe that the Irish were xenophobic too. The second tenant had abandoned the catholic morals of Ireland by giving birth to a bastard son at the age of sixteen. Society devalued her as another state subsidised whore. Tanya was stigmatised as being a welfare-absorbing single mother, but there was no judgement of the catholic man that had ejaculated and abandoned her to such brutality. The third tenant was a middle aged Catholic, who prayed with immense reverence in Saint Francis Xavier Church in Upper Gardiner Street, but other than that Mr. Molony disclosed nothing about his life. Judging by his accent he was definitely from County Kerry, his shabby appearance revealed that he survived in profound hardship and it was clear by his chronic alcoholism that he had become severely entangled in the web of the Irish drinking culture. Each difference

was the root cause of great social exclusion, but those that were judged by the good Catholics of Ireland were clement in their regard to my homosexuality and didn't bear judgement. To my greatest astonishment the impoverished Catholics of Dublin didn't have a problem with homosexuality, contrary to the discrimination against queers that I had witnessed in the socially attractive parts of Ireland. Whereas the upper class that I had always frequented tended to catholically judge me, the lower class had tolerance and acceptance. I was liberated from the dark dusty closet of silence, I flourished in poverty and I tasted the freedom that I had always dreamed of.

Poverty was now my everyday foe and there was no dancing under the flashing disco lights of gay clubs anymore. I battled in a hand to mouth existence, silenced my destitution from the world and became completely asocial. In the supermarket I carefully analyzed the advantages of special offers and reduction coupons, which made certain necessities more affordable for me. The price now determined what I bought, I wiped my ass with the toilet paper that I had stolen from Burger Queen and I discovered that the super market brand was rather efficient in nourishment and in taste. Irish customers eschewed products in close proximity to the best before indicator, but I particularly appreciated such bargain food, which was severely discounted to render it more attractive for sale. Malnutrition and starvation contaminated the world, but the majority of shopping trolleys discriminated against fruit and vegetables that didn't conform to cosmetic perfection. Customer requirements preferred more pesticide residues rather than a blemished apple or a wonky shaped carrot and such prejudice had a direct impact on the substantial quantity of comestible food trashed by producers and retail outlets. A militant shop assistant distributed the unsellables and his recycling enabled me to balance the diversity of my diet, but a few weeks later his store implemented a radical solution against scavengery. Bleach was systematically poured over all discarded food, regardless of the fact that it was edible and perfectly fit for consumption. Ireland had become a haven for civil court compensation and the effectiveness of such a measure exempted stores from all liability. Virtuous Ireland was devoured by the consumption society that the Celtic Tiger had created and had certainly forgotten that it had risen from the ruins of the Great Famine. The urban littered streets of chronic shoppers represented what Ireland had now become. The poverty that the holy bible mirrored was abandoned, catholic morality was forsaken in the social conquest to acquire more and more materialism, the Irish had become blasé and an abundance of affluence was

worshiped more than the catholic god. Ireland had sacrificed its national identity to become Americanized and Irish men and women became entangled in the prison of a credit consumption society in total ignorance of the imminent economic crisis that was to come. I believed that dreams nourished freedom and I certainly knew that the pleasure of money was a double edged sword. I had seen the gold and diamond rings that glittered on her fingers ensnarl my mother in the rollercoaster of ephemeral happiness. Her passion for her treasures had enriched her to abandon all human values and the contamination of money had strengthened me to hate the world of materialism from an early age.

I did not rebel in a militant homosexual fashion, but I didn't live in the dark dusty closet of homosexual silence either. I believed that the key to advance social acceptance was the normalisation of homosexuality, but in my utopian vision I had forgotten the wrathful intolerance of the catholic god. Burger Queen was certainly an enriching experience and I learnt about the importance of productivity, marketing strategies, reaching sales objectives and the sufferance of being a queer. The standardised baloney used to oppress gays became the weapons that my manager actively voiced to belittle me. The holy heritage of Ireland had contaminated her to believe in the effeminate mannerisms that stereotyped gays, but I didn't have a condom filled pink handbag, a Madonna collection nor a fetish for high heels either. Caitriona believed in the catholic judgement that homosexuality was an abnormal practice and I battled the brutality of another crucifixion. She overtly highlighted the grotesqueness and ungodliness of homosexuality. I survived among the derogatory remarks that had transcended from catholic generation to generation and her prejudice generated the contagious spread of repugnance against my immorality. Some first names were never forgotten; Gareth sniggered and enriched her pleasure by mimicking "gay behaviours", while Simon laughed like a hyena in collaboration with her. Some employees acted as if they had heard nothing. They were certainly indifferent towards homosexual sufferance. Others lowered their eyes to the ground to ignore such injustice. Their silence enforced the sensation of my social solitude further. Nobody dared to defend me, which cultivated the liberation of her homophobia even more. Bartlomiej looked directly in my eyes with his silent compassion, but he didn't speak the language of Shakespeare well enough to communicate what he really thought. Should I have had the bravery to battle and defend the homosexual culture against the stigmas which dehumanised homosexuality? Irish gays had been slaughtered for my freedom, heroic queers had been crucified for my liberty, but I betrayed

the freedom of Irish homosexuality instead. Each homosexual had the potential to fight against intolerance, but I didn't understand that march towards equality yet. I didn't react to her deplorable behaviour in order to avoid total destitution, but Ireland also gave me no other choice. Hostility against queers in the workplace went completely unpunished. There was still no recognition of homosexual rights under the Irish Employment Equality Act and she was not liable for legal sanctions. I wanted to revolt against that fucking bitch, but silence was the price of freedom if I wanted to survive in the fascination of liberty in Dublin alone. The brutalisation of a queer didn't destroy me and I found little sufferance in being called "a fucking queer", the brutality that had crucified me in rural catholic Ireland had certainly strengthened my emotions.

An effeminate homosexual entered Burger Queen, his camp behaviour sharply contrasted to that of the virile looking heterosexual that he queued behind, but there was certainly no difference between the colour of his pink money and the colour of the heterosexual customer's money that I was serving. Close inspection indeed revealed that there was the Irish hero Daniel O' Connell on one side of both banknotes and his 1845 pledge to Irish freedom printed with the Dublin Fore Courts in the background on the rear of each £20 note too. There was no apparent reason to discriminate against either of them, except that one was handed to me by a heterosexual and the other by a queer. Caitriona turned to Gareth, who was standing behind the cash register next me. She did not silence her judgement of the "arse fucker" that I was now serving and rather than whisper into Gareth's ear with discretion, everyone heard the brutality that she should never have said. They both sniggered as if they were alone in private conversation, but each customer looked at them in total disbelief. Some acted as if they had heard nothing and looked away in a different direction, while others lowered their eyes to the ground in silence. One courageous woman and her boyfriend boycotted and left; they must have had tolerance for homosexuality. I looked into the tearful eyes of the homosexual that had tasted sufferance and my enragement resurrected. I certainly needed the job to pay my rent and electricity bill, the free burgers and greasy French fries that nourished me also sheltered me from total starvation, but I could not silence such injustice. My fist clenched tightly and I directly it towards Gareth. Its potent force made him stumbled and he fell to the tiled floor in defeat. Caitriona screamed "You're fucking fired". I tossed the Burger Queen logoed cap directly towards her face, "Stuff your fucking job up your fucking ass you fucking bitch" and the public behind the counter loudly applauded me. "You can't walk out in the middle of your shift".

"Fuck you", I grabbed my coat and voyaged into poverty. The "queer fucker" followed me into Grafton Street leaving the food that he had paid for behind him. We talked for hours on a park bench in Saint Stephan's Green. I was not a gay militant, but he sweetly called me his hero. I learnt that he tasted the sufferance of homosexuality in secondary school every day and that he was labeled "a bender, fag, faggot, fairy, nancy, poofster, queenie, queer and sissy". He had the legal right to practice homosexual freedom, but he only knew the brutality of catholic Ireland since the beginning of time. I solaced his tears and promised him that life would get better in the changing colours of the seasons. He disclosed that nobody until that day had ever defended him and that from the ashes of destruction I had given him a vision of hope. I kissed him on the cheek and he told me that he would never forget me. "Never abandon your dreams" I disappeared in the horizon of homosexual pride and I never saw him again.

The Creation of Eternal Brutality

Caitriona didn't have the legal right to withhold my P45, but the enraged bitch didn't liberate it from her claws immediately. Each time she regurgitated another far-fetched excuse, but what really destroyed me was the vengeance that I hadn't foreseen. It was the beginning of September, my fridge was almost empty, my money hungry landlord threatened me of eviction and there was still no sign of my wages in my bank account. I certainly didn't want to abandon my fascination for freedom, but poverty forced me. Caitriona had ravaged my dreams and in total desperation I implored my holy mother for help. Devoured by tears of emotion she believed that my love for her had resurrected. Indeed my bruises had faded away, but I relived the crucifixion that had destroyed me. She solemnly swore that she would never queer bash me again. I knew that in the creation of forgiveness that there was certainly perpetual sufferance to come, but I foolishly had the clemency to absolve her brutality. She contaminated me with her ephemeral love and ensnarled me in the prison of silence again. A few hours later the abandonment of my liberty came; my brother smugly handed me an envelope with £700 and a train ticket for the next day. I had promised to visit her, but she really didn't give me the choice of deciding when. My homosexuality reverted to the dark dusty closet of sufferance, but my landlord was enriched with £480 and there was food in my fridge again.

Portlaoise, Templemore, Thurles, Limerick Junction, Charleville, Mallow and my mother was waiting for me on the platform in Cork Kent Station. There was sincerity in her tears when she embraced me; perhaps the almighty catholic god of Ireland had really enriched her with the strength to love me again? She enlightened me that she had changed, indeed normally it was forbidden to pronounce the word homosexual in her presence, but she evoked the subject and liberated her deep fears and her profound sufferance too. She believed that there was perpetual social

solitude in homosexuality, but I reassured her that there was a world of acceptance beyond the intolerance that she practiced. She rephrased that the mental disorder of homosexuality condemned me to be alone in the barren dream of love forever, but there was nothing immoral about homosexuality and to her greatest dismay I had already tasted "queer love". I was banished from the kingdom of heaven, which totally broke her heart, but the god that she loved preached forgiveness and not rancour. She had heard the sermons on the pulpit condemn homosexuals, but where in her bible was it written "thou shalt not be a queer"? There was absolution of sin if I reverted to heterosexuality in repentance, but if her prayers were silenced it was god's will that I was gay. Homosexuality was innate and ingrained in me forever. What would her sisters say about her if they knew that she had mothered a "fucking queer"? I retorted that it was forbidden by the catholic god to cast a stone of judgement and added that her vocabulary needed to be more politically correct. I certainly knew my catholic bible more than she had thought and nourishing her with my holiness seemed to console her. She wanted me to live her dream and father some beautiful children, but homosexuality had made me sterile. There was nothing in the words of god to appease that sufferance for either of us. She didn't want to read RIP on my gravestone, but "queer fuckers" were promiscuous and condemned to die of AIDS. "Do you arse fuck men"? I didn't want to cultivate her with all the techniques of homosexuality that I practiced or enrich her with enragement either, so rather than confess that I condom fucked with an abundance of homosexual lovers, I prudishly moved my head from left to right in silence instead. "I don't want you to disgrace me with a coming out". I solemnly promised to live in the silence of my homosexuality forever and in return she accepted not of sprinkle me with holy water to hetero-sexualise me anymore. I was enslaved in the profound silence of homosexuality again, but that was the imposed condition for the resurrection of our love. She deluded me to have faith in her, but the savagery of her intolerance was only ephemerally silenced.

I wanted to experience the sensation of itinerancy for one last time, but my decision to defer my final university year encountered immense opposition from my catholic mother. She highlighted that the statistics indicated a low probability rate of an eventual return to the educational system in the aftermath of a gap year. Perhaps she was right that the attainment of fruition never came from reveries, but I retorted that the liberation of dreams was far better than having eternal regret. Her brutality resurfaced in her hostile glance and she silenced my insolence. I needed to be enriched

by the taste of an espresso on a crowded café terrace and to touch the colourful fragrance of baguette that floated in the air, while being seduced by the sound of the language of Molière in the background, but she didn't give me the liberty to journey back into my dream. The restaurant waiter job in France was forbidden to accept, because my pompous pretentious mother believed that the position of "a glorified slave" was far below my social status. She belittled the value of those that contributed to the rich diversity of services that society needed and had clearly forgotten that I had survived alone in the poverty of Dublin cleaning the puke, piss and shit that decorated the walls and floors of the Burger Queen toilets. I wanted to abandon my sufferance before the colourful leaves of autumn began to fall, but I was ensnarled to live in the catholic culture of Ireland. Her iron hand betrayed my vision of freedom and she destroyed my dream. I never saw the milky green colour of the river Arve, the divine splendour of the Mer de Glace or the abundance of perpetual snow that eternalised the season of winter in the Chamonix Valley. I silenced my enragement to honour the bible instead and did not revolt against the Fifth Commandment of god.

My mother was a martyr, she now housed, fed, clothed and educated me again, but it wasn't very catholic of her to incessantly throw it in my face like shit. In her desperation for social recognition she proclaimed to the world that she provided the luxury of all my needs and that she overly bestowed me with everything I desired. She sang in self-praise that my intelligence was thanks to the hard years of her sacrifices, which condemned me to live in the immense debt of her generosity forever. There was a profound and complicated web that entangled the corruption of money and the sentiment of affection in the core of my rural Irish home. My father's affluence was a two edged sword that certainly liberated the different steps of my dreams, but it also granted her the almighty power to silence my homosexuality. Poverty was forgotten, her money became pink and I socialised under the flashing disco lights of urban gay clubs in Dublin again. I was no longer a forgotten part of the consumption society of Ireland. Indeed, the abundance of food in my fridge that their catholic money bought symbolised that I had resurrected from the ruins of destitution. My despair intensified as the colourful leaves of autumn began to fall. The mountain of books in the library in UCD concealed an ocean of knowledge on the pages inside, but it was too much of an emotional challenge for me to even open them. Every student had pinpointed clear objectives about the professional direction awaiting them, but my greatest endeavour was to survive each day in an Irish world that I didn't want to belong to. I walked on the stone beach of Bray dreaming of freedom rather

than attending my university lectures. I mourned in regret and lamented for the reveries that I had forsaken. My Rwandan neighbour Gahiji complained that Paula Cole's "Where have all the cowboys gone?" was on replay again, but I needed that to solace me.

After an atypical job interview I was hired to become a member of staff in a prestigious gay venue in Dublin. Being highly organised I had rehearsed all the potential recruitment questions, but much to my greatest dismay it simply sufficed to engage in an un-catholic act to be hired. I was not very attracted to the flirtatious manager, his beauty was relatively limited, but being promiscuous I knelt before him in accordance to his unholy desire. He lowered his white faded coloured cotton underpants to his feet, inserted his virile erection profoundly into my mouth and my cold emotions sucked it lustfully. In the belief that mankind needed salvation the mythical son of god had accepted a crucifixion, in desperation I completely abandoned the righteousness of all catholic Irish virtues and a contract was signed in the immediate aftermath of his ejaculation. I needed to live savagely in the fruitful abundance of my dreams and I didn't justify my immorality. A cloud of cigarette smoke distended in the air and the flashing disco lights liberated me, but working unsociable hours as a barman became highly incompatible with early hour lectures. The mountain of books in the university library soon became completely forgotten. I didn't want to enrage my holy mother, so I silenced that I worked in the homosexual culture. I didn't want her brutality to destroy me, so I didn't enrich her to learn that I tasted the sensation of itinerancy for one last time. In total disobedience I deferred my university year, but was the creation of such silence a sin? My betrayal certainly mirrored the catastrophic emotional state of my mind.

Working in the core of the pink market enriched me with an insight into the operational mechanisms of homosexual seduction. Gay men preyed, devoured and certainly fucked in over abundance. Licentious queers believed in the dream of eternal love, but there was only despair in promiscuity. The passion of one night stands was an ephemeral victory for all interchangeable lovers, but as the light of dawn conquered Ireland lecherous men were betrayed by the sensation of eternal solitude again. There was no fruitful virtue in such a prison of homosexual lust, but there was profound social solidarity among all gays. Tolerance flourished among the different colours, religions, social statuses, professional standings, fetishes and sub-cultures of the homosexual world. Homosexuality did not

discriminate, but reunited all minority groups in a haven that protected all differences from the brutality of catholic Ireland. There was no distain against the effeminacy of camps, the virility of dykes, the flamboyance of drag queens, the butchness of bears or the eroticism of the leather community. Transsexualism and transvestism were stigmatised by Irish heterosexual judgement, but both naturally found acceptance among the mainstream gay community. There was absolutely nothing intrinsically immoral about the different branches of homosexuality, but the righteous straights of Ireland dehumanised our enriched beauty more and more. Step by step I disconnected from the heterosexual world of holy hypocrisy and in extremity I began to frequent only gays. In my desired isolation my estrangement alienated me from my dream of homosexual normalisation, but in such a disequilibrium of seclusion the homosexual culture defended me from homophobia. Behind many smiles there was sufferance and tears, but under the flashing disco lights all queers befriended to forget their persecution.

All staff members respected the strict dress code which applied to Thursday night Karaoke; hence I adopted the drag queen culture to become a voluptuous feminine creature too. An Event Organiser, who regularly frequented the bar, noticed my potential and generously proposed to hire me for some cash in hand services. Intrigued on the idea of earning a substantial sum of money effortlessly I zealously accepted. A gorgeous tight fitting sparkling blue dress clung to accentuate and feminise my slim body. Heavily applied layers of make-up de-masculinised me even further. The final touch of a Geri Halliwell style wig enhanced my total transformation into a beautiful goddess and I became completely unrecognizable. My mission consisted of tottering in O' Connell Street for three hours in silver stilettos, flirting with the ordinary people of Dublin and distributing flyers for the inauguration of a female shoe shop. I had a nostalgic thought for the Irish martyrs of the 1916 Easter Rising as I sheltered from a downfall of rain under the portico of the G.P.O. The monumental building had been a strongpoint in their rebellion against English colonisation and the injustices that had subdued Ireland. The heroic foundering fathers of Eire were condemned to capital punishment for the crime of their bravery, but in the sacrifice of their bloody deaths Ireland tasted independence. Ireland had lamented its heroes and had forgotten the value of their slaughter too, but the legendary bullet impacts that pockmarked the columns of the G.P.O eternalised the destructive nature of Ireland's violent birth. Every Irish schoolchild was led to believe in the irrefutable truth that St Patrick had banished snakes out of Ireland,

that oppression was still visible in the bombs that terrorised a divided nation and that the immorality of homosexuality was an eternal sin. In certain myths there was Irish beauty, in others the creation of animosity, but was catholic Ireland totally contaminated with brutality against queers? A homosexual in drag didn't symbolise veneration for the forefathers of Irish freedom. I waited for the outcry of Irish Catholics to stone me for my audacity, insolence, irreverence and profanity, but I was enriched by the sensation of liberalism in the streets of Dublin instead. Had Ireland changed utterly or was such an amazing sensation of tolerance ephemeral? What if homosexual sufferance became a forgotten memory in Irish history and the holy nation of Catholics liberated queer love in the sacrament of a pink marriage? I wanted perpetual freedom from the dark dusty closet of silence for all homosexuals, but did such freedom only exist in my dreams? Ireland embraced homosexuality with more and more acceptance, but there was certainly another catholic judgement to crucify me later that day.

I scrubbed away the pink nail varnish, the scarlet lip stick, the layers of heavily applied foundation, the hint of rosy blush and the marine blue eye shadow. I totally erased the feminine traces of the drag queen that had enriched my pockets with £200. I reverted into catholic virility and Ireland enslaved me in the prison of homosexual silence again. It was a fifteen minute walk from MountJoy Square to Smyths in Jervis Street. Teletubbies was the top-selling toy that year, so I knew exactly what I wanted for her birthday present; however I hadn't anticipated the long pre-Christmas shopping queue. I bought Tinkey Winkey, Dipsy, Laa-Laa and Po. Of course, buying all four of them in a consumption society was OTT, but being a homosexual bitch I targeted extravagance in order to outshine her godfather's gift. A ten minute walk followed to catch the number 42 Malahide bus. I hadn't forecasted so many traffic jams, but with all the colourful balloons and a houseful of people my hour lateness was completely unnoticed. One candle on a homemade pink iced sponge cake was blown out. I kissed Naomi tenderly on her forehead in the aspiration that one day she would truly know me, but the long battle to love my niece had just begun. Jerry Morey cuddled her affectionately and a cloud of smoke distended above his head. It didn't bother anybody that a cigarette dangled from his mouth, but it certainly enraged me that his passive smoking was contaminating my one year old niece. I politely informed him to go into the garden like every other smoker present that day, but my brother silenced me. My hand moved mechanically towards Jerry's lips and I denuded him of his cigarette. I recognised that glance of fury in my brother's eyes. "I'm going to give you five seconds to..." he didn't have

time to finish his sentence, the cigarette now floated in his pint glass. Molly had seen everything from the corner of the room and abandoned her chat with her sister Jacintha. The pack was taken out of his shirt pocket, a flame from his lighter appeared, with a few short puffs she brought life to a cigarette, glared at me with an air of judgement as she exhaled some smoke and placed the John Player Black in Jerry's mouth. Enriched with a smug smile of satisfaction he inhaled it deeply and a cloud of toxicity distended above Naomi's head again. My fist clenched, but the baby in his arms was shielding him. It was a typical family reunion; "You fucker", my mother sounded so wicked. Normally she would have called me "a queer fucker", I was more used to that, but there were too many people present for a coming out.

My brother summoned me to follow him into the garden. "You fucking insulted my guest......" I disconnected from reality; with my eyes fixed on his moving lips it gave him the impression that I was attentively listening, but I was a dreamer floating in and out of his monologue instead. I further justified "Dad's asthmatic", after all how many times had we seen him gasping for breath? He whispered in my ear that I was a "deviant-minded queer bastard with a mental disorder". There was a certain consistency in my coldness that made me become totally indifferent to sufferance and with a haughty laugh I sincerely thanked him for the compliment. He then labeled me as being 'a fucking pedophile", which was unforgiveable. My brutality resurrected and there was an emotional dysfunction inside of me; "An eye for an eye, a tooth for a tooth and certainly a bruise for a bruise". I had femininely walked in drag in O' Connell Street earlier than day, but I fought with masculinity in his garden and each mighty blow I received from my brother I returned to him another one. All the guests were stupefied spectators behind the net curtains of the sitting room window. My holy father intervened and with catholic obedience my enemy retreated. He tenderly wiped my lower lip and his handkerchief reddened with the colour of my blood. The physical dispute in the garden had severely soiled my shirt and my father's hand kindly brushed down my grass stained trousers too. With his arm affectionately around my shoulder he smiled, but did he really condone my violence? "I'm proud of your right hook" was discretely whispered in my ear as he closely embraced me in a hug. Had I inherited his passion for boxing or did I merely imitate what he practiced when he crucified his homosexual son? Perhaps I had forgotten, but it was the first time in my life that I actually felt that I had a father. Jerry was now standing by the front door, the cigarette still dangled from his mouth or perhaps he had even sparked up another one. "You're a

fuckin' bastard" my father's eyes transpierced him like daggers. My foe fled back inside and I proudly kissed my father on the cheek. Only my father heard me say that my departure was imminent, but "fuck off", not even a second later my catholic brother threw my coat at me. My father did not defend me further, but lowered his eyes in defeat. With tears in my blue eyes I walked into the horizon alone. Molly arrived with the Teletubbies in the Smyths Toys bag, "we don't want your fucking present", but I pretended that I was too far away to hear that.

The drag queen culture enriched my pockets with an abundance of money towards the last days of 1997. Companies had their Christmas parties and the social trend that year was drag queens dancing on stage under multi-coloured flashing disco lights in heterosexual clubs mouthing either Abba or Spice Girls on playback. Scarlet lip stick, layers of heavily applied foundation, a hint of rosy blush and marine blue eye shadow transformed me into a flamboyant feminine entity and the taste of pink money corrupted me more and more. My silver glitter nail varnish, which I had discovered in the pound shop, coordinated with my silver stilettos, but if I practiced the art of drag it was for money and certainly not the development of another fetish. That Christmas everyone received expensive presents, but especially Alexander. I still hadn't fallen in perpetual love with him, but I certainly didn't forget all that he had done for me in my hours of need. The leather jacket that he had much admired when shopping together in Brown Thomas was under my Christmas tree in Mountjoy Square. "Away in a Manger", "God Rest Ye Merry Gentlemen", "Hark the Herald Angels Sing", "Joy to the World", "O Come, All Ye Faithful", "Silent Night" and "The First Noel", it was a typical Christmas in rural catholic Ireland and hymns blissfully resounded in my catholic house. The mouth watering ham was boiled in the salty cabbage water, the potatoes were roasted with the fresh herb and onion stuffed turkey, the overheated marrow fat peas denuded of their transparent skins and my mother moaned that they were too mushy. The spiced beef was baptised with Knorr Savoury Gravy and her Brussels sprouts were still my favourite. It was the first Christmas without my brother home and there was certainly too much food on the table for three people. He phoned just after we had finished the homemade banana and pear custard trifle dessert, which my holy mother had made especially for me. She was very pissed off that his Christmas was with his in-laws instead of having the traditional one with us and she coldly accorded him only one minute of her precious time. She lied "with all the preparation I don't have a second more to chat", that wasn't very catholic of her. My father watched football TV and

simultaneously engaged in a ten minute conversation with my brother. It was my turn in the hierarchy next, "Merry Christmas" there was sincerity in my words, but he retorted "Fuck off". Apparently he hadn't forgotten the birthday party fiasco and he directed his telephone handset back to its cradle. A vacant beep beep beep sound followed, but not wanting to enrich my parents with enragement I didn't enlighten them. I continued speaking into the void on the phone alone for another minute. "I love you too" the exaggerated words of my conclusion greatly surprised them; it wasn't the fraternal vocabulary that was normally used. It was an atypical Christmas in my catholic home with peace and goodwill to heterosexuals and homosexuals alike. Their catholic judgement of queers was silenced and their intolerance didn't crucify me that Christmas Day.

New Year's Eve was celebrated in a prestigious urban club in Dublin under the flashing disco lights of heterosexuality and catholic Ireland liberated another homophobic blow on the road of my sufferance. The dance steps to "Stop" had been practiced several times that day, the blond streaks dyed into the flaming red hair of my wig had the desired effect that I wanted and a Union Jack dress Geri Halliwellise me further. "The Spice Boy Drag Queens" performed on stage, but my virile aggressor thrust his way through the crowd as if he had preselected me. The powerful force of his masculine fist collided with my face in a repetitive fashion. The other drag queens fled the brutality of such slaughter in screams of terror. I staggered with difficulty to regain my feet, but another kick was directed with vigour to my stomach. In the beginning the public thought that the aggression was part of the act, but when they saw the bouncers react their laughter became sighs of horrification. The music momentarily stopped and an abundance of enraged shouts were directed towards my assailant. He was escorted towards the door and ejected from the straight club in punishment for his disorderly conduct. The venue manager arrived "The show must go on". He offered me a bottle of champagne and fifty quid extra if I accepted. I gloriously resurrected from the brutality of Ireland and smiled in total agreement. He then made a nod sign to the DJ, silence was abandoned and music played again. "You just walk in, I make you smile..." the other drag queens joined me on stage "you don't even know me". "Geri, Geri, Geri" resounded from every wall in the club at end of the performance. It was my curtain call; Geri Halliwell certainly would have been proud of me. I removed the silver glitter nail varnish, the scarlet lip stick, the layers of foundation, the hint of blush and the marine blue eye shadow for the last time. £250, a bottle of champagne and a black blue eye had enriched me. I reverted into catholic virility again, my drag queen voyage had come to an

ultimate end and my dancing on stage under the flashing disco lights was eternally forsaken.

Three women standing by the bar were still taking about the violent scene even after I had changed clothes, but they didn't recognise me now. Brendan or should I say "Baby Spice" opened the champagne, Peter Posh Spice glanced in amazement at the price list; "Jesus fucking Christ, lads, we're drinking a hundred quid". Stephen Scary Spice laughed "Did you see your shiner?" and Jeremy Sporty Spice then raised her glass in my honour; "Cheers Geri" and our five glasses touched in salutation. They abandoned me to meet their boyfriends in "The George". Perhaps I should have forsaken the heterosexual ambiance too, but I didn't feel like walking the short distance. Ten, nine, eight, seven, the countdown to 1998 had begun. Three, two, one, "Happy New Year" and there was "Auld Lang Syne" in the background. Happy New Year my ass I thought, the bruise under my eye that the mirror behind the bar reflected was the brutality of 1997. The heterosexuals around me passionately embraced in kiss, but my life was an emotional roller coaster and I was fucking single. There wasn't a homosexual in that hostile environment of straights for me to seduce that night, but to make things worse a pissed guy bumped into me and decorated my plain white shirt with his pint of Guinness. What dreams did 1998 want to liberate or destroy for me? I poured another double champagne to forget all of my sufferance and I even asked the guy next to me for a fag. A few seconds later a cloud of smoke distended above my head and I felt a certain sensation of relaxation. My mobile vibrated in my pocket, "Happy New Year Alexander", but in disheartenment he replied "Derek just dumped me". I laughed; the ephemeral love had ended just before the twelve bells of midnight. 1998 was certainly a year that was never to be forgotten.

I pushed through the noise of crowded people and I was now in the cold street. "Meet me outside the Gaiety in ten minutes and..." I had forgotten to recharge my mobile phone again. I hadn't heard the end of his sentence and I certainly needed to know. The bouncer refused to let me back into the club, "I'm Geri Halliwell". "You're fucking pissed man". I justified "I'm the drag queen you saved earlier and I forgot my jacket", that changed everything and he immediately permitted me to re-enter. Alexander looked so fucking virile; he was sporting the leather jacket that I had bought him. "What the fuck", his hand tenderly touched my bruised face. I suddenly needed freedom from what I silenced profoundly inside and Alexander

liberated his seduction too. I lustfully kissed his succulent lips with almighty passion. The taste of the cigarette that I had just smoked betrayed me, but I justified that I had certainly needed a calming soothing pleasure. Were we devoured by the desolation of solitude or conquered in harmony by eternal love? Perhaps the bubbles in the champagne had gone directly to my heart rather than my head? We denuded, but it was completely different from all the other times that I had mechanically fucked homosexual men. The sex that I had always practiced was emotionless in the fulfilment of a horny desire, but when I looked into Alexander's blue eyes that night, I was making love. Each sensation was in total accordance to what Aristotle had said and we were "composed of a single soul inhabiting two bodies."

The Promise Of Silence

.

15

The Infatuation of Despair

Before my eyes on the breakfast table was a luscious plate of rashers, sausages, slices of black and white pudding and a fried egg, but if Alexander really wanted me to fall in love with him forever he certainly needed to butter my toast too. "Fuck off", and he passionately kissed me instead. Under the flow of warm water in the shower he caressed my denuded body. The sensuality of each touch completely seduced me, "I love you Alexander". It was the first time in my life that I said those words with real sincerity. Homosexuality had a certain advantage that heterosexuality didn't have and from his wardrobe I borrowed a pair of socks and a boxer shorts. Alexander confirmed that soaking my stained shirt in soapy water overnight had not removed the Guinness that had baptised me. He handed me a long-sleeved T-shirt and what was tight fitting on him enhanced me with a baggy urban street wear look. Alexander wore his black leather pants. Judging by my erection he was so fucking sexy in his leather. Using what leftovers were in his fridge I created a delectable meal and candles on the table revealed my romantic touch. For dessert there was a colourful fresh fruit salad. I explained that the tulip shaped design of the Waterford crystal glass, concentrated the charismatic fragrance of the whiskey inside and enhanced the taste of the full-bodied aroma sensations, but apparently I was still a philistine concerning the whiskey culture. "That a double scotch not a double whiskey", he hadn't even tasted the decadent amber coloured liquid in the glass that I served him yet, but judging uniquely by the shade of the colour, he knew the difference already. He was a true connoisseur and his cultural passion was a journey of a palette of colours that ranged from jonquiripe corn to sun-kissed bronzes. A cigar from his humidor was guillotined and identified as a Toro. After a couple of long puffs it glowed uniformly and a cloud of smoke distended above his head. A luxury cigar was "a pleasure in life" that he granted himself more than occasionally and the passionate way that he smoked it certainly enriched his virility further. "I can't wait 17 more days for your birthday". He impatiently opened a drawer and from his

bureau and withdrew a square shaped box. What glittered on his finger I had always admired and the beautiful gold ring inside, which was engraved with my name, was encrusted with the same black stone as his. There were tears in his glorious blue eyes, "I love you so much" and Alexander immortalised his deep affection for me. I wanted to flourish in the passion of his kisses forever and I liberated my perpetual emotions for him too, but was the beauty of such love destined to be eternal or ephemeral?

On the 7th of January 1998, caller ID on my mobile phone revealed a familiar number. "Hello my sexy lover", but rather than hear the virility of Alexander seducing me in reply, it was a feminine voice that I heard instead. Indeed we had never met, but Liz had the impression that she already knew me. She didn't know how to tell me, but judging by the tears that I heard falling from her eyes there was great sufferance in what I needed to know next. In the seconds that followed I learnt what I didn't want to know. There 458 road deaths in Ireland that year and tragically Alexander was one of them. "My brother always said that he was going to marry you". Her beautiful words were the greatest sufferance of my whole life. I don't remember much of anything after that. I felt enragement more than sufferance and my mourning immortalised my perpetual love for Alexander. I walked to Saint Francis Xavier Church and prayed for hours to a god that I didn't believe in. What if homosexuals were really banished from the kingdom of heaven? If I reverted to catholic prayer could I resurrect Alexander or was his soul condemned to the burning fires of hell for eternity? The almighty god of Ireland did not answer my questions and many more tears fell from my blue eyes in despair that day. In a silent prayer I lit a holy candle, ashes to ashes, dust to dust, I loved him forever.

His funeral was somewhere in Sligo, but I didn't go. I mourned in an abundance of solitude alone instead. He was buried in a cemetery that I never visited, in a village that I have even forgotten the name of. It solaced me to think that his coffin was in the same flower covered grave as his beloved mother. It comforted me to believe that she was there for him in death. On the night of his funeral I battled to survive in despair and lamented with a bottle of Paddy, twenty Benson and Hedges and a Henri Wintermans Half Corona Cigar, the latter which I entirely smoked in homage to Alexander. I wanted to forget my sufferance and silence my emotions, but each double whiskey that I drank seemed to enhance my sufferance even further. Come the morning nothing had changed, the bottle was almost half empty, the ashtray of butts overflowed, the odour of stale

tobacco was impregnated in the walls of my flat, but I still had my sufferance. Alcohol wasn't the almighty solution to appease my grief or my hangover, but I drank another double whiskey and smoked another two cigarettes for breakfast. A few minutes later I needed to regurgitate and afterwards I cleaned the vomit that I had created from the carpeted floor. The mirror reflected a person that completely repulsed me. Alexander certainly would have been enraged if I voyaged on that roller coaster of self destruction forever. More tears fell from my eyes, but from those tears I resurrected. Portlaoise, Templemore, Thurles, Limerick Junction, Charleville, Mallow and my mother was waiting for me on the platform in Cork Kent Station. I needed to forget my sufferance and be liberated from Dublin. My homosexuality was forbidden in rural catholic Ireland, so I silenced my woe in the days that followed. My silence betrayed Alexander as if he had never existed, but I was in the dark dusty closet of homosexuality again. I didn't enrich her to learn about the brutality that destroyed me when she admired the black stoned ring that decorated my finger. In her creation of homosexual silence I was totally alone. My perpetual love for Alexander now belonged to my secret garden of silence forever.

In the following weeks homosexual promiscuity and the freedom of the queer fucking culture contaminated me with further immorality. I seduced naked men in abundance under the flashing disco lights of catholic Ireland, but one night stands ruthlessly intensified the profound sensation of my eternal solitude even more. In the destitute of love I kissed, denuded and consumed man after man, but licentiousness did not diminish that profound feeling of being alone. Devoid of affection and wanting to be liberated from my sufferance, I fucked an umpteen quantity of interchangeable lovers. I consumed so many homosexuals with ephemeral passion, but there was no sentiment of affection in such despair. All the men that I seduced at night were forgotten when the light of dawn conquered Ireland again. Was my sexual enragement my revenge on Alexander? Was the practice of promiscuity my betrayal of his forsaken love? I was condemned to the solitude of loving Alexander in silence forever, but I certainly didn't want to live in the valley of tears either. Perhaps I should have lamented more, but fucking was part of my sufferance and I needed to abandon the dream of his perpetual love. An attractive man of metrosexual appearance flirted with me in Grafton Street. Judging by his cultivated accent he was of a high social standing and his charisma led me to presuppose that he was endowed with all the moral and ethical principles that Irish Catholics have.

In my judgement his eyes mirrored sincerity, his seductive smile enriched his beauty, but I hadn't tasted the brutality of his kiss yet.

As he savagely groped my erection he passionately implored me to be corrupted by his bare penis, but it was of utmost importance not to play Russian roulette in the promiscuous world of the gay culture. The spread of STDs certainly did not discriminate between heterosexuals and homosexuals, but the common practice of homosexual promiscuity did disproportionately impact the rampant transmission of HIV in the gay community. I was an absolute believer of condom fucking and my categorical refused to engage in unsafe sex aroused his rage. My denuded body felt completely repressed and imprisoned under the masculine weight of his corporal mass. I struggled to be liberated from his domination, but the more I battled the more his aggressiveness seemed to increase. Without hesitation his hand smothered my mouth to silence my resistance. The pungent smell of nicotine embedded in his fingers bewildered me; after all there had been no cigarette taste in his kisses. A fierce glance of lust glittered in his eyes to enhance the level of his determination to fuck me. He must have seen the terror in my eyes, but the more I contested to be liberated the more his force intensified. It was clear that I did not consent in what qualified as potential homosexual rape, but his persistence to penetrate me strengthened. It was certain that he wanted to attain his sordid desire at all costs. There was a sudden smashing sound of a fallen object. It had originally been a designer bedside lamp, which one had to admire when first seen, but its beauty had become a symbol of destruction in my struggle for freedom. The abundance of broken glass, which littered a considerable surface area of the parquet floor seduced his undivided attention and enabled me to become liberated. I searched for my clothes, a second later I was fully clothed, but he needed to punish me for my insolence. Under the surface of his beauty I discovered his brutality and his fist collided with my face.

I had grown up in the poverty of my father's love and in the coldness of his emotions, but I had certainly inherited his passion for boxing too. I suddenly remembered his roaring words "speed, reflex and endurance". Enragement enriched me with brutality, a warrior resurrected from silence and my ephemeral lover was now my opponent. In a fully upright stance I delivered a powerful uppercut to my adversary's chin. A close range jab to his chest destabilised him even further. I mechanically adopted the defensive position; my legs perfectly shoulder-width apart, my left hand

and foot out front, my elbows close to my ribs with my chin tucked into my chest. My ability to predict the direction of his punches appreciably lessened the potent force of the blows that he liberated. My body shifted slightly to the right in anticipation as another punch arrived in his counter attack. Once his still-extended arm had been evaded, I guided a swinging circular movement, which fissured the vulnerable layer of skin just below his left eye. In the seconds that followed my knuckles seemed to explode in agony, but my savagery had the desired victory that I wanted. Tears of blood now trickled down his face in defeat. The key turned, the door opened, the cold night air caressed me and the streets of Dublin liberated me again. I wanted to forget him, but for several days the mirror reflected the impact of his brutality.

His physical appearance didn't seduce me much, but Robert certainly knew how to resurrect my dreams from the sufferance that I wanted to forget. I saw flowers when I should have seen weeds, I forgave his brutality when he destroyed me and the passion of each cold kiss somehow ensnarled me in the prison of my need to be loved by him. To cultivate our love I accepted his desire to live with him, but it was definitely far too soon after our first kiss. Robert belonged to the convivial climate of the Irish social binge drinking culture and I learnt that he overly practiced the national Irish sport of getting pissed. He ingurgitated pint after pint; indeed he had a certain fondness for alcohol and had developed a high level of tolerance for it in the years before we had met. The mass of empty glasses in a linear fashion in front of him was an irrefutable indicator of the full extent of his alcoholism, but I was too besotted by him to have a catholic judgement. Our social life flourished surrounded by his circle of drunken friends, who accepted his generous offer to buy another round of drinks, but always forgot when it was their turn. His jovial laugh strengthened in their company, his incomprehensive words slurred more and more and a cloud of Dunhill smoke stagnated directly above his head. What the fuck had enticed me to fall in love with Robert? The virtue of alcohol was that it softened his emotions and it was at that moment that I tasted the sincerity of his love. His kisses became passionate, but that gentleness was always ephemeral and behind closed doors I tasted the enragement of his clenched fists. The entangled web of social euphoria in pubs enriched the brutality of his love, it crucified my reveries, created my sufferance, but my silence liberated him from the judgement of Ireland.

The brutality that was engrained in me resurrected, my violence responded to his violence "an eye for an eye, a tooth for a tooth and a bruise for a bruise", but the sufferance that decorated my body certainly represented that he was stronger than me. It became frequent that I walked under the beauty of the stars alone to evade his nocturnal drunken rages. The illuminated world of neon shop signs and deserted streets enhanced the sensation of solitude that devoured me. A few hours later upon my return he was placid in his sleep. My frigid body wanted to be warmed and comforted by the blazing heat that his naked body emitted, but in fear of awakening his enragement I dared not touch him. Robert was not inclined to suffer from hangovers, but he definitely suffered from a dissociative identity disorder. He had so many different distinct personalities depending on the harmony of his humour, so I never knew which man the light of dawn was going to reveal. One day I returned after food shopping, but I had forgotten to buy milk to soften the bitter taste of his coffee. I certainly felt the impact of his temper, but that valuable lesson taught me never to forget to buy a pint of milk again. Some mornings I didn't recognise him at all because of his gentleness; that was when his erection made love to me and he had completely forgotten the potent punches of the night before. His mental disposition and temperament changed in a matter of seconds, either he loved me with docility or he hated me in the liberation of his brutality. My dream of perpetual love was in the ruins, but his seductive words still enthralled me. I needed to taste more sufferance before I desired my liberty again.

I succeeded in reassuring Robert of the sincerity of my love when he was sober, but under the strong influence of alcohol he became completely unpredictable in his behaviour and even more irrational in his judgement. I thought that the green eyed monster symbolised that he loved me deeply, but there was absolutely no love in the domestic violence that debased me. Scenes of jealousy were prevalent in our relationship. He was plagued by insecurity and demented in the belief that I flaunted with all men, so I submissively began to walk with my eyes lowered. In the same way that holy Catholics confessed their sins I had to justify everything when I wasn't by his side. I basically lived in the prison of getting the third degree. There were an abundance of stipulations to abide by in the cultivation of his love and step by step I became passively enslaved in the hard conditions of his domination. It even became forbidden for me to frequent my friends without him; heterosexuals and homosexuals alike. They made inhuman efforts to tolerate his insolence, but his contemptuous regard towards me naturally increased their dislike of him. One night I liberated

my flirtatious smile on the dance floor with a really cute guy. It didn't require much to fuel the emotion of his brutality and my irreverence towards him enraged him. He raised his hand as if he wanted to hit me, but he certainly didn't display his true nature in public. It was later when alone that I reaped the hostility that I had innocently harvested and he punished me for my "straying eyes", but I still loved him afterwards.

It was to the stupefaction of my social entourage that the more abusive Robert was towards me that the more I worshipped him. A cacophony of concerned voices encouraged me to forsake him, but I silenced his flaws to passionately defend him instead. Nothing had the power to dissuade me from loving him. In time my social circle radically decreased in size because their critical judgement of his odious behaviour enraged him. What they didn't understand was that the more they revolted the more he slaughtered me and the more he hated them the more I became isolated in the solitude of his love. The rumours stated that Robert kissed, denuded and fucked other men, but in the belief that no man belonged to another man I tolerated his betrayal. Forewarned was forearmed, I had seen so much promiscuity in the gay culture of Ireland, so I gave him the liberty to fuck others in silence if he wanted. Homosexuals wooed me, I even felt a passionate desire for some, but I didn't taste their kisses in seduction. Working in the gay bar was the absolute freedom that I didn't want to lose, but it became more and more problematic. With an abundance of rage Robert implored me to change jobs, but I categorically refused to become totally enslaved in his jealousy. I did not submissively surrender to his plea, hence the scenes of his mistrust intensified, but even if I had worked in a world of Eunuchs, he still would have been jealous despite their sexual impotence. I revolted for the first time; perhaps something in me was changing? Was my love dying in the sufferance of his brutality?

His unscrupulous need for my money was entangled with my perverted need for his affection and the more I loved him the more impoverished I became. I provided for all his needs and bestowed him with everything he desired. Robert was a parasite; my labour nourished and housed him, but I soon discovered that his light-fingered hands abused my wallet to buy his Dunhill cigarettes too. In total desperation to taste perpetual love I enabled him to leech me, but I didn't care because in return I felt loved. Ireland was a paradise for social welfare benefit fraud; Irish Catholics prayed to the almighty god with reverence, but Robert preyed on Ireland to survive. As an active self-employed taxi driver he knew every street and every road in

Dublin. The world saw a hard working man, enriched with the values of Irish morality, but underneath the surface of his righteous appearance was the treachery of his silenced corruption. "Thou shalt not steal", but Robert had long abandoned the virtuous words of the Eighth Commandment. He ruthlessly ravaged Ireland and I lived in the total ignorance that Ireland sustained him. With readiness I entrusted that my money enriched the landlord each month, but the bastard that I loved had a welfare housing supplement and cultivated his alcoholism with the fruit of my work instead.

An abundance of Irish rain fell from the dark cloudy sky. His chronic eczema had become volcanic and I was condemned to what seemed like an interminable wait in the doctor's surgery. In fear of cross contamination from the other patients I had strongly set forth my desire not to accompany him, but Robert silenced my freedom again. I was now surrounded by pallid faces because I had passively accepted my affliction rather than confront his brutality. I flicked through a glossy covered magazine to give the vague impression that I was attentive to its content, but in fact my blue eyes glared around the waiting room in a silent effort to diagnose their ailments. People watching seemed to pass the time more quickly than reading, but with catholic judgement a haggard middle-aged woman stared back at me in total disapproval of my impoliteness. Perhaps I suffered from a renowned Irish disease called curiosity, but not wanting to challenge her I broke all eye contact with her. My ephemeral interest reverted to the magazine, which had become idle in my hands, but I rapidly became distracted by the tick tock sound effect of the clock just above my head. It totally enraptured all of my undivided attention and over-powered me to ponder that I was ageing fast. Another glance around engrossed me in the information on the medical posters on the wall, but they weren't sufficiently appealing enough to captivate me for very long. I then fidgeted with my stainless steel Swatch in another attempt to consume my impatience. The GP only needed to write a prescription for some topical corticosteroid creams, but I had the impression that I was waiting for Godot.

The surname of the next patient was announced by the doctor and the haggard middle-aged woman that had stared at me so much disappeared from my view. As I journeyed towards the reception I overheard the secretary request an unemployment medical card from Robert. Much to my surprise he did deliver it into her hand. My presence had ensnarled him and

I certainly learnt that the man I loved wasn't honest. The smug look that had always danced in his eyes faded as the disclosure of his fraudulent scheme enlightened me. He justified that if Ireland had the generosity to sustain the comfortable existence of immigrants, that it was his natural right to have the same equality because he was an Irish man. In the core of his discriminative discourse it suddenly became transparent where the abundance of his available money for alcohol really came from. It was now also clear why the apartment lease was exclusively under his name; not because he wanted to protect the privacy and intimacy of our homosexuality in the way he had always claimed, but because Ireland housed him too. In my catholic judgement he certainly betrayed Ireland and even if I didn't feel great affection for Ireland anymore, I was engulfed by such a sensation of hate for a social parasite that bled my country. The Irish struggled to survive in the enslavement of the Celtic Tiger, but pint after pint Robert ruthlessly ravaged their Ireland. They battled to pay high interest rate mortgages and to nourish the needs of their catholic children, but he didn't give a fuck about their problems. It was a great injustice that both Ireland and I sustained him and my righteous opinion openly disclosed my distaste of his immorality. His aggressive words silenced my abhorrence with rage, but I revolted that my respect for him was in ruins. I didn't want his brutality to destroy me again, but I needed to defend Ireland. The door of the apartment slammed behind me, which was a clear indicator of the imminent slaughter that was to come. As I removed my wet bomber jacket he lit a cigarette and puffed on it heavily. He then punished me with more aggressivity than ever before. Normally the exertion of his physical force was directly associated with the extent of his drunkenness, but it was the first time that he was completely sober. The force of his masculine punches soon became mundane. I knew that it was wrong for me to love him with such sincerity, but I had fallen in love with the need of being in love. I was completely dependent on his love in order to survive.

I was beginning to understand the patterns which nourished his brutality, so I no longer retorted against his criticism, defended my dreams from his destruction or revolted in open defiance of his rage. With what seemed to be genuine words he always begged for my forgiveness. With tears glittering in his brown eyes he implored me not to abandon him. Engulfed in an ocean of sincerity he swore with his hand on his holy bible that he would change. He kissed me with passion and I believed in his solemn promise, but his repentance was always ephemeral. Brutality was profoundly engrained in Robert since the beginning of time. He didn't

know how to be any different and he crucified me more and more. In regret he liberated his lustful desires and it was at that precise moment that he loved me the most. He denuded me to reveal the bruises that his enragement had created and in the act of fucking there was so much sufferance. The movement of his erection aggravated the throbbing pangs that invaded my whole body, as if I were slaughtered by the stabbing effect of a million daggers tearing into my flesh. As he moaned in pleasure I groaned in pain. Where was the white-picket fenced suburban home of perpetual love that I had once believed in? Perhaps in the homosexual culture that dream never came true? In the changing colours of the seasons my love was ravaged by despair. His kisses repulsed me and my naked body stiffened in cold rejection of his touch when we fucked. Our naked bodies soon became complete strangers in the double bed that we shared. I needed to abandon him forever.

16

The Destruction of Forgotten Years

Robert was liberated from his sufferance dancing under the flashing disco lights to vibrant music. The freedom of the promiscuous gay culture and the heavy consumption of alcohol enhanced the euphoria in his insouciant appearance, but beneath the surface he silenced the destruction of forgotten years. Certainly everyone in holy catholic Ireland had a promise of silence, for some it strengthened them to become warriors, for others it destroyed them in a prison of eternal tears and for Robert it created his savage emotion of brutality. In the harmony of silence there was serenity, but in the elapse of time it either crucified or liberated mankind forever. Robert's sufferance needed a heroic resurrection and one tearful night his irrevocable words revealed everything. Indeed underneath the facade of his aggressivity I discovered that there a very sensitive man. A glass containing a lot of Smirnoff trembled in his hand, but a series of heavily inhaled puffs on his Dunhill seemed to calm him a little. He ingurgitated another double vodka almost instantaneously after the first. The cigarette was stubbed out in the ashtray on the table in front of him and then his long voyage towards his liberty began. No beautiful flowers had blossomed in the garden of his youth. It was clear that the journey into his life that night was going to be extremely strong in emotion. There had always been a certain consistency in his coldness and I was beginning to understand why.

His father seduced her with kisses, he fucked her with passion and nine months later Robert was born. In the catholic Ireland of 1961 his mother was enslaved to declare the solemn vow of eternal love before the almighty god. Social and religious pressures condemned her to love, to cherish and obey till death and holy ordinance gave rise to her troth and her eternal sufferance. Coming from an Irish home of high catholic principles and social morals compelled his father to be a respectable man; hence in accordance to the strict ethics of the catholic Irish culture, he was condemned to marry her in her pregnant state. Even thought he really

didn't know her, he submitted to the sacrament of a shotgun wedding and he solemnly pledged to love her forever too. They had never had the time to fall in love, but the importance was that Robert was a real Irish Catholic and not a bastard born out of wedlock. There was no harmony between love and the savagery that dwelled in their holy home. Brutality was a banality of her everyday life and his drunken father slaughtered her incessantly. She had destroyed his dream of freedom and she certainly needed to be eternally punished by his rage. She lived in the silence of her fallen tears and his militant blows crucified her again and again. Robert never tasted the frivolous sensation of a normal childhood. From an early age it was made clear that he was the son that his father never wanted. The entanglement of brutality that had created his sufferance was profoundly embedded in Robert since the beginning of time.

His revelations enriched and enlightened me to understand that the complexity of certain social problems had escalated his brutality and his sufferance. In his flashback another double whiskey fuelled his enraged father with the courage to hit her again. He vividly remembered the fear that glittered in her eyes as she implored him to have pity. The tears that fell from Robert's eyes equally begged him to have mercy on his mother, but his rage was already liberated and he destroyed her even more. A cold paternal discipline and a militant love reared Robert and he learnt that "virile Irish men don't fucking cry". A forceful blow directly struck the six year old, but was that to silence him or to masculinise his son? His mother embraced her precious child in her arms to intercept the physical impact of the potent punches and to shield him from his father's virility, but some blows circumvented her defense and Robert prematurely became a man. Was Robert the creation of the passionate violence that he tasted in his catholic home? Was such brutality genetic or learnt? He was completely indifferent to the emotion of love because he didn't know what the normality of love really meant, but did he have the almighty power to abandon the cycle of brutality and step into the light of freedom? Robert had absolutely no control over his rage either and there was certainly nothing heroic in the way that he loved me. He slaughtered me with the same destruction and every sordid part of the violence he described was reproduced by him. I was certain that his father had created all the behavioral and emotional dysfunctions in his life, but I still didn't know everything yet.

There was a few seconds of silence as Robert moistened his lips again, but this time to increase the euphoric effect of vodka he consumed a large quantity directly from the bottle instead. He stubbed out yet another cigarette in the ashtray, which now overflowed with butts. With a couple of short firm puffs another Dunhill glowed uniformly and a cloud of fresh smoke distended above his head. The mechanism of domestic violence was deeply imprinted in Robert since an early age. The scenes of destruction and the tragedy of tears that he had witnessed were profoundly enrooted and engrained in his mind. She loved her oppressor with the same devotion to love that I loved her son and had the same emotional generosity to forgive as me. There was always the same barren hope that he would change, but his father slaughtered her again and again. Robert clearly understood that I tasted the same sufferance, but he was unable to justify why he reproduced the same potent punches. For the first time ever he did display what really seemed to be genuine regret. Perhaps Robert didn't know how to be any different, but he certainly promised me that he wanted to change. With more deep emotion falling from his tearful eyes than ever before, he disclosed that he didn't want to be like his father anymore. It had become a ritual that Robert swore with his hand on his holy bible; how many times had I seen him vow to god to abandon his brutality? An ocean of sincerity glittered in his brown eyes again, but this time I really thought that it was a solemn promise that he could respect forever. From the dark dusty closet of his despair he seemed to find a vision of hope and I had faith that he could flourish in the morality of my perpetual love. I really believed in the resurrection of his dreams from the ashes of destruction that he relived.

The light of dawn arrived and there was a promise of a new beginning, but had he really found the serenity to become different? In the weeks that followed there was a radical change, his drinking became moderated and even nonexistent on certain days. In his new founded desire to be sober his passion to socialise among homosexual hedonists faded away and he totally boycotted the Irish pub drinking culture. The green eyed monster was truly abandoned too, his suspicious presence was forgotten and I had the liberty to dance under the flashing disco lights with my social friends alone again. His abundance of alcohol was forsaken; there was no more enragement or sufferance, no more brutality or bruises, Robert didn't demean or debase me either and he now seduced me with real passion instead. Every Thursday afternoon he frequented the second market stall at the corner of Henry and Moore Street and the same scented bouquet of flowers was bought for me each week. In general I thought that red roses

were an over-used cliché to symbolise love, but it was highly romantic coming from a man that had always been cold in emotion. I was touched, but he didn't love me well enough to know that Pink Stargazer Lily was my favourite flower. His sincerity flourished and my love for him certainly resurrected. Our denuded bodies were no longer foes in the double bed that we shared and his erection seduced me again and again. The passionate movement of his penis invaded me with a profusion of pleasure and the more we fucked the more I desired him. My love for him had certainly resurrected from the destruction of forgotten tears. I believed in the white-picket fenced suburban home of perpetual love again. I really wanted to believe in the eternity of his love and to age in the changing colours of the seasons looking into the beauty of his brown eyes forever, but was his change definitive?

I listened in complete silence as Robert described all the colours, shapes and sounds of sufferance. Her screams awoke him from his sleep; his mother was certainly in difficulty again. She heard the gentle steps of her concerned son on the creaking stairs, his eyes met her glance in the distance below, but she moved her head from left to right in a repetitive fashion as if begging him not to descend a step more. She had fallen out of love, his desire repulsed her, but his enraged father desired to fuck. With brutality he pinned her to the wall, her piteous supplications implored him to stop, but he lustfully continued to denude and fondle her voluptuous breasts. In his flashback Robert advanced a few steps more as if he wanted to liberate her, but before his father's hand completely smothered her mouth to silence her resistance, "NO" came from her lips. Robert now clearly understood that she didn't want him to enter that room. Her aggressor hadn't noticed his presence and believed that she had revolted against him. His fist hardened into a clenched position and collided with her face in a repetitive fashion to bruise her again. The more she resisted the more aggressive he became and the more his potent punches slaughtered her the more passive she became. From where he was seated on the stairs Robert had a direct view of the brutality which ensued on the kitchen floor, but he didn't understand anything. Her knickers were lowered to her ankles; in that way she could no longer move. Her delicate body was immobilised under the heavy weight of his masculine corporal mass. She didn't battled to be liberated from his sordid domination anymore, but simply closed her eyes tightly as if praying in silence instead. The seven year onlooker certainly didn't know that the correct term for such brutality was marital rape.

Reliving years of sufferance resurrected his emotional need for a double vodka; Robert moistened his lips directly from the one litre bottle of Smirnoff, then his emotional voyage continued. She staggered to her feet and correctly positioned her cotton lace trimmed panties to cover her vagina. The "fucking bastard" buttoned and zipped in order to house his langer back in his pants, then casually lit a cigarette and smoked it with virility. She devoured a double whiskey and a cloud of smoke distended above her head too; perhaps both gave her the courage to silence her tears? Robert later heard his father drunkenly singing and her loud laughter echoed with gaiety; everything was alright again. The next morning she served his father breakfast and he kissed her tenderly on the forehead, they had forgotten the brutality, but nine months later Cain was born and that was the son that she never loved. There was a huge discrepancy in how she reared her two sons. Robert flourished in the abundance of her affection, but an entanglement of destruction had created Cain and she nourished him with sufferance instead. Brutality was his heritage; she destroyed him and most certainly created the behavioral and emotional dysfunctions that escalated the violence that ravaged his life. In the resurrection of sufferance I learnt everything about Cain. "Thou shalt not kill" was the forsaken Commandment of god in September 1996. The neighbours had heard the savage passion of his enragement, but silenced her tears; it was her normal journey into brutality again. Indeed, it was common practice for his potent punches to crucify his girlfriend, but enriched with the emotion of destruction Cain liberated too much rage that day and a few minutes later Janice walked into the valley of the shadows of the death. He kissed, denuded and fucked her limp body and as he ejaculated blood spewed from her mouth. For two days he consumed whiskey after whiskey, until her petrifying corpse was found on the kitchen floor by Robert and every newspaper in Ireland lamented. Robert wanted liberation from all of his sufferance, but I feared that what he had unearthed had the almighty power to destroy him with a vengeance too. Was the silence he betrayed too emotional for him? He reached for some more vodka, but the bottle disappeared from his temptation. I didn't want him to get pissed and thought that my insolence would enrage him, but in despair he smiled and kissed me instead. Robert had certainly changed forever.

"Thou shalt not be a queer fucker" was certainly not a Commandment given to Moses by god and the more I unriddled the bible the more underlying ripples of homosexuality I discovered. Had there been a certain promiscuity among Jesus Christ and the twelve apostles? Had he been crucified for the eternal resurrection of mankind or to silence

homosexuality? Was there a parallel between my crucifixion in rural catholic Ireland and his death of the Hill of Golgotha? I believed that the son of god had been devoided of homosexual liberty and that he was really persecuted in order to grant humanity the perpetual right to condemn queers. What also resurrected in my reading was the misogyny of god. Adam was banished from the Garden of Eden, but it was clearly indicated that Eve had enticed him to succumb to temptation. Mary didn't remember having an orgasm in pleasure and was condemned to become an eternal virgin; but perhaps Gabriel had used GHB to impregnate her? Women were enslaved in silence; she was betrothed to Joseph without freedom of choice and enriched by the sufferance of childbirth in poverty instead. The biblical history of womankind was entangled with brutality and sufferance and the myths of the pulpit sermons created the submissiveness of the catholic women of Ireland. There was the forbearance of freedom; the Irish god wasn't so barbaric as to conceal them behind a veil to completely bereave them of their liberty, but the solemn vows of marriage did enchain women in kitchens and enslave them in bedrooms. There was the sin of contraception; their divine role was to reproduce and rear an army of catholic preaching children. There was the forbiddance of divorce; the righteous politics of Ireland condemned them to the prison of love and god repressed their emotions in eternal obedience to men. The catholic bible was renowned for the teaching of love, but in the parables that I read god was definitely a misogynist. The catholic silence of Ireland destroyed women in the solitude of such brutality. Robert's mother was betrayed by her loyalty to god, her catholic forgiveness deluded her and she survived in the destruction of so many forgotten years. Nothing had the almighty power to liberate her, until she dressed in unadorned black clothing for his catholic funeral in 1989. She was totally overwhelmed by a deluge of tears the moment her husband's casket was lowered into the grave, but was it genuine tears of mourning or crocodile tears that fell from her eyes that day? "Ashes to ashes, dust to dust, the fucker was dead", there was so much rancour, animosity and hostility in the coldness of Robert's words. She never betrayed the promise of eternal silence and his brutality was never unearthed by her. His potent punches were silenced away from human judgement forever, but perhaps it was for the catholic god to judge him if the kingdom of heaven really existed? It was in the beauty of his death that she found her salvation, but catholic Ireland still silenced the sufferance of many other forgotten holy women.

17

The Desertion of God

His father was full of smiles and sanctimonious spirituality in public, he prayed with reverence on the Sabbath Day, but underneath the facade of his catholic piety was his silenced brutality. His pious mother was a fragile minded soul, the bible and the sermons fuelled her to believe in the wrath of god and as she prayed for everlasting life she found the compassion to forgive the banality of her husband's violence. She evangelised Robert with biblical dreams, she contaminated him with her passion for all the holy myths and her faith strongly influenced him to become an altar boy. I didn't know that so much sufferance could be liberated from the love of god, but Robert disclosed that god was the most destructive force of all evils. In the beginning his subtle touches seemed normal; Robert's surplice needed to be perfect if he wanted to serve god, but step by step his platonic affection became lust, his desires became unholy acts and in the changing colours of the seasons god denuded Robert. In the Sacrament of Confession she had enriched the priest with an insight of the sufferance that ravaged her catholic home. Knowledge was his absolute power to ensnarl Robert and he overly befriended her cherished son. He seduced with positive words of encouragement, he flattered with the greatest of admiration and naturally Robert appreciated the kind attention of a man; after all such kindness was a sharp contrast to the militant brutality he had always known. It was a common known fact that all children loved sweets. In his great generosity he always put some directly in Robert's pants pocket and touched his penis. With a rural accent he justified that his accidental intrusion was normal in such a confined space. It was the first cunning step to gain total trust and once obtained there was always a new objective to reach in his strategic corruption. The next level of abuse was that Robert emptied holy pockets, which contained an abundance of sweets. In order to retrieve his booty the young boy zealously put his delicate hand into the priest's pants pockets several times. It was now still relatively playful, but the degree of sordidness soon intensified. The love

of god betrayed Robert and the catholic culture of secrecy and self-preservation silenced that holy sin.

"Jesus fucking Christ" were the natural words that betrayed Robert. The chalice that had been entrusted in his hold had fallen from his grip to the floor. "Thou shalt not take the name of the Lord thy God in vain" roared the enraged clergyman. An ocean of tears fell from Robert's brown eyes believing that he was condemned to the eternal fires of hell. The slamming sound of the sacristy door echoed throughout the church, which intensified his fear of receiving a severe bashing. Robert's emotional development certainly knew the sufferance of the repetitive strokes of a hard leather belt strap, after all his militant father had always practiced an abundance of potent blows to lead him onto the road of morality; however the compassionate priest comforted his tears with a kiss on his forehead and graciously embraced him in his holy arms instead. The warm feeling of human affection certainly offered Robert great solace; it completely differed from the strict militancy that he had always known. The holy priest smiled lovingly, which further reassured Robert and the key turned to forbid anyone from entering the sacristy. God was on the verge of severely punishing Robert for his violation of the Third Commandment.

The catholic man placed a burning candle in Robert's hands, knelt before him in prayer, but the almighty god didn't want to grant forgiveness. He then paced the room in total silence to intensify Robert's fear. A glance of terror glittered in his tearful eyes, but was it the wrath of god that he should have feared at that moment or the perversion of a corrupt priest? Robert was ensnarled in god's rage and needed to be purified. He implored and begged to be saved from eternal damnation. From the oak cupboard a bottle of holy water was removed; raising it towards the stained glass window the colourful light enhanced the impression that it was divine. Robert was denuded; the clergyman anointed him in a second baptism, the coldness of god's love sanctified him and his soul was cleansed from the corruption of Satan. The hands of god had strayed to an area of intimacy that was normally forbidden to touch, but the silence of catholic Ireland tolerated that. The special blessing liberated Robert from an eternity in hell and he became a worthy follower in the eyes of god again. Robert placed a kiss, as requested to do so, on his cheek and thanked the man of the cloth for the serenity of forgiveness that he had bestowed upon him. His small hand was firmly placed on the holy bible and a solemn vow of eternal silence was sworn. Forewarned was forearmed, Robert learnt that the

betrayal of God was punishable by banishment from the kingdom of heaven and he then kissed the bible in a pledge of perpetual silence. Coins replaced sweets from that day forth and church money led to further corruption. Robert certainly did not disclose such enrichment to anyone; in the impoverishment of his home there was not an abundance of money and such affluence granted him a certain liberty; but indeed it condemned him to eternal sufferance more and more. Step by step Irish innocence was being lost forever and the holy priest continued until there was no more innocence left.

Certain words were forbidden in front of an adult, but the priest claimed that it was an injustice because adults used the same obscene language too and that even Shakespeare was replete with vulgarisms. Robert immediately thought that Shakespeare was a biblical hero or a disciple of Jesus that he had never heard of. The ignorance of the young boy was humorous and made the holy man laugh, but it wasn't of importance to rectify such an error. Robert was exempt from normal social conduct in the discretion of the sacristy or elsewhere if they were completely alone. He ordained him with the right to curse, all restrictions concerning profanity were abolished, but a strict inflexibility concerning the Third Commandment was enforced; "Thou shalt not take the name of the lord thy god in vain". Robert was granted the almighty freedom to say a multitude of bawdy words, the degree of vulgarity included shit, bastard, bitch, cunt and all the different variations and conjugations of the word fuck. God fondled and groped his penis afterwards, that method of divine absolution was certainly more efficient than Saturday morning confession. There was no queue of sinners, no penance to recite and god's forgiveness even forgave the sins that he hadn't even committed yet. To banalise was to befriend, so his tactful predator equally indulged in the flow of indecent foul language too. It naturally conquered Robert's total trust that they shared another secret. In the same way that the Ten Commandments silenced humanity from revolt, a strict cardinal rule was imposed to entangle Robert in the web of corruption. Nobody was ever to know of god's special affection because if disclosed the wrath of god would fall upon him. Perpetual silence was a sign of the profoundness of his faith. Robert didn't want banishment from the eternal kingdom of heaven, so he kissed the bible in a pledge of holy silence again and again. Robert was the servant of god, chosen for the salvation of humanity, predestined for miracles in the biblical land of Ireland, but he had to silence the realm of god's love or face the sufferance of a crucifixion like Jesus. The ingenious priest preyed on Robert and enslaved him to become the lover of god. The

gullibility of a child's dying innocence believed everything that the priest said; after all it was renowned that virtuous clergymen didn't lie.

One day a nun from the nearby convent discovered Robert with no surplice and no underwear in the sacristy. The priest immediately justified with a reprimanding voice, "shameful for a boy of his age to urinate in his pants" and the glance of disgust that glittered in his eyes enriched the value of his words to sound even more plausible. "Sarry for the disruption Father, I'll put fresh flowers on the altar and leave ya change the boy alone". Apparently the situation was credible enough to entrust the semi naked boy to the holy man or if she had had any doubt she certainly didn't disclose it. In his flashback Robert vividly remembered each specific word of her abandonment. He strangely stated that it was clear from her musical rural accent, which still echoed in his mind, that she must have originated from Cork. He believed that her silence had willingly condemned him, that the crimes that took place only a few metres away from the catholic tabernacle, which housed the Eucharist, were renowned, but silenced. The catholic culture of secrecy and self-preservation enabled paedophiles to remain active within the clergy, perhaps she simply hadn't wanted to liberate the truth? Priests molested the innocence of Ireland, but there was no punishment for such immorality. The silence of Ireland raped Robert again and again and the treasure of his Irish innocence faded away in ruins forever. Freedom was now in the beautification of condemning injustice, deliverance was the serenity to battle resurrected tears, survival was a question of learning to advance from the ashes of destruction, but was Robert resilient enough to survive all the disclosed truths of his emotional journey? It was certain that he needed liberation from silence, but such holy brutality resurfaced with a vengeance to destroy him again. So much emotion fell from his tearful brown eyes as he liberated everything. He definitely didn't need to justify why he ingurgitated a double vodka and instantaneously another large double vodka again and again that day. That was his effort to forget, but his sufferance was profoundly engrained in him forever.

Robert developed severe and radical behavioral changes at the age of twelve, which was a clear indication that something was wrong. He overtly manifested a high level of aggression, brutality and violence to his peers and he revolted against all adult authority with insolence. What was diagnosed as turbulent syndrome and attention seeking was indeed the cry of his silenced tears imploring help, but his sufferance continued in the

destruction of many more forgotten years. The church was in such proximity to Robert's house as to enable his pious mother to tread to the sacristy in her slippers to confess her distress. She lowered her eyes in emotion and the man that sexually abused her precious son gently consoled her in her hour of need. The rosary was recited; not knowing that the holy man that prayed with such reverence beside her also preyed on her naked son. In total ignorance of his sins she erroneously requested his valued help. His godly empowerment to judge her disclosed that the brutality in the core of her catholic home was the root cause of Robert's emotional instability. Believing that spiritually was the only solution, she gladly accepted his generous proposal to guide Robert along the right path of life, but in doing so she unwittingly granted him an abundance of liberty to further corrupt the catholic innocence of her favourite son. Robert began to frequent the priest nearly every day after school and sleeping in the Roman Catholic presbytery during certain weekends was totally tolerated by his mother. She didn't know that Robert and the holy man shared the same bed or that they had become inseparable and dependant lovers. The religious man that read sermons from the pulpit nourished Robert with his morally debased kisses. The servant of god that tasted the blood of Christ directly from the chalice denuded him. The holy hands that distributed the body of Christ from the altar on the Sabbath Day fondled his penis. The man that forgave sinners in the Sacrament of Confession destroyed him in the obscure silence of Irish catholic child abuse. There was no truth that the blood of the covenant was poured for the forgiveness and the remission of sins, because the man that raised the Eucharist to god in front of the congregation every Sunday was the same man that raped the innocence of Ireland. Robert was betrayed by god and was ensnarled more and more to become the priest's lover.

The changes and challenges of puberty began and Robert's penis elongated, darkened and pubic hair surfaced. In parallel he had violated the Eighth Commandment to steal a cigarette from his father's freshly opened pack and without much discretion he smoked his first Dunhill in the field near his home at the age of thirteen. By total lack of chance his father had seen him and severely punished him with brutality to encourage him to deter from such an addictive habit. His catholic father equally made him promise on the holy bible to abstain from cigarettes for eternity and he furthermore condemned his son to the mercy of god by informing the priest. The door of the clergyman's house opened, "Thou shalt not fucking steal" retorted the man of god with a mischievous smile. Robert clearly understood that his father had honoured his word to denounce him. He

disclosed his wrongdoing to god, but there was no supplementary punishment to chastise him. There was certainly no need for penitence to repent; to absolve his sins it always sufficed for the holy man to denude and fondle him. The priest overtly criticised the hypocrisy of adult behaviour and highlighted that his father didn't practice the forbearance he preached. With a couple of short firm puffs a cigarette glowed uniformly and a cloud of smoke distended above the priest's head. That completely bewildered Robert; it was the first time that had ever seen him smoke. Despite all the time that they had spent together he didn't recall having ever seen the man of the cloth direct a fag to his lips. His arm stretched outwards, the red and gold coloured box leaned in a forward motion towards Robert, who glared longingly at a cigarette which dangled alluringly from the pack. He enticed Robert to the temptation of smoking with him in the same manner that the biblical serpent's temptation had seduced Eve to succumb to the forbidden fruit. The virile sight of a man smoking with such gratification tantalised Robert more and more, but he hesitated not wanting to disrespect the solemn promise that he had made to his father. The priest openly condemned his father's false sense of morality; after all it was an injustice that he smoked and denied Robert of the same manly pleasure. Smoking was a rite of passage that would make Robert become a real man and he justified that it was not a sin in the eyes of god as it certainly wasn't forbidden in the bible. It was not virtuous to encourage Robert towards such a vice, but it was a necessity to constantly adapt to Robert's changing needs if he wanted to corrupt him more. It was even for that particular reason that the priest had zealously started smoking again after many years of self-restraint, self-denial and total abstinence. He exhorted Robert to go forth; it was only to be another secret that was to befriend them more. The priest glamorised that smoking was the epitome of sensuality, sophistication and masculinity. His words of encouragement increased the allurement, until Robert was no longer able to resist both the pressure asserted on him and the fascination of his desire to smoke again. A cigarette was directed towards his mouth, a match was struck and the priest smiled with a certain satisfaction as Robert sucked inward and inhaled each drag passionately.

Robert particularly liked the almost immediate calming sensation that he felt after each deeply inhaled puff. In the beginning it was a drag of the priest's cigarette in the sacristy whenever he wanted to feel lightheaded. In the liberty of god's tolerance it became an occasional cigarette in the Roman Catholic presbytery. Then, smoking together became an everyday banality, which actively contributed to Robert's eternal dependence. In a

relatively short period of time, Robert systematically smoked several cigarettes a day because his addiction to nicotine was beginning to manifest itself. Irish sinners struggled to survive in poverty, but they generously enriched the collection box at weekly mass and it was with such holy money that Robert bought his first twenty pack and the others that followed. Of course, it was totally illegal to sell cigarettes to a minor in catholic Ireland, but many local grocery stores only abided by the laws of god and not by the laws of Ireland. Mrs. Byrne was a rigorous churchgoer, who disclosed everything in the Sacrament of Penance and Reconciliation. She confessed that she had sold Dunhills to the angelic looking altar boy, but the priest informed her that it must have been an errand for him as he had started smoking again or even a service for his father, who smoked exactly the same brand. Of course she believed the virtuous clergyman; but even if she had had any doubt, she definitely didn't voice or disclose it again. Robert was instructed to only buy Dunhills from Mrs. Bryne's shop from that moment on; it was the only way that he could cover his ass.

Smoking was romanticised and sensualised by movie stars like Humphrey Bogart and James Dean, which created a platform of social acceptance and ensnarled Robert even more. It was an intrinsic part of the Irish culture; a cloud of smoke distended above heads in cinemas, pubs, restaurants and even on public buses too, but in that forgotten era it was normal that smokers had the liberty to expose non-smokers to the toxicity of second hand smoke. There was complete tolerance for smokers worldwide and the affordable price of cigarettes in Ireland enhanced its accessibility. The tobacco industry mastered all the parameters of marketing; the glossy pages of magazines made the attractiveness of smoking a common practice, flashy commercials on coloured television popularise cigarettes further and the world of sports from Formula One to Snooker, under the guise of sponsorship, drove brand loyalty forward even more. The only dissuasive measure enforced was from overly rigorous catholic parents, but the banality of chain smoking in Robert's home had already made him an indirect smoker since an early age. Coming from a home of regular smokers statistically multiplied the probability that he was to become a heavy smoker, but the almighty priest had certainly nailed his coffin. Step by step anti-smoking campaigns changed Irish attitude, not with the objective to restrict liberty as smokers claimed, but in the necessity to educate and discourage. The blanket smoking ban in March 2004 was the major stepping stone to liberate Ireland from passive smoking. Ireland was the first country worldwide to forbid smoking in enclosed public spaces

and the ripples of Ireland's legislation influenced the whole world to implement the same effective measure of dissuasion too. The freedom to advertise had already been abolished for donkey's years, but the multitude of colourful cigarette packs on the market still acted as "mobile bill boards' to enhance the sensuality of smoking. On March 10th 2015 President Michael Daniel Higgins signed the Standardised Packaging of Tobacco Act and Ireland became the first country in the European Union to battle against "the recruitment of young smokers". The deglamorisation of smoking was certainly the beginning of forgotten allurement. The cowboy succulent Red of Marlboro, the glamorised glittering gold of Benson and Hedges and the seductive royal blue on white of Rothmans were now forbidden. The rainbow coloured packaging of all brands became impoverished looking without colour, while large printed warnings and graphic photographs further denuded each pack of its attractiveness. Perhaps the march towards a cigarette free world had begun, but eternal victory would only resurrect if the now relatively affordable price of cigarettes skyrocketed to become totally unattractive to the pockets of consumers. The example of Ireland was once again the start point of the domino effect and country after country followed.

It was an early morning in 1976 that Robert turned his head away from holy kisses in revolt for the first time. He specifically remembered the hoarfrost covered pavements on that cold day. He was beginning to understand that catholic Ireland had abandoned him to his silenced sufferance and his abhorrence to manifested god's affection was a clear indicator that the priest's empowerment over him was coming to an end. In the flowery month of May, Cain became enriched with catholic values in the Sacrament of Holy Communion and to further develop his spirituality his mother equally entrusted him to the love of god. The holy man no longer demonstrated tenderness for Robert after that, but displayed a particular fondness and preference for Cain instead. Robert had naturally become too old to be his favourite toy and was discarded like a sperm filled condom. In such rejection he felt a certain sensation of wrath. His enragement that his young brother had become an altar boy was interpreted as jealousy by all, but it really represented his oppressed fear that history would repeat itself. He assigned himself the mission to save Cain from the brutality of a destructive god, but it became a more and more difficult task to ensure his constant protection. The priest found a million plausible excuses to separate them, but Robert knew what solitude in the sacristy really meant. He revolted against the holy man in blatant refusal to abandon Cain alone, but one day it simply wasn't possible. Robert

immediately identified what the sweets that the generous priest had given Cain signified. The colourful leaves in the church grounds had fallen; he now believed that the immorality of the servant of god needed to be punished and not reproduced.

With immense difficulty he confessed all the obscure years of abuse, but his catholic mother didn't want to believe him. He desperately longed for her to solace him, but she did not liberate him from his sufferance. Total disbelief glittered in her eyes and she dismissed the corruption of the holy man as a figment of her wicked son's vivid imagination. She repudiated that such a serious accusation was completely untrue and her hand collided with his face to silence his insolence. Robert implored her to believe him, but she coldly silenced his tears with brutality again. The silence of Ireland and her profound faith in the catholic god were stronger than her love for her son and she directly went to the sacristy with her head lowered in shame. The priest had serenity; if the compassion of the almighty god forgave such a blatant lie, she needed to find the catholic strength of forgiveness too. The rosary was recited and the holy man that had preyed on her naked son prayed with such reverence beside her. Then, he justified that the dramatic situation represented the social level of Robert's emotional instability. Without hesitation she willingly accepted that the brutality in her catholic home was the key contributing factor to Robert's evilness. The priest caustically informed her that Robert needed her love more than he needed god's prayers and with tears in his eyes he informed her that it was no longer possible to evangelise her sons. She agreed that Robert was far beyond god's divine salvation, but begged the holy man not to exile Cain from the love of god. If the compassion of the almighty god forgave all sins he needed to find the catholic strength of forgiveness too, but he silenced her tearful supplications and discarded both Robert and Cain as dishonourable. The next day Robert went to the sacristy to return the delicately washed and neatly ironed surplices to the priest. He clearly remembered that the colourful leaves that he trod on in the church grounds were wet from the Irish rain. The clergyman imposed a solemn promise of eternal silence on the holy bible, but Robert stated that he no longer believed in his "fucking bollocks of a god". There was so much rancour in his hate for god that the holy man didn't recognise Robert anymore. Brutality had destroyed his faith in biblical dreams, in all the myths of the catholic sermons and in the divine love of the almighty god. A virile fist collided with his face to brutalise Robert in physical punishment for his irreverence, but no emotion of repentance resurrected. Robert was liberated

and savagely hated him, but he still felt a sensation of affection for the man that had destroyed him.

Robert never sought vengeance, his agony was silenced forever and Ireland enriched him with spirituality instead. He was force-fed to believe that if the compassion of the almighty god forgave all sinners that he needed to find the catholic value of forgiveness too. He recited creeds and sang hymns of praise in the same church by his mother's side at weekly mass. It was not out of reverence to god that Robert closed his brown eyes tightly as the priest placed the communion host upon his tongue, but in total repulsion. He understood that there was no truth in the biblical myth that the blood of the covenant was poured for the forgiveness and the remission of sins, because the holy hands that had fondled his penis continued to raise the Eucharist to god in front of the congregation. The judgement of churchgoers never crucified his predator, but grieved several months later when unexpectedly a new priest stood on the altar to replace him. Robert saw a smile of silent victory glitter in his mother's eyes that day; the holy man that everyone loved now served god in a different church in rural Ireland. Other altar boys, before and after him, certainly tasted the same destruction, but the catholic culture of secrecy and self-preservation silenced their sufferance too. The lips of the religious man that had kissed Robert read the sermons from another pulpit. The hands that had denuded his body continued to distribute the body of Christ on each Sabbath Day. The holy sinner that forgave Irish sins in the Sacrament of Confession certainly abused other Irish catholic children in the sacristy of another parish. The years of silence that followed destroyed Robert even more than the seven years that god had abusively betrayed him. Catholic Ireland didn't want to be enlightened by his tears of sufferance and it now enraged him that the brutality of the servant of god was never punished.

Was his homosexuality the creation of the almighty catholic god or had the holy priest bestowed Robert with the immorality of homosexuality? Society needed to know what factor had influenced his "homosexual choice". Did "queer fuckers" resurrect from the love an over-powering mother, the militant blows of an enraged father or the psychological trauma of an emotional childhood factor? It was certain that Robert had been reared with brutality and much sufferance too, but his homosexuality was not born in the sacristy. Many altar boys had been sacrificed by the catholic silence of Ireland and their revenge on god now enriched Ireland with the unwanted truth. Normal functioning heterosexuals were coming

out of the closet of catholic silence; in the sacristies of catholic Ireland their innocence had been destroyed, but homosexuality was certainly not created. His passion for men was engrained in him since the beginning of time and Robert believed that the emotion of homosexuality was innate. He ingurgitated a second double vodka and to further forget his sufferance he reached for some more, but in despair I removed the bottle of Smirnoff from his temptation. His fist clenched in enragement that day and he liberated the brutality that I thought he had forgotten. Robert certainly wasn't resilient enough to rise from the ashes of destruction and to survive amid all the demons of his emotional journey. The past resurfaced with a vengeance and the ripples of the agony that he had unearthed destroyed him more and more. Just when I was beginning to believe in the eternity of his love he began to drink more heavily than ever before. My dreams withered away like the last bouquet of red roses from Moore Street and in the resurrection of his brutality my love faded away forever. His savage rage slaughtered me again and in my desired battle for my freedom I didn't love him anymore. The silence of god crucified Robert for eternity.

The Promise Of Silence

18

The Emotion of Revolt

It was impossible to survive in his passionate rage forever and I began to submit to the defeat of my dream of everlasting love. There was certainly no affection in the physical brutality of my relationship and I knew that it had come to an end. I thought that I had fallen in love with Robert forever, but in the consistency of his hostility my emotions became totally indifferent again. The sincerity of my love had faded away, our naked bodies no longer fucked in the double bed that we shared and in the silence of my thoughts all I wanted was liberation from his destruction. Was it better to be alone than suffer eternally in the prison of his love? Was it better to resent the tragedy of defeated love than never to have loved at all? Of course, I didn't want to be alone again, but blow after blow I realised that I was already alone in the solitude of his brutality. I was alone in my sufferance when his cold glance intensified the velocity of his potent punches. I was alone in his enragement and no beautiful flowers bloomed in the abundance of my fallen tears. I was alone in my solitude when I walked the streets at night fleeing the forceful aggressivity of his drunken violence. I was so alone in the crumbs of his affection when he consumed and fucked other men. I believed in the resurrection of dreams from the ruins of his cold kisses. In despair I was beginning to understand that I needed to abandon him in order to cultivate and nourish my freedom again.

One wet Irish night I was completely seduced by an amazing American. The crowded balcony overlooking the dance floor enabled me to admire every rhythmical movement of his body as he danced under the flashing disco lights below. Stars glittered in his dark brown eyes at the precise moment that he saw me and something just happened that had never happened to me before. I became totally enchanted as if he was the prince charming directly out of the fairy tale of my dreams. I was completely besotted by him, but even if I wasn't in love with Robert anymore, it was never my intention to betray him. I turned my head away to silence my

attraction, but the irresistible sensation to look for just one second more was stronger than me. My blue eyes lowered to roam the dance floor again, but to my greatest dismay he was no longer there. Perhaps he had only been a figment of my silenced desire to become promiscuous again? Perhaps the alcoholic drinks that I had ravenously consumed, in order to forget all of my problems, had enhanced my mind with the volatility to imagine him? "Fishing for someone nice", laughed the sexy accented voice, which had just awkwardly squeezed into the few vacant centimeters of remaining space on the balcony next to me. I was so engrossed in my lustful hunt that I completely refrained from reacting to such a quip. What actually distracted me was the Christian Dior fragrance that abundantly floated in the air. I immediately identified the woody floral musk scent as being Fahrenheit, which was a seductive odour that I particularly liked. Who was the virile man that had given my sense of olfaction such immense pleasure? A glorious smile resurrected in his dark brown eyes, which in the obscurity of the club lighting seemed to be almost black. He blurted out that he found me highly attractive, even if I had been somewhat arrogant towards him. He was extremely awkward in the maladroit fashion that he communicated his flirting, but I certainly found him very alluring. A cute moment of silence followed, but everything about him aroused me so much; the sublime charm of his eyes, the succulent lust of his lips and the sensuality of his amorous disposition. I immediately knew that I was to be denuded by him before the end of that night.

A Gloria Gaynor drag queen on stage mouthed "I will survive". The already vibrant ambiance of the flashing disco lights was enhanced further by an onward wave of gay men, which in great abundance invaded the dance floor. It was at that precise moment that Justin leaned forward to kiss me in a passionate way that no homosexual had ever kissed me before. Was the divine feeling of such profound ardour a new discovery on my lips or had I merely forgotten the romantic value of a perfect kiss? Perhaps such a sensation only existed in the freedom of promiscuity or in the treachery of love? Each kiss contaminated me more and more with a natural desire to betray Robert and a sentiment of revenge resurrected. The more I kissed Justin the more I forgot Robert and the more I forgot Robert the more I kissed Justin. The desire that glittered like stars in his dark brown eyes seduced, corrupted and liberated me. The same sensation of seduction, corruption and liberation glittered in the lust of my blue eyes too and my glorious voyage into freedom began. Justin and I denuded and I liberated my immorality in the harmony of his love on the softness of the crisp white linens in the Clarence Hotel. There was so much passion in that

ephemeral love that I never wanted it to end. Was there betrayal in fucking another man, when Robert fucked a profusion of other men? Perhaps catholic Ireland judged me as a promiscuous sinner, but I certainly didn't feel the emotion of guilt. It was clear that I no longer belonged to the barren desolation of Robert's love. I didn't love Robert anymore, but had my affection faded away in the brutality of his rages or in the beauty of the kisses that I tasted that night?

I wanted the abundance of passion in his kisses to corrupt me forever and ever, but the brutality of promiscuity punished me for my betrayal. The destructive light of dawn illuminated the luxury of the spacious hotel room, which over looked the river Liffey and I knew that our kiss had to touch in harmony for the last time. I belonged to the prison of catholic Ireland and the enraged brutality of Robert's love, but the charming accent of Justin certainly belonged to the world of American dreams. He enticed me to abandon everything for the rest of his stay, but was it really possible to live a lifetime of love in just three days? Did I have the emotional strength to fall profoundly in love, knowing that the eternity of that love was never to be? Was it better to know the sufferance of ephemeral love or regret forever the defeat of never having loved him? I was lured by the beauty that glittered in his glorious brown eyes. The passionate taste of another lustful kiss liberated my emotions from hesitation and his seduction totally conquered me. He promised me that it would be the most sensational love that I had ever known, but did such passion justify my desire to taste promiscuity again? It was certain that we were star crossed lovers, but I agreed to meet Justin in the hotel lobby at precisely 11a.m.

I walked the early morning littered streets of Dublin filled with the joys of life, but there were a lot of fuck words among the numerous text messages and voicemails from Robert waiting to demoralise me. The brutality that echoed in each message I deleted on my mobile phone was more aggressive in nature than the one before. I prayed to Eros, the god of love, to compassionately inspire me with a fish story credible enough for Robert to swallow, otherwise I was to be destroyed by his potent punches again. Before having the time to put the key in the apartment door, it abruptly flung open. It was clear that a double vodka had already moistened his lips, even several judging by the low quantity of Smirnoff in the bottle near the box of Kellogg's Corn Flakes on the kitchen table. "I thought you were fucking dead"; he bellowed with such dramatic rage that all of Dublin must have heard him shout. I didn't care enough about him to react; I was

beginning to understand him more than he thought. It didn't seem plausible coming from the monster that had pounded me a million times with his fist that his concern was genuine, but he lovingly proclaimed that the thought of a plastic wreath on my grave and a marble headstone engraved with my name had plagued him with an ocean of tears. Apparently, he hadn't closed his eyes to sleep that night, but that too was difficult for me to believe. I discretely looked at my reflection in the mirror; there was so much rancour in my silenced hate for him that I didn't recognise myself anymore. There was a moment of hesitation as I frantically searched my mind to defend my nocturnal absence from our bed, but I simply stated that it was too emotionally difficult to explain all the details immediately. I looked at the clock on the kitchen wall to suddenly realise that I needed to justify more profoundly if I wanted to abandon him, but I had always been too rigorous and overly prude to lie. Suddenly, my mouth blabbed in a mythomaniac fashion that the long night had been with my brother in tears of deep emotion and that my return to rural Ireland for three days was imminent. Robert always believed what he wanted to believe. A flow of tears filled his tender eyes and he hugged me to soothe away all my sufferance. I almost laughed when he offered his sincere condolences for the deceased, but at no precise moment I had indicated that anyone was dead. It was not problematic that I silenced his error because it was the perfect alibi for my betrayal. Then, he kissed me; it was a rather nice kiss, even if it was embedded with a strong taste of Dunhill, but all I wanted to do was wipe his affection from my lips. Perhaps if I had had a real problem the warmth of that kiss would have naturally enriched me with a sensation of love, but after the sincerity I had found in Justin's kisses it was certain that I didn't appreciate Robert's lips touching mine. The more he became gentle in his emotions the more I became cynical in my silenced thoughts. He followed me from room to room with his hands dug deeply in his idle pockets. In my hour of need he repetitively reassured me of the consistency and reliability of his love. I could definitely count on him to brutalise, destroy and crucify me for certain, but he was not reliable for anything else.

It was more fashionable to don in unadorned black clothing for mourning, rather the rainbow of coloured clothes that I carefully selected for my amorous adventure. It was blatant that flashy colours were not exactly appropriate for attending a traditional Irish funeral, but Robert didn't contemplate any different. On such a melancholy occasion I didn't have a real need for Calvin Klein One either, but for my coming seduction it was a must. A voyage into "The Odyssey" enhanced my credibility by giving the impression that I needed something to read on the train to Cork Kent

Station. Knowing that homosexuals regarded a high importance to physical attractiveness, I paid particular attention to optimise my beauty after my shower. A dollop of medium-hold gel was delicately applied to enhance the shiny aspect of my blond coloured hair. Its viscidity hardened to strengthen the gravity-defying spikes of the messy but yet sophisticated look that I wanted. I even applied anti-wrinkle moisturiser to hydrate my face; all that I wanted was to be beautiful for Justin. I desired to enchant his brown eyes to fall in love with me more and more. I definitely looked too sexy for someone lamenting a death, but after another double vodka to calm his profound grief, it was sure that Robert didn't even notice the difference. One critical task remained, but Robert believed that it was too emotionally difficult to do it alone. He was relatively well enough acquainted with my employer, so I accepted his insistence to phone on my behalf. From the bedroom I clearly overheard the conversation. I was surprised to learn that my beloved grandmother suffered from poor health and that a sudden death had seduced her. His vision of reality must have been impaired by the years of Vodka that he had overly consumed, because I had certainly not indicated that she was dead. My manager must have sympathised, because Robert gracefully accepted his condolences several times, which made it even more believable.

I indiscreetly glanced at my watch again; it was precisely eighteen minutes before my rendezvous with love in the Clarence Hotel lobby. With my brisk urban walking pace I needed nine minutes to arrive there, three minutes more if I wanted to make a good impression by arriving early and five minutes just in case I needed more time for something unforeseen that I hadn't thought of. It was typical practice for me to calculate every second of my life. Basically, my departure had to be more or less immediate if I wanted to respect the rigour of my planning, but my sudden impatience to prematurely abandon Robert seemed to arouse his curiosity. Heuston station was a common destination for taxi drivers to drop off and pick up passengers, so he naturally knew the train timetable off by heart. The next train was just before midday, but such precision was impossible for me to refute. The purchase of a black funeral tie in Dunnes Stores was another lie in my stratagem. It seemed like a very plausible excuse to justify my evasion, but it didn't give victory to my ruse; Robert heroically handed me one from his wardrobe. The clock on the wall now indicated that I had only seventeen precious minutes left. I had so much difficulty to think of something credible enough for him to believe, but fortunately there was nothing in the fridge to make a good sandwich. Robert knew that I categorically refused to buy the expensive food that was served on the train

and that my ritual was to always shop in Centra in Capel Street before each journey, but he removed a neatly folded twenty pound note from his pocket to pay for an Iarnród Éireann lunch. A James Joyce would have largely covered the cost of a cheese sandwich, a bag of Tayto and a fizzy drink on the train, perhaps even a bar of Cadbury's chocolate too, but a Daniel O' Connell was twice that value of a James Joyce Irish banknote. It was the rareness of such generosity that enticed me to abuse the compassion of his charity. I justified that he had bled my wallet dry a million times before, so without a second thought I gladly accepted the plunder. The tragedy of death had become a real comedy of revenge.

My stainless steel Swatch indicated that I had less than fifteen minutes left, but in accordance to the logic of his calculation I had at least another forty five spare minutes before my obligation to leave; after all it only took twenty five minutes to walk to Houston station from where we lived. Signs of agitation must have become visible on my face; because he allured me to believe that I needed a Dunhill as an effective means to calm my stress. I had casually smoked a few cigarettes now and then with him, but I didn't need or want one, or even if I did feel like one I certainly didn't have the time to waste. After a couple of short firm puffs his cigarette was lit. He sucked in some smoke anxiously and exhaled a cloud of tension. The Dunhill was then directed towards my lips with lure and I needed the same gratification as him. I deeply inhaled a few puffs again and again partially to satisfy his insistence, but now mostly to yield to my sudden need. Tick, tock, tick, tock; smoking the cigarette completely enhanced me with a relaxed sensation and I became lightheaded, but a glance towards the clock on the wall reminded me of the importance of time again. More valuable seconds were lost in the bathroom as I refreshed my mouth with an abundance of toothpaste. I wasn't mourning a river of tears in lamentation, but he really believed that it was my hour of need. He wanted to accompany me to the train station, even if that meant walking in total silence. I comforted him that everything was alright and coldly informed him that I needed time to grieve completely alone. Another Dunhill glowed uniformly and a cloud of fresh smoke distended above his head again. The door of the apartment opened representing the certainty of my escape, but just as I was about to leave he grabbed my arm firmly. My heart pounded; perhaps he had suddenly understood that everything was a lie? No, I had simply forgotten to kiss him goodbye.

I had the impression that I had a million things to live before my death, but that life wanted to steal the valuable seconds that I needed to fulfill my dreams. An indiscreet glance at my watch indicated that I had lost a substantial amount of minutes being overly nice to him. There wasn't a moment more to lose; but Robert corrupted me with the taste of another repulsive kiss. I kissed him with passion; it was to subdue the arousal of any suspicion before he liberated me to betray him. From the balcony he waved goodbye, not knowing that he had given me the freedom to fuck another man. He flicked his cigarette butt; it descended to litter the street below, but such indecent behaviour was completely habitual for him. With only seven minutes remaining it was almost a certainty that my punctuality was to be completely forgotten. I quickened my pace, which enhanced the impression that my steps had become leaps. The moment I was out of sight, my feet slapped the concrete pavement and I ran faster than I had ever run before. A warm sensation of energy seeped into my quadriceps muscles. The wind I created violently whipped my face and gently caressed my blond hair. The journey became a blur of flashing images before my blue eyes. I didn't wait for the green pedestrian light before crossing Ormond Quay. A bus abruptly slammed on its breaks, a taxi swerved a few centimetres to avoid me and the aggressive sound of a few horns echoed as agitated drivers beeped to voice their rage; but I didn't care about the residues of anger that I abandoned on the road behind me. An elderly man stepped out of my way on Grattan Bridge. I distinctly heard 'ya fucking bastard' emerge from someone in the background; but I most certainly didn't stop to identify which holy Irish Catholic had rightfully insulted me. I was ready for seduction and I really wanted to kiss Justin again. Perhaps Ireland judged me as a sinner, but I didn't repent. I coldly justified that to sin for a taste of true love was not a real sin. It was the beginning of the abandonment of all my sufferance. In the art of treachery there was no turning back to Robert's love ever again. The emotion of revolt had awoken from deep within me.

A casual plain white T-shirt, a black leather jacket and a rip and repair style blue denim Jeans enhanced his profound beauty in the distance. He was definitely the most sensual man in the lobby and by far the most attractive man that I had ever seen in Ireland. The lust that glittered in his dark brown eyes immediately justified my desire to taste promiscuity again. The Pink Stargazer Lily bouquet in his left hand seduced me and certainly conquered my love even more. It was my flower of passion and romance, my absolute favourite flower, but I had never mentioned that to him. I was relatively prude concerning all types of public displays of

affection; either coming from homosexual or heterosexual lovers alike, but the passion of his kiss freed me from the prison of hesitation. I thought that catholic Ireland was repulsed by homosexuality, but nobody crucified us for the liberation of our gay kiss. It was not problematic in the Clarence that Justin had overtly displayed his affection towards me. There was no glance of disapproval from neither the concierge nor the middle aged woman that had clearly seen our seduction. The receptionist smiled in total acceptance too, but perhaps she wasn't catholic in her sexuality either? Was Ireland developing a tolerance for queers? Perhaps homosexuals had the right to be normal actors in society too?

The changing colours of so many seasons have passed, but my passion for Justin never faded away; as if I had the eternal liberty to live that yesterday again and again. I clearly remember the taste of every kiss, the sensation of every touch and the love that glittered in those dark brown eyes that denuded me. If Justin was everything that my dreams desired why was our profound love condemned to be so ephemeral? Why were we star-crossed lovers when our profound love wanted to be eternal? Perhaps the catholic god of Ireland really wanted to punish me for my betrayal? Rather than dream we fell in love and rather than accept the tragedy of falling in love we both dreamed of being in love forever. There were genuine tears in his dark brown eyes as he beseeched me to accept his everlasting love. "Abandon Ireland, I will give you the eternity of my love and all of your dreams", but Ireland was my prison and our fate had been adverse since our first kiss. Perhaps I should have forsaken Ireland to love Justin forever, but I still didn't have the bravery to battle the changing tides of life. I loved him more than I had ever loved Robert and certainly more than any man that I had ever been in love with before, but I didn't love him enough to abandon Ireland. I wanted to live the different colours of every season in the passion of his undying love, but it was certain that his perpetual love was to be shared with another man and not with me. The vastness of the Atlantic Ocean forbade the survival of our love and forced our lips to touch in tearful harmony for the last time. The roads of our lives diverged in different directions and Justin returned forever to the world of American dreams. I mourned in the ashes of his love, but it was definitely better to have known the taste of doomed love rather than regret forever the defeat of never having loved him at all. My dream of true love had been liberated for three days, but I now had a sensation that I was dying alone in despair. There had always been a certain consistency in my coldness that made me indifferent in my emotions, but my sufferance revolted in the liberation of my tears.

19

The Lamentation of Abandonment

The waves of the Atlantic Ocean bereaved me of Justin. His forbidden kisses were not forgotten, but I still silenced my betrayal. I intently admired the magnificent bouquet of Pink Stargazer Lilies, which reflected all the passion that had glittered in his brown eyes. The flowers now decorated a cheap looking plastic vase on the mahogany nest table in the sitting room, which certainly didn't do their beauty any justice and it enraged me that Robert believed that I had bought them to seduce him. I had completely fallen out of love with the bastard, but for the moment he didn't know that I wanted the promiscuous freedom of the gay culture to corrupt me again. I wanted to relive all the beauty of life; to kiss, denude and fuck other men, even if that meant being condemned to the solitude of homosexuality forever. I had been liberated by a taste of what love should really be and my dreams now needed a glorious resurrection.

I wanted to abandon Robert; "I don't fucking love you", but he rebelled that his profound love for me still existed. He smiled at me with a destructive glance in his cold eyes. I knew that his potent punches and strenuous kicks would escalate his savage brutality, but I didn't care. In despair I believed that he needed to taste the sufferance of my betrayal and his rage certainly resurrected then. The Stargazer Lily flowers were now in ruins on the carpeted floor; he had ravaged their beauty. The masculine weight of his corporal mass became my coffin and the firmness of his hands tightened around my neck in strangulation. The pressure he applied induced my difficulty to breathe and I had a foreboding sensation that the fucker wanted to kill me. Was he enriched with the same passion of enragement and the same coldness of emotions as Cain? Was death to liberate me from the prison of his destructive love forever? It was not my desire to walk into the valley of the shadows of death and share the same fate as Janice, but Robert's hands tightened more and more. Tears fell from his eyes and he implored me to love him again. He begged for my

forgiveness with the threat of his hands still wrapped around my neck. I didn't want to know if queers were condemned to the eternal fires of hell or if heaven was gay friendly. I wanted a two fingered gesture of revenge, but it definitely wasn't the right moment to forsake him. After my repentance he had the serenity to forgive me. I recited a solemn vow on his holy bible and swore that I wanted to love him forever again. A double vodka moistened his lips, a cloud of Dunhill distended above his head and he passionately kissed me. I felt the sensation of a million daggers stabbing my flesh in sufferance, but he believed that our denuded bodies had fucked in harmony again. I feared that I would not survive the brutality of another aggression. The silent battle for my liberty from the prison of his enraged love had just begun.

My bruises had faded and I needed liberation for a few days; Portlaoise, Templemore, Thurles, Limerick Junction, Charleville, Mallow and my mother was happily waiting for me on the platform in Cork Kent Station. What normally repulsed me now fulfilled me with serenity. The sound of my holy mother turning the discoloured gilded pages of her aged bible in prayer was harmonious and I even found the oily smell of the industrial machines in my father's workshop relatively pleasant too. In the dark dusty closet of homosexuality I soul searched to find my forgotten dreams and in the balance of silence I resurrected from the ashes of my destruction. Robert soon understood that my promise to love him forever was ephemeral. I had no sincere affection for him, my kisses were cold, my emotions were distant and I stiffened in distaste of his touch. Robert battled to survive in the ruins of my love and he still punished me to live in the prison of his love, but I was now ready to rebel for my eternal freedom. I didn't particularly want to share a bathroom with three other tenants again, but beggars can't be choosers. My previous landlord laughingly informed me that "the price of poverty" had increased by £80 a month in rent. In desperation I didn't argue with the conman; some fool had to enrich him and his ardent love for Ferrari. I didn't view the basement studio in Belvedere Place as it was still occupied for twelve more days, but in any case I already knew what the austerity of a heavily stained mattress and the peeling paint on a studio ceiling was. Robert desired to believe in my love and I desired my freedom, but if I wanted my revenge I needed to feign my love. I kissed him with passion in the silence of my abandonment for another few days. Robert certainly had faith in my love again, but my vengeance was silenced in each kiss that I liberated.

The Promise Of Silence

A cute looking leather queen drank his Guinness with a thick cloud of cigarillo smoke distending above his head. Judging by the flirtatious smile he directed towards me I could have seduced him if I had wanted. A cute looking lesbian couple kissed in a dim lit corner of the bar, it was the first time that I had ever seen them. I counted ten homosexuals dancing under the flashing disco lights on the spacious dance floor, wow there wasn't much seduction in what was normally the most promiscuous queer bar of Ireland, but all the homosexual hedonists of Dublin had frequented the opening of a new gay venue that night. The manager decided "We'll just keep Jurassic Park open". Seconds later the disco lights didn't flash anymore, the bouncers escorted everyone into the small lounge instead and a free cocktail thanked each client for their valued cooperation. There were certainly too many workers behind the bar now, so the manager liberated a few of us and I placed a kiss on his cheek in great appreciation. Robert didn't use the nitrate based liquid, but the pungent smell of poppers invaded my nose as I entered our apartment. The half empty bottle of vodka on the kitchen table didn't really surprise me much, but why there two empty glasses? As I neared, the sound of breathless moans echoed from the bedroom. Robert was arse fucking with so much passion. I had never seen such desire when he fucked me, but in his betrayal I tasted my liberation. Robert glanced towards the bedroom door, smiled at me with a cold air of revenge and with his eyes locked in the silence of my blue eyes he continued to fuck his promiscuous lover. Perhaps he wanted to create my enragement, but there was no resurrection of sufferance. There was always a consistency in my coldness that made me indifference in my emotions and I believed that there was no treachery because I didn't love him.

The moonlight glittered on the statue of the Children of Lir and a soft wind rippled on the water of the reflective cross shaped pool in the Garden of Remembrance. I pondered that my journey of freedom had begun on the same park bench there. So much in my life had changed since then, but I still hadn't found my serenity yet. I certainly drank too many double whiskeys in a heterosexual bar in the hour that followed, which liberated my real sufferance. Alexander had abandoned our perpetual love and I still hadn't forgiven him. A sensation of profound despair consumed me as I walked the streets of Dublin alone. I had battled to be liberated from the memory of Alexander, but my forgotten tears resurfaced with a vengeance and my eternal affection for him resurrected. I lamented in the ruins of his destruction and I mourned for the lost dream of my eternal love with him. I still needed to learn how to journey in the solitude of life without him. I

kissed Robert with passion as if nothing had happened; perhaps I needed to feel the sensation of human emotion? I saw his Dunhills on the table and a cloud of smoke distended above my head. "You're fucking pissed", Robert certainly didn't recognise me. He implored me to love him, but I silenced him. He really believed that I wanted to love him, but "I don't fucking love you" resurrected in my enragement. He begged for my forgiveness, but a few seconds later I regurgitated and decorated the tiled kitchen floor. "Fuck, Fuck, Fuck" I heard Robert retching again and again as he cleaned the ocean of vomit that I had created. I must have fallen asleep, because there was a complete void after that, but I certainly had a killer of a hangover in the morning.

I suffered from an emotional dysfunction that made me cold and I silenced Robert when he begged me to love him. He was defeated by the abandonment of my love, but he still battled for the resurrection of my affection 'an eye for an eye and a tooth for a tooth" with so much brutality. My brother had banished me from his life because I was "a queer fucker", but in my hour of solitude I phoned him. I implored, begged and beseeched him to liberate me from the brutality and the sufferance of love. A lot of vodka had already enraged Robert that day and I feared that his enragement would escalate more after his return from the pub that night. My holy brother heard my despair and must have still had a sentiment of affection for me. He revolted in rage "if that fucker is there when I arrive I'll kick the fucking shit out of him". I passionately kissed Robert for the last time and the aversion I felt in that kiss consumed me with an even greater desire to forsake him. I peeked out the window to be certain and watched his silhouette fade away into the distance. The moment he was out of sight, I went from room to room, throwing my worldly possessions into plastic bags without feeling any emotion. A palpable tension suffocated me in fear as I opened the door, but indeed it was my heroic brother to liberate me. It was a considerably long time since I had last seen him. He smiled at me in a loving way and hugged me tenderly as my tears fell. Had he changed in repentance of his catholic judgement or did my dream of his tolerance delude me again? I wanted to believe that he really loved me, but his hate of homosexuality was certainly engrained in him forever. The door slammed behind me without regret and I tasted my freedom. I no longer belonged to the prison of love. I was liberated from the brutality of Robert's enragement forever. There were no more potent punches to destroy me ever again.

The Promise Of Silence

Robert tasted the solitude of my silent revenge, but did his tears fall lamenting my love or did my abandonment consume him with rage? My life seemed to be an abundance of despair and I cried myself to sleep on the contemporary leather sofa in my brother's living room that night. Dawn conquered Dublin and a bewildered face was staring at me in total fascination when I opened my eyes. It was an eternity since I had last seen her and it was certain by her hesitation that she didn't exactly know who I was. It was whispered into Naomi's ear that I was her uncle. I closed my eyes tightly pretending that I was still in the world of dreams. The exaggerated sound of my false snores made her giggle. Her timid finger prodded my head in a child-like fashion to verify if I was really asleep or not and before my feet touched the carpeted floor her ocean of kisses enriched me. Morning breakfast was singing Teletubbies to the sound of her laughter, gaiety filled the air and I hugged her preciously again and again. I wanted to engrave and immortalise that moment in my mind forever. I had found a vision of hope in the beauty of a new beginning, but there was a mountain of different challenges in the hours of the days that followed. Little did she know of my battle to love her and my niece became the powerful weapon in my brother's war to destroy me again. I battled for the forbidden right to love her, but there was the resurrection of his intolerance and she became his revenge on my homosexuality. He believed that I had the almighty power to contaminate his catholic daughter with lesbian immorality and he crucified me for being a queer. My brother had the catholic compassion to grant me three days dwelling in the comfort of his Malahide home. He believed that such generosity was largely sufficient to enable me to resurrect from the ashes of destruction, but I needed a week more. I implored him to house me until the studio in Belvedere Place would be vacant and available for me, but in his coldness if I became famished in the streets of Dublin it wasn't his fucking problem. "Reap the fucking shit that you harvested". On the third day, Jesus rose from the dead for the salvation of humanity, but I was evicted from his holy home in punishment for my homosexuality. I began to hate catholic Ireland with even more and more rancour.

I encountered my university professor by chance in O' Connell Street. Everyone believed that he was heterosexual, but I knew that the intolerance of catholic heteronormative Ireland was not a prison for his homosexuality. I had seen him dancing under the flashing disco lights in the gay bars that I frequented and indeed he seduced, kissed, denuded and fucked an abundance of ephemeral homosexual men. A different moral sense of human values was ingrained in his self-culture; he certainly liberated me

from my despair and housed me in Crumlin Road for the days that I needed. Did we liberate a desire to fuck that we had always silenced? Was the emotion of fucking in the homosexual culture cold or practical? After the passion of his luscious kiss another ephemeral journey into homosexual promiscuity began, but for breakfast it was tea and toast again as if nothing had ever happened. There was the sufferance of more crucifixions in my life to come, but an eternal friendship had flourished either before or after our ejaculations. JP believed in my homosexual freedom and in the resurrection of my dreams and I never tasted solitude again. My Dublin accented landlord handed me the key and the Celtic Tiger took £560 from my pocket to enrich him. I opened the door, but before having the time to discover the poverty inside my mobile phone rang. How many enraged fuck words did Robert want to pollute my freedom with this time? I heard his tears beg for my forgiveness, but my emotions were cold. He promised me that he would change, but I certainly didn't believe him. He implored me to love him again, "Fuck off Robert". I didn't want to return to his brutality and I silenced him forever.

I had always seen an abundance of sadness glitter in her wild eyes and I certainly believed that Molly had a secret garden of silence. Indeed she concealed the brutality that had destroyed her from catholic judgement, but in tears she betrayed her promise of silence and all of her sufferance resurrected to me. Molly enlightened me that she was engrained with an aversion for all men and that if she revolted against me with so much distaste it because I was a man and not because I was "a queer fucker". During the early years of her childhood, his lips had kissed her with passion, his hands had fondled and denuded her with lust and his penis had penetrated her again and again. Her catholic mother was so contaminated by the pulpit sermons that she didn't want to believe her. She should have crucified the bastard that raped her daughter, but she enriched Molly with the spirituality of the bible instead. It was such religious brutality that escalated all the emotional and behavioural dysfunctions in her life. Molly never resurrected like Jesus Christ, but faded away in the eternal ruins of silence. Her anxiety attacks surfaced with more and more vigour, her profound depressions deepened and she was ravaged in the prison of her perpetual sufferance. Her catholic mother prayed to god in awe and reverence, "god be with ya, god bless ya", god was in every fucking sentence that the holy woman said, but the bitch had coldly abandoned Molly to total solitude in her hours of need. Perhaps she prayed to the almighty god of Ireland in repentance, but was it possible to forgive her catholic silence now? No beautiful flowers bloomed in Molly's past. I

consoled her ocean of tears and accepted that she needed to punish all men. I now knew everything, even the silenced name of the uncle that had fucked her for so many forgotten years.

My brother had fallen out of love and desired his liberty. His kisses had become cold, caustic and distant in a marriage that he no longer wanted to belong to. He didn't want to survive in the prison of Molly's love forever and his naked body stiffened in total displeasure of her touch when they fucked. He was completely destroyed in an ocean of despair and he needed me to resurrect him from the ashes of destruction. The brutality of his intolerance had betrayed me again and again; perhaps in revenge I should have informed him to reap the shit that he had harvested, but I practiced catholic love and forgiveness instead. How many times did he punish me for being "a fucking queer", but I had the strength to forget all of that sufferance. I had rigorous moral values ingrained in my self-culture, I wiped away his tears as he lamented and I didn't forsake him in his hour of need. My dank basement flat wasn't well appointed; the 1970 style wallpaper was severely stained with age, a growth of mould spots decorated part of the ceiling, years of dust was heavily embedded in the carpeted floor and my Chlorophytum Comosum struggled to survive in the lack of natural light. My brother dreamed softly in the comfort of my bed for as long as he wanted and I slept on the faded red velvet and stone hard armchair that decorated the corner of the room. I was also the hand that wiped away her tears, I didn't understand her empathy of his sufferance, but Molly told me to be charitable in my neutral judgement. She believed that it was best that I housed my brother, perhaps she feared that otherwise he would fall into the arms of some Irish whore instead? She wanted me to contaminate his dream of liberty with an insight of what his life was to become without her. She certainly understood the mechanism and complexity of his mind more than I thought, but would the desolation of poverty really entice him to revert to her perpetual love again?

Molly mourned his dying love and battled in an ocean of despair. Her pious mother implored god to nourish my brother with the solemn promise of eternal love, but her prayers didn't touch Molly with the emotional support that she really needed. Her sister justified with toxicity that she had only tolerated him for years and that she had never liked him much. She even believed that the bastard had liberated Molly, but rather than enriched Molly with her deep aversion she should have silenced her disdain. Stone casting was forbidden in her holy bible, but she gleefully condemned their

marriage to perpetual doom. The bitch certainly should have scrutinised the betrayal of her adulterous husband more closely instead. Molly's dreams were in ruins, but for her catholic friends it wasn't their fucking problem either. Her tears savagely destroyed her in solitude more and more and she lowered her head defeated by everyone's catholic judgement. My father systematically tossed a coin to the beggar on the church steps on the Sabbath day, with a smile the narthex door was held open for an elder and he also prayed for the resurrection of my brother's love. My mother's condescending righteous opinion had always criticised Molly; her blonde peroxide hair was distasteful, the abundance of rings on each finger was a vulgarity, the slovenliness of cleanliness in her catholic home wasn't next to godliness, but my mother now stepped into the light of tolerance. She befriend her so much in her hour of need that it seemed that she had even forgotten that Molly originated from the lowest stratum of underclass of a certain urban Dublin area. My mother knew all about the sufferance of a roller coaster marriage and she defended Molly from all the social judgements that crucified her. The almighty catholic god of Ireland believed in the prison of eternal love, but I allured my brother to taste the freedom that he really wanted. My holy father enticed him to revert to her love, after all coming from an Irish home of high catholic principles and morals he needed to be an honourable man. Step by step my brother was enslaved forever in a catholic marriage that he certainly didn't believe in. Molly completely forgave him, but was her revenge nine months later when Sorcha was born? Was she the desired fruit of their passion or the fertilised seed that sealed my brother's fate?

It was beginning of great social change in Ireland; the poverty of the Great Famine was forgotten and a consumption society enriched the urban streets with an abundance of affluence. The Irish didn't want to slave in certain jobs and the Celtic Tiger didn't discriminate against the different colours, cultures or religions that invaded catholic Ireland. A swarm of job hungry new comers arrived with a dream of belonging to that Irish El Dorado, but my reverie was to forsake Ireland again. I needed a voyage of freedom and I wanted to be enriched by the taste of an espresso on a crowded Parisian café terrace and to live among the colourful fragrance of baguette that floated in the air. Under the Franco-Irish Cultural Agreement there were fifty five positions in the English Language Assistants Scheme that year. It was of great importance to master all the techniques of classroom management, but working under the flashing disco lights in a gay bar hadn't enriched me with the pedagogical practices that I required for teaching English in a French secondary school. My drag queen experience

had enlightened me with an insight into make-up and the harmony of matching a glittery dress with silver sparking high heels, but I certainly needed more than the accessory of a Geri Halliwell wig to perform efficiently in the core of a classroom. The almighty catholic god of Ireland must have heard my mother's prayers or perhaps god wanted to banish my promiscuous homosexuality from Ireland because as the colourful leaves of autumn 1998 began to fall, Ireland faded away in the distance. The tides of my serenity changed to liberate me from my sufferance and the gentle rays of the October sunshine caressed my face in Saint Maixent l'École. It was a remote world far from the homosexual freedom that was practiced in Paris, but I resurrected and blossomed there resplendently.

My spacious apartment was well appointed; it was a total contrast to the dank basement flat, the dust embedded carpeted floor, the mould spotted ceiling and the severely stained wallpaper that I had known in Dublin. My monthly rent, including all bills and for a substantially larger surface area, represented the equivalent of biweekly rent in Ireland. Believing that proficiency was through practice, I had trained for my classroom performance reflecting in front of a full length mirror for hours. I now felt a room of staring eyes focus on me as my teenage students regarded me with total judgement from head to toe; I was most certainly the only teacher in the school that wore a shirt and tie. I feared that my discourse was to fall nervously from my mouth in a stutter of incomprehensible words. My stress was palpable in a slight moment of hesitation; such silence was unnoticeable by them, but in my thoughts it completely betrayed me. Perhaps I needed a double something to relax, but instead a few deep breaths discretely conquered the sea of nervous tension as I paced before a class for the first time. Then, my smile totally enshrouded the overwhelming sensations of jitter that devoured me and I discovered an intense passion to conquer dreams that I had either never known or that I had completely forgotten. I found such fulfilment in disseminating the English language and I finally knew what direction I wanted on the road of my professional life. Far from the labyrinth of books in the UCD library it was a challenge to undertake my final university year via the field of distance learning, but there was no better place to absorb Balzac, Baudelaire, Flaubert, Molière, Rimbaud, Stendhal and Voltaire than directly in the country that had created and inspired them. All of my dreams were paved with certainty from that moment on.

It was socially forbidden to be homosexual in certain jobs and coming out of the closet in the core of the teaching vocation in France was still viewed as gay propaganda. If humanity believed that homosexuality was learnt and not innate, queers were predators to enlighten innocence with a corrupt passion for immorality. I did not want to taste the sufferance of discrimination or the accusation of indoctrinating homosexuality in the minds of my students. In fear of intolerance I didn't parade in the battle for queer freedom, but silenced my homosexuality instead. Silence certainly did not propagate the social acceptance of homosexuality that I dreamed of, perhaps it dehumanised queers further, but in a heterosexually dominated society sometimes there was no other choice. Perhaps my silence betrayed the march for homosexual liberty, but it was about survival among the strict rigours of a heterosexual world. France was liberty, equality and promiscuity, but I didn't practice homosexuality. I didn't seduce, kiss, denude or fuck any licentious lovers. I needed solitude to resurrect me from the desolation and sufferance of love before I had the serenity to believe in perpetual love again. My holy father posted me two Douglas Hyde banknotes at the beginning of each month, perhaps that symbolised his love for me, but it certainly enraged me instead? Each time I opened the envelope I hungered for a hand written sign of his affection, but there were no paternal emotions in the neutrality of empty words. He had had the generosity to house, feed, clothe and educate me for years, but I still longed to be enriched with the sentiment of his love. I never really knew if my father loved me or not.

The season of autumn faded and "Away in a Manger", "God Rest Ye Merry Gentlemen", "Hark the Herald Angels Sing", "Joy to the World", "O Come, All Ye Faithful", "Silent Night" and "The First Noel" passionately resounded; I had returned to rural catholic Ireland for another homophobic Christmas. A tell tale sign of my homosexuality was liberated in something I had said or done and my holy mother needed to hetero-sexualise me again. Due to my age there was no brutality in her enragement, but she crucified me with the hostility of words instead. "Birth to a fucking monster", she enlightened me that if had known that the foetus she had carried inside her for nine months was a queer, that she would have killed it. Death by an illegal backstreet abortion should have destroyed me and liberated her from the sufferance of mothering a "queer fucker". The Brussels sprouts on my plate, which were my favourite vegetable, didn't taste the same after that. Did she want me to be found hanging in lifeless suspension from the century aged sycamore tree at the end garden instead? I rebelled with insolence and I asked her for a rope. The catholic culture

had enriched her to believe that without everlasting repentance that I was condemned to the fires of hell. "Bless you for you have sinned", but I didn't desire to journey into spirituality or repent for my homosexual immorality. There was harmonious peace to heterosexuals in the prison of the cold churches where she prayed, but certainly no tolerance for a homosexual son was found when turning the discoloured gilded pages of her aged bible. There was more sufferance preached from the pulpit sermons than love, but I didn't believe in the myth of the almighty catholic god. The coldness of winter had denuded the sycamore tree, but did I have the strength to survive to see foliage gloriously conquer it again? Did she have the power to abandon the wrath of god and walk into the light of tolerance forever? I did not genuflect in need of forgiveness before her god and I didn't believe in the fruition of my dream of homosexual freedom either.

Diane Forde's brown eyes glittered with such beauty that they should have seduced all heterosexual men, but their testosterone was more lustfully attracted to her voluptuous breasts instead. We met in a promiscuous heterosexual bar of seduction in Niort, but I certainly didn't want to denude her. My homosexual eyes looked directly into her heterosexual eyes and I didn't journey into her cleavage. Diane was highly tolerant to all difference, which enticed me to liberate my coming out. In her judgement homosexuality wasn't a felony against god or a contamination in society. In the freedom of her tolerance she liberated me from the prison of silence, the ocean of despair and the profound sufferance that still destroyed me. In the social structure homosexuals were more sensitive in emotions than heterosexual men, that enhanced her attraction to me and a beautiful friendship flourished. To celebrate my 23rd birthday my Geri Halliwell wig resurrected from the profound depth of my suitcase. A heavily applied layer of make-up de-masculinised me and a black tight fitting sparkling dress from her wardrobe was used to effeminate me further. We socialised under the flashing disco lights in her favourite heterosexual nightclub in high heels on that cold night. There was vivacity in her laugh because Jerome was so heavily pissed that he didn't realise that I was endowed with a penis. In the belief that I was a feminine creature "my gorgeous Jerome" passionately kissed me. There was so much lust in his heterosexual kiss that the taste of his sumptuous lips was engrained in me forever. On the crowded dance floor his erection caressed my leg and betrayed the horny thoughts of his silenced seduction. He clearly wanted to fuck me, but Diane forced him away to dance in a different direction. My

freedom was certainly ephemeral, Ireland needed to crucify me and the seasons changed colour again.

With so many books in my luggage it was impossible to imagine my return to Ireland alone, so with catholic charity my parents battled the long journey. My father was cold in his emotions, it was certain that the trip had exhausted him, but in the days that followed their touristic visit of Poitou-Charentes his emotions for his queer son were still caustic and distant. Tears fell from her beautiful blue eyes as my holy mother kissed me, which ensnarled me to ponder that she had changed. Judging by the alien display of her maternal behaviour it was blatant that she had sincerely missed me, but my enthusiasm to taste the eternity of her love was certainly an oversight of the ephemeralness of her affection. I really wanted to believe that her love had resurrected from the ashes of forgotten sufferance, but was her intolerance to betray me again? The last thing that I saw as the glorious days of Saint Maixent l'École came to an end was my students mourning my departure. I gazed wistfully through the rare windshield; some chased after the car waving, a handful were blowing kisses in a amicable fashion, others were crying in woe as I disappeared from their sight forever, but all had boycotted attending their philosophy class to bid me adieu. An ocean of tears fell from my eyes knowing that the rigour of catholic Ireland was probably going to consume my liberty and destroy me again.

A brief stop-over in a supermarket on the road to Roscoff began in the pleasant ambiance of wine shopping, but her brutality turned the clemency of that day into a homosexual crucifixion. She needed to hetero-sexualise me and any sign of homosexual immorality was a well-founded reason for her to massacre me again. There was no flirtatious seduction in the smile of the cute looking man that had merely glanced at me, but my mother was certain that my homosexuality had betrayed me. She imposed her social definition of heterosexual behaviour, but in resistance I rebelled to piss her off. I deliberately admired his ass, which enraged her even more. The softness of her tender emotions faded away, the gentleness of her smile completely withered and her hand collided with my face with no forewarning. The holy sermons had overly contaminated her with eternal aversion, distain and repugnance and there was still no tolerance for "a fucking homosexual". Nothing had changed in her catholic judgement; I still didn't have the right to be a queer and my sufferance resurrected again. So much rancour consumed me that I retorted that I wanted her to

die. I staggered to and fro in an unsteady fashion as my father punished my insolence by a series of forceful blows. The eyes of the other shoppers cast a second glance in complete disbelief, but the banal aggressivity that had horrified them had enslaved me for so many years in silence. There was so much solitude in the abundance of despair that followed.

As the ferry departed the distance enlarged to abduct my beloved France away from my sight. Each second of the journey denuded me of my liberty and each breathe contaminated me more and more in the prison of Irish repression again. How many catholic Irish homosexuals had been seduced in despair by tears and walked into the shadows of the valley of death? I really needed to abandon the prison of homosexual sufferance that she created and I wanted the perpetual silence of death to liberate me from the brutality of her catholic judgement forever. In total desperation her homosexual son mechanically climbed over the rails that lined the Val de Loire promenade deck. The hypnotic movement of the waves below lured me to taste my desired freedom. The soft moonlight, which reflected on the cold sea, incited me to plunge into the liberation of death rather than revert to an eternal homosexual crucifixion in rural catholic Ireland again. My lustful desire was to die. I prayed to the almighty god to forgive me. I feared an agonising death, but my need to embrace death was stronger than my passion to live. The wind caressed the woe that fell from my eyes and I loosened my grip to abandon the sufferance of homosexual life. I was ready to be banished from the kingdom of heaven, but in a last second of enlightenment I somehow discovered that I had the strength to survive. An ocean of emotion fell from my blue eyes as I cried in the lamentation of my abandonment of death. I had almost forsaken my dreams, but I resurrected from the ashes of tragedy instead. If I wanted my revenge on her I needed to forget the desolation of her brutality. If I wanted the fruition of my reveries I needed the serenity to conquer one last Irish battle. My judgement was not before the almighty catholic god that night, but before an exam jury in Dublin a few days later. As the light of dawn conquered the sky Ireland appeared on the horizon, but I believed in the changing colours of freedom again.

The Promise Of Silence

20

The Hesitation of Love

Homosexual love was a myth, created in desperation by libidinous queers to justify the promiscuity of the gay culture. In the social sexual liberty of homosexuality men kissed, denuded and fucked in abundance, but there was no ripple of love in such freedom. Forgotten nights of passion with a multitude of interchangeable lovers had forced me to understand that there was no sincerity in the ephemeral kisses of homosexual men. Robert's brutality had completely defeated my belief in love too and the poverty of his love had enriched me to believe that the fruition of love did not come from reveries. Perhaps the almighty catholic god had created homosexuals to be eternally loveless and I was deemed to such holy penance and silent repentance forever? I didn't have the faith to battle for the liberation of love or the strength to taste the sufferance of falling in and out love again and in despair I coldly silenced all of my emotions. On May 27th 1999 the road of my life began to change, but I was totally unaware that he was seduced by my beauty. He silently desired to liberate his lustful passion for me, but that night his discreet glances in the distance on the dance floor did not meet my eyes under the flashing disco lights. The eternal lover that I had always dreamed of was a kiss away from my lips, but I hadn't seen the ocean of beauty that glittered in his profound ocean blue eyes yet. Did the savagery of homosexuality really condemn me to be alone forever? I needed to conquer my hesitation if I wanted to taste his perpetual love.

The moment I entered the most reputed urban gay club in Dublin on May 28th 1999 our eyes interlocked. It was absolute love at first sight; a sensation that I had never known before and a myth that I certainly didn't believe in. I knew all the fundament steps of homosexual seduction, but he was the most pulchritudinous man that I had ever seen. He was certainly far too beautiful for me, so I didn't dare to flirt. I also didn't want to taste the despair of queer promiscuity again, so I turned my glance away in an arrogant effort to ignore him. I struggled so hard to forget him, but neither

the rhythmically disco music nor the rainbow coloured lights distracted me from thinking of him. I battled to forsake him before he conquered my emotions further, but it was the strongest desire of lust that I had ever felt. I didn't want to be contaminated by love ever again, but he was deeply engrained in me forever. I wanted to silence my deep attraction to him, but my eyes needed to be nourished by his lascivious beauty again. His physical appearance had certainly allured me, but it was the discovery of his moral values that really seduced me, especially the colour of sincerity that glittered in his profound ocean blue eyes. I needed to taste his passion and his sublime smile enticed me to liberate a succulent kiss. I certainly rebelled to betray the hesitation of love and from that moment on I was besotted, but did his love really want to flourish and blossom in the changing colours of each season with me? Had Philippe battled the waves of the Atlantic Ocean to heroically conquer the eternity of my love in the promiscuous land of Ireland?

The intense sound of the disco music became silent; some devoured their Guinness with serenity, others went to "The Boiler House" to fuck in desperation, but in the alley off South Great George Street a considerable number of homosexuals still lingered. They certainly needed to hunt quickly if they wanted to seduce an interchangeable lover for the night. A promiscuous guy of average beauty preyed on Philippe, but I did not battle to defend my seduction. I believed in the liberty of betrayal if he wanted, but he desired to fall in love with me. I had tasted the brutality of love, the desolation of love, the tears of love and the sufferance of love had certainly ravaged me too. I had forgotten the sensational beauty of love, but my dream of love resurrected from the ruins of despair again. We kissed and denuded under the stars on a roof top garden and the sensuality of our entangled bodies liberated a profusion of love in harmony. I wanted to immortalise each sensation of each emotion forever, but the colours of dawn conquered the sky to betray me and the waves separated our worlds in different directions. Catholic Ireland was my almighty prison and in the hours that followed he returned to a never heard of place called Thiers. The taste of his passion was engrained in me forever, but was it love or infatuation that devoured me again? Each letter that he wrote seduced me more and more, but was his perpetual love for another man and his ephemeral love for me?

The Promise Of Silence

Philippe paced the train station platform in Vichy on July 2nd 1999. His smile then liberated me from the hesitation of love and his profound ocean blue eyes most certainly mirrored that he was "Quelqu'un de bien". Thiers flourished in medieval architecture, but the affluence of industrialisation had long abandoned the shabby town where he resided. The virile men that mastered fire and water had forsaken the valley, the factories that had once symbolised the prosperity of an industrial civilisation had become ruins and the savagery of time had destroyed the tenacity of generations of knife makers along the banks of the river Durolle. The glittering sun enhanced the beautiful view of Auvergne below with such magnificence and it was among the volcanic peak of Puy de Dome that I understood that he was to become my everything. For three glorious days he nourished all of my dreams with the sensual taste of his kisses. For four nights our desires denuded and in harmony we practiced the art of making eternal love. I wanted the sensation of his passion to be perpetual, but it was ephemeral again. Time betrayed my freedom to love him and I still belonged to the prison of catholic Ireland. Passengers dragged their suitcases in a frantic rush. The destructive sound of a whistle blew and the doors of the train closed to imprison me. "Je t'aime", each tear enhanced his sufferance of being in love with me. His dream of love had resurrected, his home was still enriched with the fragrance of my Calvin Klein, but I had faded away into the horizon and a sensation of despair marred Philippe.

The Irish rain lashed down as my plane landed and catholic Ireland consumed me in woe. Nothing had changed in Dublin, Daniel O' Connell still towered over shoppers near the river Liffey, Molly Malone still resided among the tourists in Grafton Street, but the city that I had once loved passionately for its freedom now crucified me alone. The musty air in my studio enhanced my solitude, the incessant hum of the rush hour traffic enraged me and there was so much despair in looking at the flowers that I had bought on Moore Street for three pounds, which had withered in the vase where I had left them. I wanted to be enslaved in his profound ocean blue eyes forever, but the hesitation of love clouded my mind again. Did Philippe really want to liberate my dream of love? I had never felt so much passion for a man before, but what if the sufferance of love was to defeat me again? Was the deep sentiment of his love to fade away in the distance? Was I to become forgotten in the changing colours of the seasons? I believed in the eternity of his love, but perhaps I was only a dreamer? A sentiment of incertitude devoured me, but his love wasn't ephemeral and Philippe promised me the stars and the moon, but he liberated all of my reveries instead. August 28th 1999; he conquered the

waves of the Atlantic Ocean to seduce me in Dublin again. He certainly discovered that my world was under the flashing disco lights of urban gay clubs. Certain social friends believed that my homosexual love was a myth, others condemned it as infatuation, all judged Philippe as ephemeral, but he enlightened me that they were contaminated by the green eyed monster. He enriched me to understand that a consumption society had lured homosexuals into a promiscuous culture and that in the queer tolerance of fucking there was almighty freedom, but that in despair their jealousy had surfaced. In the passion of his kisses I abandoned the desolation of their judgement. On the stone beach of Bray Philippe revealed that the seed of his eternal love was fertilised. My love resurrected and I now had the faith to battle for his perpetual love.

I eternally silenced that death had almost seduced me and that the hypnotic movement of the waves had incited me to plunge into the reflected soft moonlight on the cold sea just a few days before our first kiss. I thought that my smile was more enriching because flowers didn't grow from tears, but he needed to know about the holy brutality that had created me. I didn't want to taste his judgement, but in the changing colours of the seasons my past resurrected from silence and he knew me profoundly. Whereas I saw weeds Philippe saw beauty and I learnt that in fuelling my passion to survive that the crucifixions of catholic Ireland had enriched me to become the amazing man that he had fallen in love with. I always believed that no lover ever needed to know about my sufferance, but I found my resurrection from silence in his love. There had always been a certain consistency in my emotions that made me indifferent to feelings, but Philippe changed me. In the Garden of Remembrance I disclosed that I was enslaved in his love and that I was alone in the prison of an almighty catholic country that I strongly resented. I needed to forsake Ireland in the name of love and Philippe desired the liberation of the same reverie too. He wanted to love me in abundance forever, but his kiss was ephemeral again. Passengers dragged their suitcases in Dublin airport. "Je t'aime", each tear enhanced my sufferance of being in love with him. My flat was still enriched with the fragrance of his Jean Paul Gaultier, but he had faded away into the horizon and a sensation of despair marred me. I closed my eyes to pensively relive the intensity of each second again, but when I opened my blue eyes he wasn't there to kiss me. Promiscuous homosexuals certainly wanted to seduce me under the flashing disco lights, but my love didn't wither away in the taste of another man's passionate kiss. I could have fucked an abundance of queers in the silence of betrayal if I had wanted, but too much beauty blossomed in the garden of my dream. My

faith in love had perpetually resurrected. I wanted to age with Philippe forever.

Mrs. Murphy was a renowned fortune teller in Henry Street; some reasoned that she was endowed with a vision of the future, but I was more skeptical in my thoughts. I didn't believe in the biblical myth of god and certainly not the words of a Dublin accented woman that was to read my palm for £20. "Born to be fruitless with no children on the path of your life", perhaps an effeminate gesture had betrayed my homosexuality and enlightened her that I was a barren queer? "There will be victory after the agony of silence", it was true that I wanted liberty from the dark dusty closet of silence, but didn't all homosexuals have the same dream? "I foresee great sufferance, but freedom in your survival", I smiled; it was a mundane fact that the gay culture was contaminated with tears and battled for eternal freedom from catholic judgement. "Everlasting love will be over the sea in a land of a foreign tongue", but didn't travel stream deeply in Irish blood since the beginning of the Great Famine? Then, the haggard old voice disclosed "your perpetual happiness is with a blue eyed man". Perhaps the statistic probability of blue eyes was higher than any other colour? "A name beginning with P will love you forever"; was Mrs. Murphy really endowed with an irrefutable gift of foresight or was it just by chance that Philippe loved me? "Death will take you as an elderly man", perhaps the Catholics of Ireland didn't want to crucify me for the immorality of homosexuality after all? Had I survived the brutality of an Irish god to be liberated by the kisses of Philippe forever? Was the power of his love to liberate me from the holy judgements that had destroyed me for years? I certainly had to forsake my dear Ireland if I wanted to live all of my dreams.

My catholic mother prayed to her almighty god to hetero-sexualise me and her barbaric judgement still crucified me for my homosexual immorality. Ireland had splendidly risen from the ashes of poverty, but the Celtic Tiger had completely forgotten me. Did I want to abandon my holy Ireland to taste homosexual freedom, to forsake the preposterousness of a consumption society or to flee the prison of catholic brutality? I needed to be enriched by the taste of an espresso on a crowded café terrace in the land Molière again, but enragement did not entice me to passionately desert Ireland. Philippe had liberated the fruition of all of my dreams and I merely wanted to cultivate his perpetual love. A vodka party in my Dublin studio was a relatively original idea to enrich my pockets and lighten the

load of my suitcase. It was with a James Joyce banknote that someone impulsively bought my rollerblades. A Daniel O' Connell for the fetish handcuffs that had never been used despite the vast number of interchangeable lovers that I had had. Martin's glorious drag queen days were beginning and my silver bling bling high heels sold for a Catherine Mc Auley. For some of my social friends it was an affordable way to ornately furnish or decorate their flats, but for others it was the purchase of another dust collecting object that they really didn't need. A few envisaged that my zeal to sell everything was to become an eternal regret, but in desperation for cash I didn't believe in materialism or sentimental value. A Douglas Hyde banknote was promised by Michael, but I never saw the colour of his money; he certainly cherished his booty more than my friendship. The more elated everyone was the more attractive everything became in the pissed ambiance that Smirnoff created. An hour later my wallet was £268 more corpulent, condoms improvised as balloons and a neighbour threatened to phone the Garda Síochána "if that fucking queer music doesn't fucking stop". It was not socially incorrect that Christopher puked in the street as we walked to "The George". Homosexuals were crucified, but there was no vulgarisation in binge drinking and his drunken demeanour encountered no hostile judgement from the pious Catholics of Ireland. It was an unforgettable night dancing for the last time under the flashing disco lights with the promiscuous men of the gay culture; but I didn't belong to that world anymore. The beauty of Dublin had liberated my homosexual freedom, but Ireland had not conquered my eternal love.

My alarm clock had sold for £2, so the next morning the door bell ringing disturbed me from my sleep instead of an acute buzz sound. The floor was still littered with empty vodka bottles, the ashtray overflowed with butts, but Aunty Annie, the cleanest woman in the length and breadth of Ireland, reacted in a normal fashion as if she hadn't even seen or stepped over the mess. The calamity that ravaged my studio was everywhere; judging by her smile the Geri Halliwell wig suspended from the lightshade certainly bewildered her, but she disclosed no sign of intolerance. Kathryn categorically refused all my hospitality, but I didn't dishearten. An abundance of panic-stricken glittered in her eyes as I carelessly rinsed a lipstick stained glass, which had squatted in the kitchen sink overnight. Annie's giggle became a loud laugh in anticipation as I generously filled it with Coke. I handed it to my cousin, but she dared not put the drink to her lips in fear of contamination. I wanted to disclose to Annie that I had fallen in love, but my catholic mother had deluded me into believing that there was no tolerance for "homosexual fuckers" in the eyes of Annie, so I did

not liberate my lover from the dark dusty queer closet yet. I wanted to parade my love in total freedom, but I was condemned to survive in a prison of silence for another eleven years. To love in silence betrayed the battle for homosexual acceptance, but there was certainly no rainbow coloured gay flag waving to liberate me in my hours of need either. Nobody ever revolted against my mother and the brutality of her holy judgement forbade me to become her "fucking queer son".

Naomi danced in her Malahide garden and an abundance of sunshine glittered in her golden coloured hair. The air filled with gaiety the moment that she saw me arrive, but nothing had changed in my battle to cherish her. I waved in a friendly fashion to my brother, who beckoned his daughter away from me and he forcibly seized the gifts that I had given her from her hands. The teddy bears were thrown to the ground in a display of his rancour and he slammed the door in my face. If his catholic religion proclaimed the love of god, he certainly forgot to practice it. He listened to the sermons from the pulpit with awe, he genuflected with spirituality before the Eucharist and he tasted the body of Christ with reverence on the Sabbath day, but he crucified me for the immorality of homosexuality again. There was no tolerance for 'a queer fucker" in the immaculacy of his catholic family and Naomi was his weapon in my sufferance. In the rigour of his beliefs he didn't want me to contaminate his holy heterosexual home with homosexuality. From behind the net curtains Molly peeped, but she did not defend me and I tasted her almighty betrayal. She had clearly forgotten that I had wiped away her tears in her hours of need. My niece stared from the upstairs bedroom window. I waved a kiss and she smiled. My head lowered in defeat as I walked down the road and my tears resurrected in solitude. Such was the vision of despair that destroyed me that day. I hated the biblical brutality that enriched Ireland; if I wanted to survive in the freedom of homosexuality I had to forsake catholic Ireland forever.

October 19th 1999; the bright light of dawn enlightened the egg shell colour of the walls in my bedroom in rural catholic Ireland. The gentleness of her hand touching my face awoke me from the profoundness of my sleep. Tear after tear conquered her blue eyes and moistened her pale white cheeks with emotion. She kissed me with the passion of a mother that would die for her child. She displayed her profound love for her son as if she had completely forgotten that I was "a queer fucker", but such love was always ephemeral. That morning I wanted to believe in the eternity of her love

again, but I sincerely think that that was the last time that she really loved me. Her face was to be ravaged with the signs of ageing, her vitality and vigor were to fade in the desolation of time and in the changing colours of the seasons she was to perpetually forsake me. Perhaps she loved me in the sufferance of her silenced thoughts forever, but her hate against the homosexual race was engrained in her intolerance and she never resurrected in repentance. I still loved my mother, but she did not know that I had fallen in love. I didn't want my love to be crucified, so I enslaved Philippe in my dark dusty closet of silence. I certainly silenced that he seduced, kissed, denuded and loved me. Did my silence betray the battle for homosexual freedom or was silence a double edged sword of despair? Silence was the freedom to love Philippe without a crucifixion and also the prison that liberated my dreams. Before my departure she sprinkled me with holy water from the font by the front door knowing that I hated that catholic contamination. In prayer she implored her almighty god to escort me on the glorious journey of life, but I didn't believe in the myth of her god. Not wanting to liberate her rage I did not rebel and my silence enriched her with serenity. My pious father was totally dispassionate for his homosexual son. He was devoid of affectionate emotions for me and his coldness enraged me with hate. I abandoned the promiscuity of the homosexual culture, the flashing disco lights of the gay scene, the brutality of her catholic judgement and the solitude of my crucifixions. I abandoned my dear Ireland forever. The suitcase that I dragged behind me, not only contained my dreams, but also the silence of all my sufferance.

21

The Fruition of Reveries

I abandoned Ireland for the fruition of my reveries and Philippe certainly created all of my dreams. From that moment on I was liberated from my Irish sufferance and the glorious beauty of my life reflected in his profound ocean blue eyes forever. Intolerance imprisoned him in the dark dusty closet of silence, but he flourished in my love and now wanted to parade for his homosexual freedom. Knowing that his father didn't believe in any form of social tolerance I justified that I didn't want him to taste the same crucifixion that had destroyed me. I didn't want him to be contaminated by the emotional tears of a destructive coming out, so I betrayed his battle for gay liberty and enslaved him in silence instead. I believed that our love needed to develop more deeply under the dormant volcanoes of Auvergne before waving his rainbow coloured flag to the world. I deluded him to believe that he needed to survive in silence among the strict rigours of a heterosexual culture for a little longer. To her greatest dismay I was not in Ireland to attend my university graduation ceremony, but whereas my pompous mother wanted me to be under the spotlight of honour to enhance her self-importance, falling deeper in love with Philippe was more my cup of tea. She had battled to rise from the ashes of destitution, belonging to a consumption society was her revenge on poverty, she prayed with vanity and she indebted me in the fact that she had housed, fed, clothed and educated me for twenty three years. With a pretentious air she disseminated to every Catholic in rural Ireland that the abundance of her affluence had cultivated me with a Bachelor of Arts degree, but her grandiloquence had strangely forgotten to disclose that I was "a queer fucker". My virtuous holy catholic mother continued to crucify my homosexuality in the changing colours of each season. Philippe believed that I was too cold in my judgement of her and enriched me with the clemency to forgive her, but he hadn't tasted her brutality yet.

I believed our love didn't need to flourish in the myth that all gays were fans of Madonna and that if heterosexuals did not need to justify their heterosexuality that queers equally didn't need to justify their homosexuality either. I desired to rupture the pink stereotyping that slaughtered the gay culture since the beginning of time and live without judgement, so we did not harbour the beauty of our love in the dark dusty closet of social intolerance or parade for queer freedom either. We certainly did not rebel in a militant fashion, but did our silence betray the homosexual battle for acceptance? The balance of silence was our freedom to love, but was there more sufferance than freedom in the prison of silence? I tasted the arrogance of certain adverse opinions; some of his social friends believed that my love was ephemeral, others thought that my affection was entangled in a need to be liberated by his affluence, but I didn't love Philippe to belong to a consumption society. The Celtic Tiger had forgotten me, poverty had enriched me, one suitcase definitely contained everything in the world that I possessed, but I hadn't abandoned Ireland to be enslaved in the injustice of their unfounded beliefs. The green eyed monster deluded them to think there was economic interest and not sincerity in my love, but I battled even more against the culture differences of being Irish. They also condemned me as being savage and barbaric because I didn't speak with flowers or master the language of Molière. The changing colours of autumn denuded the trees, winter covered the volcanic peaks in an ornate blanket of snow, spring flourished and our love blossomed in abundance, summer deepened our passion further, but Philippe had abandoned them in punishment of their cold judgements.

The Celtic Tiger had certainly forgotten to enrich me, but France liberated all of my dreams. Madame Adrienne, the Commissioner of Education in Auvergne, believed in the fruition of my reveries too. A few deep breaths conquered the sea of nervous tension that devoured me at the beginning of the job interview and a profound discussion on the techniques of classroom management and pedagogical practices began. Believing in my proficiency she kindly interrupted my passionate discourse and retorted that she didn't need more time to ponder because she was already certain of my efficiency. I now felt a classroom of staring eyes focus on me as teenage students regarded me with total judgement from head to toe again; after all I was probably the only teacher in France that wore a shirt and tie. The prestigious Lycée Blaise Pascal in Clermont Ferrand became my workplace for seven months and I resurrected and flourished in the vocation of teaching the elegant language of Shakespeare again. France was a world of liberty, equality and promiscuity, but under the surface of

tolerance there was still a certain brutality towards homosexuality. Was there more sufferance in the dark dusty closet of silence or in coming out? Some believed in the myth that queers could revert to heterosexual love; in my forgiveness of their ignorance I became more compassionate in my judgement of them. Others thought that homosexuality was a social contamination, but in their aversion I became a warrior. Words that enriched generation to generation with intolerance destroyed me, but in their hate I became a survivor. There were also holy Catholics that thoroughly believed in the freedom of homosexual love. There was no wrinkle of distaste, no flinch of horror, no disgust in her eyes and no emotion of repulsion in her body language. Claire Desthomas cultivated her faith in the almighty god in total harmony with the liberty that enriched her with homosexual acceptance. In her heterosexual bible it was not problematic to befriend "a queer fucker". The pulpit sermons in Ireland preached that "arse fuckers, benders, fags, faggots, fairies, nancies, poofsters, queenies and sissies" were eternally banished from the kingdom of heaven, but the sculptures that Claire believed in practiced the love of god instead. Homosexuality was not a felony against god or a savagery that destroyed the moral values of society. Whereas some focused on who I fucked rather than who I really was, Claire became an eternal friend that loved me for me. Was there more tolerance in the catholic doctrines than I had thought?

Our first Christmas tree was relatively naked. It was with a shoe box of decorations that it was beautified, but year after year the branches were enriched with more and more abundance. There were no catholic carols in the background, but with Andy Williams "It's the Most Wonderful Time of the Year", Brenda Lee "Rockin around the Christmas tree", Dean Martin "Let it snow", Eartha Kitt "Santa Baby" and Nat King Cole "Chestnuts Roasting on an Open Fire" it was a very gay Christmas instead. There was Mariah Carey "All I Want for Christmas Is You"; Philippe made a heart shape with the fairy lights and I kissed him with a boa of tinsel garlands around my neck. Wham "Last Christmas" played too; indeed I found George Michael rather attractive, but he hadn't been smoked out of the closet yet. It was so romantic dancing to Bing Crosby's "White Christmas", but Philippe certainly didn't understand why each decoration had to be placed in an impeccable fashion with such delicacy and precision. In the silence of my thoughts I desperately needed his love to liberate me from the sufferance of every Irish Christmas that I had had. My father had always moaned as he lowered the boxes from the dusty attic with resentment. Child like happiness always glittered in my mother's blue

eyes finding sentimental value in each decoration that she treasured. Every year it was the rediscovery of our favourite objects, as if we had forgotten their existence and seen them in admiration for the first time again. With tenderness she unboxed the crib and venerated the baby Jesus with reverence. To holy hymns she sang glory to god and our catholic home became a multitude of rich colours. Each year my mother and I elaborately and sumptuously embellished the tree, but rather than adorn it with us my father sat alone in another room. He never practiced our Christmas rituals; watching virile sports on television was of more importance to him. In the serenity of Christmas my mother provisionally forgot my homosexuality. In the euphoria of her emotions she disclosed a profusion of love, but in doing so she contaminated me with her ephemeral affection. When each decoration had enhanced the splendour of the tree, her brutality resurrected and I became her "fucking queer son" again. Philippe now learnt that Christmas for me was not about the birth of Jesus Christ, but the crucifixion and the deep sufferance of a gay man. I betrayed the silence of Ireland and he now understood why each decoration had to be placed in an impeccable fashion with such delicacy and precision on our tree.

I knew that rural Catholic Ireland had not changed, but I had the compassion not to abandon my mother to a lonely Christmas without me. My holy father tearfully implored me to worship his catholic god in Saint Josephs Church on Christmas day, but I strongly declined to fulfil his desire. I justified that there was no forgiveness for "a fucking queer" in the kingdom of heaven. He enticed me to repent to the almighty god for my immorality, but I didn't believe in the myth of god. That insolence enraged him further, but he needed to tolerate that I had faith in the freedom of the gay culture and not in the prosperity of prayer. His brutality resurrected to ravage me in punishment for my parade of irreverence, but I certainly had no repentance for the sin of my homosexuality. I was crucified by the savagery of catholic Ireland again and dehumanised by same destructive force that I had always known since my coming out. An hour later he genuflected before the Eucharist; everyone saw the vision of bliss of a righteous catholic man, but underneath the surface of his pious appearance was a real sinner. Irish families silenced homosexuality with so much aversion. Some holy Catholics believed that it was better to have a gay son decaying in a cold grave amid a social mass of flesh eaters rather than dancing in a smoke filled nightclub under flashing disco lights amid promiscuous homosexual men. Some queers died in the catholic sacrament of suicide, but I certainly didn't believe in their resurrection. Ashes to ashes, dust to dust; the abundance of intolerance in catholic judgement

silenced Irish homosexuals forever. Was there less sufferance in bereavement than in the acceptance of homosexual love? Did Irish homosexuals really need to taste the eternal silence of death or was homosexual liberty possible in the heterosexual catholic culture?

I was born into a catholic family that systematically venerated god with so much reverence. My father had the generosity of a catholic with three coins on each Sabbath day, one for the collection box, one for the candle box and one for the beggar outside on the church steps. Intolerance in the sermons resounded from the pulpit and my father prayed for my repentance, but rather than hetero-sexualise me, his almighty god banished me from the kingdom of heaven and condemned me to eternal promiscuity among the burning fires of hell instead. I believed that there was no holy justice in catholic Ireland; "Thou shalt not commit adultery" was the seventh Commandment of god, but my righteous father had most certainly ripped that page directly out of his bible. He always made the sign of the cross when he drove passed a church or a cemetery, he genuflected in awe before the tabernacle in prayer, he crucified me for the practice of homosexuality, but he gloriously fucked other women and my catholic mother still tasted betrayal in his kisses. Sister Mary Magdalene was a virgin bride of Christ that had taken the perpetual vow of poverty, chastity and obedience to god. She uttered thanksgiving for the abundance of nourishment that represented our Christmas dinner, but in my humble opinion the Brussels sprouts tasted exactly the same before and after her benediction. "Amen" my enraged father glanced at me with wrath, but I still rebelled and closed her prayer in total silence rather than voice the four letter word that I didn't believe in. He didn't crucify me in punishment for my insolence because he certainly needed to be politically correct in her holy presence. After the delicious mouth watering meal my asocial father sang a harmony of hymns with the nun; such a masquerade of holiness totally repulsed me. It was of more importance to cultivate a friendship with her rather than love his homosexual son; after all her habit and her starched white wimple enhanced the social reputation of his sanctity.

Philippe phoned me later that day; the first snow had fallen in Auvergne. I silenced that the brutality of Ireland ravaged me again. For a few minutes I survived in the freedom of his love and forgot all of my sufferance, but the pale egg shell colour of the bedroom wall in rural catholic Ireland was certainly my prison. I still silenced that I had fallen in love with him, but the smile that glittered in my blue eyes must have betrayed me. My holy

mother enforced to know in a peremptory fashion if another queer fucker corrupted me? I knew that there was to be no clemency in her counter reaction, but in despair I revolted with the truth. I begged her to have the strength to love me, but the almighty god had died on a crucifix for the salvation of Irish heterosexuality and she liberated her wrath instead. My virtuous mother didn't step into the light of tolerance and after that coming out she destroyed me more and more. She belonged to a heteronormative catholic society, venerated god with total reverence in her morning prayers and passionately read the scriptures from the discoloured gilded pages of her aged bible each day. She listened attentively to the monotonous Sunday sermons, which condemned the immorality of homosexuality and preached a resurrection for heterosexuals in the eternal kingdom of heaven. Her faith was so admirably profound that even in the darkest moments of her life she still believed in the myth of god. Materialism glittered in her catholic eyes and another diamond ring sparkled in abundance on her finger that Christmas. She still silenced the taste of adultery that was deeply embedded in my father's kisses and she coldly punished me for practicing the sin of homosexuality.

Utter desolation devoured me as I crossed the fields of rural Ireland in the rain that night. Those with the same blood had crucified me with brutality and in my hour of need I knocked on another catholic door. Her children were playing blithely with their toys on the carpeted floor; Santa had come. Ann Casey and her husband were engulfed in an American movie on television and it was not unordinary that she seated me on the sofa between them. It did not enrage him with jealousy that I cuddled her in deep affection; homosexuality was certainly engrained in my behaviour and Terrance deduced that I had no desire to denude her voluptuous breasts. In her usual tender fashion she consoled the abundance of my tears and her love became my sanctuary again. In the silence of her eyes there was tolerance, but in the belief that there was no homosexual freedom in catholic Ireland I still feared to disclose my immorality. Ann understood all the sufferance that was behind my prison of silence, but her silence bewildered me into thinking that she thought I was straight and in fear of another catholic judgement I silenced my homosexuality. In the belief that queers inculcated homosexuality and not catholic virtue my holy brother always attentively scrutinised me and forbid me to be alone with his children, but Ann gave me the total freedom to love hers. I climbed the high wall in the Middle Glanmire road to trespass in the Orchard playground a million times with them, but Catholic Ireland forced me not to liberate my homosexuality and they aged in the silence of my difference.

The Promise Of Silence

The pulpit sermons preached against the immorality of the queer race, which fuelled my holy mother with wrath and enriched her with intolerance. She deluded me to believe that silence socially hetero-sexualised me, but in the changing colours of the seasons I learnt that such silence had greatly betrayed Ann too.

The storm of December 26th 1999 left a spectacle of desolation behind. The force of the winds had deracinated the forests of France. A debris of pylons littered the landscapes as if nature had demonstrated a revolution of revenge against mankind. The ruins of fallen chimneys defaced the streets like the aftermath scene of a deadly warzone. My eyes were enriched by the ruinous scars; total destruction was everywhere, but the brutality of rural catholic Ireland was the real destruction that was deeply engrained in me. Underneath my euphoric appearance and behind my frivolous facade so much silenced sufferance consumed and devoured me. I wanted eternal liberation from the intolerance that my holy mother practised, but her immortalised brutality always resurrected to crucify me again. I desired to journey into the freedom of my dreams, but I lamented in tears and survived in the savagery of my crucifixions instead. The glittering snow that covered the volcanic mountains allured me in admiration and the coldness in Auvergne penetrated me deeply for the first time. The denuded trees abandoned their hibernation and an abundance of foliage and multi-coloured flowers emerged from the barrenness of winter's despair. In the changing colours of the season I flourished in the sincerity of Philippe's perpetual love; I certainly blossomed in the beauty of his profound ocean blue eyes.

Diane's voyage to Auvergne was the discovery of the Puy de Dome, which gloriously towered over a plateau of volcanic landscape. A historical walk in Clermont Ferrand followed and she prayed to the almighty god with reverence in Notre-Dame of the Assumption Cathedral. We ascended the 150 steps of the Bayette church tower, which majestically enriched our eyes with a divine view of the city below. Diane belonged to a consumption society, so a few hours in a multitude of shops in Place de Jaude followed. I still needed to taste the sensational flashing disco lights of the gay culture, but it definitively wasn't Philippe's cup of tea. In the belief that love was a freedom and not a prison he incited me to socialise in a queer club with Diane if I wanted. Her beauty allured all heterosexual men, but her heterosexuality certainly didn't attract the desires of the homosexual men in the Zyzy Folie that night. All flirtatious eyes turned

from the bar to devour me, but it was the thick cloud of cigarette smoke and the pungent smell of poppers, both which heavily contaminated the air, that engrossed my thoughts. The music was techno rather than gay divas, which certainly didn't inspire me to dance much either. The web of social races, which enriched France with different colours, creeds and cultures, knew that the revolutionary heritage of liberty, equality and fraternity was just a myth. The distinctive cheek kissing nation radically practised racial discrimination instead. Society mirrored a forbiddance to tolerate Niggers, Arabs and Muslim and I was condemned as being savage and barbaric because I had a Shakespearean accent when I spoke the language of Molière. Heterosexuals in general were cold, distant and distrustful of others, but the aloof homosexual world was composed of the most caustic creatures that I had ever encountered. Perhaps I had changed, but it was certain that I didn't belong to that homosexual community of promiscuity anymore, so I abandoned the hostility of the homosexual urban clubs forever. The heterosexual bouncer didn't want to denude me and judging by the seduction in his eyes Diane had utterly besotted him. He smilingly remarked that there was charm in my accent and it emerged in the conversation that followed that the local wiper factory sought to employ a native English speaker. I didn't know where Issoire was located geographically, but it was to colour my life with the dreams that I had never even dreamed of.

A sea of nervous tension devoured me as the train from Thiers moved closer and closer in the direction of Issoire. I flicked through the Montagne newspaper, but people watching distracted my eyes instead. Rather than enrapturing my thoughts in something productive I dissected the physical appearance of each passenger, which certainly captivated my mind for a substantial length of time. With my brisk urban pace it was more than a fifteen minute walk along the main road to the factory, but if I had known of the short cut through the housing estates at the back of the train station, it would have only taken me eight. Being overly punctual definitely made a good impression, but it also prolonged what seemed like an eternity of a wait in the reception area. The odour of the rubber from the manufacturing process enriched the air. A pool of stress transpired under my armpits and began to moisten my shirt. It was clear from the beginning of the interview that the training manager had strong human values and her smile immediately made me feel at ease. A profound discussion on the techniques, management and pedagogical practices of teaching English began. The level of enthusiasm she voiced reflected a certain interest. Her pen moved incessantly from left to right in her notebook judging my

performance and perhaps even scrutinising my body language too. The two month mission was to implement an E-learning resources system and to provide intensive training to the mainstream team that needed to be efficient in business English communication. The meeting concluded with a brief tour of the factory, which clearly signified what hadn't been disclosed yet. Then, I was introduced to Rondel; the wild red headed P.A. welcomed me to the team in a warm fashion. In Ireland my dreams had been famished in the world of the Celtic Tiger and destroyed in an abundance of despair, but France liberated the fruition of reveries that I had never imagined.

The 6:06 a.m. train from Thiers to Issoire became part of my quotidian routine in June and July 2000. The three hour daily trip enabled me to increase my productively and be highly assiduous before and after the workday. The industrial world was certainly a challenge with a level of autonomy that I had not envisaged. There were no concise step by step instructions to guide me on the road of my mission and I was entrusted with the total responsibility to manage the project alone. My office was isolated on the second floor, but it was better for my concentration rather than being in the open space. That August we holidayed in the Côte D'Azur because my pockets were enriched with an abundance of money. La Promenade des Anglais in Nice, Le Palais des Festivals in Cannes and the famous Gendarmerie Nationale in Saint Tropez; everything enchanted my eyes with resplendence and Philippe liberated all of the reveries that I had never dreamed of. As the colourful leaves of autumn began to fall Madame Adrienne renewed my seven month teaching contract and I disseminated the glorious language of Shakespeare in Lycée Blaise Pascal again. The wiper factory hadn't forgotten me either and strongly incited me to become a Business English Language Consultant. French administration was renowned as a fearsome minefield of bureaucracy, but to cultivate the venture of self-employment the URSSAF system was surprisingly simple. With the promise of a highly reputed firm as a client I did not hesitate to seize the profusion of challenges that October 2000 granted me. Philippe believed in the fruition of my reveries and I was devoured by my need to have a two fingered gesture of revenge on the Celtic Tiger, which had always forgotten me. I wasn't overly ravaged by the years of the economic crisis and the butchery caused by the different training reforms didn't destroy me much either. In a competitive business world my tailor made services battled to survive, but from that moment on I flourished as a warrior.

Drinking alcohol was a learnt appreciation in France, a collective pleasure consumed in moderation, but puking in Place de la Victoire vulgarised the customary practice of binge drinking, which was the common mechanism among the Anglo-Saxon community that I frequented at that time. There was an impressive quantity of flamed Tequila shots and a prosperity of pints consumed in Café Pascal. A cloud distended with liberty among a forgotten civilisation that had social tolerance for passive smoking. There were no flashing disco lights if I remember correctly, but an abundance of vibrant music that enhanced the ambiance of many a night. It was the place to be for a certain generation and conviviality was the common religion of all. The overly friendly marketing strategy of the barmen and the attractive prices seduced the Arabs, Atheists, Catholics, Jews, Muslims, Niggers and even the queers of Clermont Ferrand. It was in such a heterosexual world that I befriended Maarika Matveeva in November 2000. The moment I heard that there was a Russian in the pub it became a must to meet her. Even though the strict rigors of her culture preached the immorality of homosexuality, liberty was deeply engrained in her self-values and she believed that homosexuality was not a profanity against god or a social contamination. Joey Murray was certainly the most liberal heterosexual I had ever met. The Australian had seduced Maarika with the promise of his perpetual love and he conquered my eternal affection too. We blossomed in the glorious years of our youth and we aged in the changing colours of the seasons together. They wiped away the tears of my sufferance in many a moment of need and enriched my life with the dreams that I had abandoned. In rural catholic Ireland I was too fucking queer to be a godfather, but was the fruition of that reverie silenced in my despair forever?

22

The Corruption of Appearances

Underneath the surface of her holy appearance my mother silenced her intolerance with a kiss and she welcomed Philippe into her catholic home in August 2001. I forewarned him that rather than smile in appreciation of her insincere acceptance that he should perhaps ponder about the betrayal of Jesus Christ by Judas Iscariot, but his biblical ignorance had deluded him and her facade had certainly seduced him too. Her masquerade of catholic virtue resurrected and he rebelled that I was too cold in my severe judgement of her. Philippe always dreamed of glorious flowers rather than weeds, but he battled in the belief of a dream that he was never to taste. My righteous mother hated "queer fuckers", but she delusively misled him to believe in the harmony of her love for homosexuals. The pulpit sermons condemned the immorality of homosexuality, but he simply hadn't tasted her venomous rancour yet. Her enragement wasn't liberated from the prison of silence that day or in the days of our holiday in rural Ireland that followed, but in the changing colours of the seasons he tasted her savagery. Everyone knew that I loved Philippe, but in the corruption of appearance they hetero-sexualised me and silenced my homosexual love. They certainly recognised the passion for me that glittered in his profound ocean blue eyes, but in fear of her wrath society never rebelled to liberate me. The brutality of their silence crucified me in despair, destroyed me in the dark dusty closet of homosexuality and betrayed my freedom.

I didn't believe in the myth of god, so it certainly wasn't to honour her almighty catholic god that I decorated the crib with a garland of sparkling tinsel. The touch of colour was intended to further enhance its sentimental beauty in her eyes and to conquer her admiration, but criticising the aged wallpaper that decorated all the walls of our apartment enraptured her thoughts more than venerating the birth of Jesus Christ. Her face cringed to display her utmost displeasure as my holy mother went from room to room. I wanted her to be proud that I now battled to survive with a hefty

mortgage, after all it hetero-sexualised my homosexuality, but her judgement crucified the lack of luxury that lingered in my home. She belonged to a consumption society and had certainly forgotten that she had originated from an abundance of poverty. I didn't want the resurrection of her enragement, so in my clemency I forgave her, but her insolence gave forth to Philippe's intolerance; "Rome ne s'est pas faite en un jour". I silenced him and rather than revolt further he wrapped gifts with immense delicacy and placed them under the "poorly decorated Christmas tree". Indeed, my fairy lights didn't glitter in a profusion of wealth, a shoe box of decorations had dressed the denuded branches, but it profoundly mirrored Philippe's love for me. It was the first year that the big wheel dominated the Place de Jaude and a deep layer of snow covered the peak of Puy de Dome. The cold air deeply penetrated our bodies as we towered above the city, but the colourful luminosity of the streets below filled all our faces with enchantment. In the belief that god punished my immorality she unearthed her rancour from silence. I silenced her brutality with silence because I didn't want Philippe to taste sufferance, but he remarked that wrath gleamed in her eyes when she looked at him. Her emotions were caustic too, Philippe was beginning to understand that my holy mother wasn't a Catholic that practiced the love of god, but I didn't disclose that she hated him.

Medium beige foundation invigorated her pale complexion, a resplendent rosy coloured blush enhanced the seduction of her cheekbones, eye shadow, eyeliner and mascara brought depth, dimension and harmony to beautify her blue eyes further, pale red lipstick made her even more alluring and an abundance of lacquer stiffened her blonde highlighted hair. The destructive signs of aging had completely forgotten her and crow's feet, frown lines and wrinkles were completely absent on her face. My mother looked so radiant; her beautician had plucked and shaped her eyebrows into a perfect arch and dye had even darkened them in colour. She smiled with utter admiration at her reflexion in the bathroom mirror, perhaps in the silence of her thoughts she wanted to immortalise that moment of her beauty forever. I revered that her clothes were outlandishly stylish, but to her dismay my father didn't raise a glance away from the television. She thrust forward her affluence and forcibly protruded that her fingers sparkled in gold and diamonds. It certainly repulsed Philippe that she flaunted in such a pompous fashion. It was difficult for him to understand that such a pious Catholic belonged to a consumption society. With his eyes still glued to the football match, my father retorted that to decorate her with ornate jewellery was the symbol of his perpetual passion,

but if he believed in the eternity of love why did he practice promiscuity? It was Christmas Eve 2001; he overly displayed his generosity as she ravenously bustled from shop to shop like a headless chicken. He nourished all of her desires again, but the sumptuous taste of his lovers' lust still devoured my mother's lips like poison. Underneath the surface of her ephemeral happiness she survived in the silence of his heterosexual immorality and materialism was her cry of despair to forget his betrayal. Philippe innocently smiled at me in the street, the waves of her gay intolerance began to surface again, but in desperation to spend more and more money she silenced her disdain. With tears in his eyes my father implored me to worship the naissance of Jesus Christ on Christmas day. He still didn't accept that I had forsaken the beauty of his religion. It enraged him that I didn't believe in his almighty catholic god, but to kneel in reverence before the altar when the sermons crucified homosexuals would have been pure hypocrisy on my behalf. Rather than be contaminated by hymns of praise with my holy parents in l'église Sainte Jeanne d'Arc I boycotted the local church and I was condemned to peel a mountain of Brussels sprouts, carrots and potatoes instead. There was peace and harmony for the rest of the day; my mother severely criticised everything and slaughtered my homosexuality, but I silenced my sufferance in the belief that rural Ireland would not destroy me forever.

Society systematically hetero-sexualised all men, but did Philippe really need to rebel in a militant fashion and parade his homosexuality overtly? He long nourished the dream of liberation from the dark dusty closet of silence, but did I have the right to force him to forsake all belief in tolerance? There was certainly nothing intrinsically immoral about being "a queer fucker", but I didn't want him to battle the sufferance that I had known and I needed to defend him from the tears of a homosexual coming out. I still believed that silence did not betray the beauty of homosexual love, but shielded it in harmony away from slaughter. He reluctantly abandoned his desire for freedom, but stipulated the terms and conditions of his passiveness. I was given no choice in my acceptance to meet his parents, but it was clearly defined that it under the pretence of a platonic friend rather than as his lover. What struck me most when I met his father was that his eyes really protruded from their sockets. Philippe explained that he had had a nuchal cord problem, but my medical culture didn't know what that term meant. The umbilical cord had wrapped around the foetus' neck and although John had survived asphyxia, hypoxia had resulted in blindness to his right eye since the day of his birth. Shortly after his retirement, an elbow collided with his left eye as he laced his shoe in a

queue and eternal darkness began to conquer his world after that. John's vision was fading away when I first met him, but he still saw the outline of what he called shadows. A few months later his severely impaired sight completely faded and he mourned all the beauty that he was to never see again. He was totally blinded in his judgement of colour, origin and creed too. With barbaric discrimination he denigrated Niggers, belittled Arabs, disparaged Jews, defamed Muslims and he even besmirched holy Catholics. Queers also faced the same crucifixion; I believed that the intolerance that Philippe tasted condemned him to despair and eternal silence.

Colette blossomed in vivacity when I first met her, but the waves of ageing soon began to surface in her physical appearance. In the changing colours of the seasons time ravaged her body and savaged her mind without forbearance. Tears of agony fell from Philippe's profound ocean blue eyes as the natural brutality of life completely destroyed his cherished mother. Her hostile reencounter with age was certainly a foudroyant battle; a few months later a Zimmer frame retrained her mobility and independence, but then the muscles in her frail legs no longer supported her weight and fall after fall she became wheelchair bound. She slowly withered away into a world of deep silence too. Step by step her memory faded and I lived in the pangs of his sufferance. There was great social isolation of the elderly in their hours of need in France and an abundance of solitude devoured Philippe as he battled alone. Colette completely forgot how to manage domestic chores, but for a blind man John was really remarkable. Her profound ocean blue eyes had become his vision. He stumbled to clean, he floundered to cook and with the exception of some crumbs under the kitchen table the house was always impeccable. Laundering, ironing, food shopping and maintaining their house and small garden certainly consumed all our time each Saturday, while his self-absorbed brother as a passive onlooker drank coffee and puffed passionately on a cigarette. Was a homosexual more virtuous in emotion than a heterosexual son?

In the belief that silence shielded our love from judgement Philippe didn't rebel in a militant fashion and the silence we cultivated enabled me to befriend John and Colette for years. The freedom of our homosexual love was enslaved in silence, but his father certainly believed in the pink triangle of the gay holocaust. He overtly discriminated against the richness of all cultural diversity and wanted a universal genocide of Niggers, Arabs, Jews, Muslims and the public execution of queers. Life had endowed

Philippe with all the social graces of ethical behaviour and political correctness, but his tolerance was limited to a handful of forced polite words in her company. The abundance of aversion he displayed towards his sister-in-law originated in the irreverence that she had always manifested to his parents. In the belief that silence was better than the liberation of rancour Philippe did not parade his homosexuality, but was it in ignorance or in vengeance that she denounced his immorality to John? Blindness had forbidden him to see the gay passion that glittered in Philippe's profound ocean blue eyes, but the bitch enlightened him and smoked Philippe out of the dark dusty closet of silence. John's wrath towards me was liberated without restraint. All the kindness that I had always shown and all the friendly moments that we had shared were completely forgotten and I became "a homosexual fucker". Philippe revolted to defend me from a catholic crucifixion by a man that didn't even believe in god, but John crucified me with more of a catholic judgement than the catholic judgement that my holy mother practiced. The language of Moliere that he employed to tag me as "an arse fucker" didn't exist in my lexicon yet, but later in the car Philippe explained exactly what his father's words really meant. Tears fell from Colette's blue eyes, in her judgement it didn't make a difference that I loved her son, but another reverberation of anger from John silenced her insolence forever. His repugnance banished me with even more brutality than the brutality of the almighty catholic god of Ireland. John didn't see the beauty of homosexual love or the daffodils dancing in the wind outside that day and I never saw him alive again. Life had bestowed me with very cold emotions, but Philippe tasted the sufferance of homosexuality for the first time. Consumed by enragement he swore to forsake them forever. He wanted John to reap the shit that he had harvested, but I had the clemency to silence his revolt. I did not need John's benediction to love his son, but Colette definitely needed her son's love to survive. The tides of life didn't change much after that; his onlooking brother still drank coffee and puffed passionately on a cigarette each Saturday, but Philippe now struggled to do everything alone. There was no redemption; the distaste for queers was deeply ingrained in John and he never repented. Homosexuality reverted to the profound prison of silence again and Philippe never found the serenity to forgive his father.

In the harmony of his heterosexual bible the immorality of homosexuality was forbidden, but my righteous brother now wanted to meet Philippe. Homosexuality was banished from the kingdom of heaven and he hated "queer fuckers", but perhaps some television programme had cultivated

him to understand that gays were normal individuals of different profession, social class, colour and religion? Had he rebelled against the pulpit sermons and with irreverence desired to liberate me from the prison of silence forever or was I still a dreamer? He thoroughly believed in the myth of homosexual effeminacy and had really expected to meet a Madonna fan in high heels with a pink condom filled handbag, but Philippe mirrored so much more virility than my heterosexual brother. He even found that my lover was a gorgeous looking man and was glad that I didn't belong to the promiscuous culture of homosexuality anymore. That night we went to his local pub and an astronomical abundance of Guinness was consumed by him. His profound passion for alcohol manifested in the shots that followed, but not wanting to enrage him I silenced my judgement. Philippe normally didn't practice the sport of getting pissed, but so many pints elated him quickly and he later decorated the streets of Dublin with his vomit. Tears filled my brother's eyes; under the surface of his gay appearance he wasn't very happy, but the almighty catholic god of Ireland believed in the prison of eternal love. He was enslaved forever in a catholic marriage that he certainly didn't believe in and he liberated his silenced sufferance to me in an ocean of despair. Nine months later his fate was sealed and Darius was born, perhaps his perpetual love for Molly had resurrected? I believed in the fruition of my reveries, but catholic Ireland didn't liberate my dream and betrayed me again. Under the surface of tolerance that my brother now practiced I believed that he had abandoned his hate of homosexuality, but in his holy judgement I was still "too fucking queer" to be a godfather.

Being in love had totally changed me; I had forsaken the flashing disco lights of urban gay clubs, forgotten the art of homosexual seduction and certainly abandoned the promiscuity of the gay culture too, but was perpetual love forever or dying in a fading passion? He walked closer and closer towards me in the street near Place de la Résistance and judging by the intensity of passion in his eyes I was led to believe that he found me attractive. As he passed his head turned in my direction, his face enlightened with a flirtatious smile and his eyes devoured mine. Jean Luc was charming, affluent, cultivated and alluring. He desired to immortalise his youth, but wrinkles enriched his face and the strong signs of ageing already betrayed him. From the beginning I befriended him with sincerity and disclosed that there was no freedom to kiss, denude or fuck me. A profound platonic affection flourished, but one night he did kiss me. Each second of that lustful kiss implored me to forget Philippe, but it contaminated me with rage instead. I did not see him for seven days after

that, not knowing was it me avoiding him or that it was Jean Luc avoiding me, but when we met again he acted as if he had completely forgotten. The colours of the seasons changed; leaves littered the pavements in Clermont Ferrand, the ubiquitous volcanic rock, which darkened the city's architectural facades, sharply contrasted to the luminosity that reflected in the abundance of snow that had fallen and there was still no treachery to corrupt the eternity of my love. I believed in the asexuality of a homosexual friendship, but in silence Jean Luc had fallen in love with me. In the prison of his thoughts he wanted to seduce me, but was there hope or despair in such a dream?

Philippe still denuded me with lust, but since the moment of his seduction in Dublin everything had changed. The sensuality of our entangled passion was a now profusion of ardent love. He knew each fissure and crevasse of my body and his every touch fulfilled my erotic desires. I really needed ten minutes of silence first thing in the morning and even a mere glance in my direction during breakfast risked exposing him to my grunt, but rather than forsake me he saw my virtues and loved me for me. He liberated me from the sufferance of catholic Ireland and on the voyage of perpetual love he nourished and conquered all of my dreams. The sincerity that glittered in his profound ocean blue eyes enriched all of my reveries with faith, but his love was not a prison that devoured my liberty either. Jean Luc kissed me again, but rather than corrupt me with betrayal, the touch of his insipid lips on mine repulsed me. Rather than abandon his desire to denude me he revolted with another forceful kiss and battled to seduce me again. He began to unbutton my shirt and the silhouette of his erection protruded from his pants. He inanely disclosed that he had fallen in love with me, but was promiscuity to conquer me again? I certainly was not made in the image and likeness of my adulterous father and in total repugnance I abandoned his preposterous seduction. I saw Jean Luc in the street a few days later. His eyes were caustic, distant and still enraged with despair. I smiled in a social fashion in his direction, but to my dismay he did not smile back. Our platonic friendship didn't have to wither away, but judging by the cold way that he completely ignored me, I was led to understand that if he couldn't fuck me that he didn't want to know me anymore.

I worked in close social contact with a group of nine children in Mendes France primary school for two years. My interactive pedagogical method enriched each Wednesday afternoon with songs about alphabet, animals, colours and numbers. I animated the lessons with an abundance of smiles

and my positive words of encouragement fuelled my pupils with enthusiasm to learn the language of Shakespeare. "Faire la bise", the ubiquitous French norm was profoundly embedded in their culture, so it wasn't problematic that eight year old Djibril, Loic and Thomas cheek kissed me each week. Seven year old Audrey had developed a further tendency to hug me too, but would tolerance have been the same if their parents had known that I was a queer? If homosexuality was envisaged as learnt, gays were potential predators; hence my dream of homosexual freedom needed to be abandoned and I certainly did not enlighten them with my homosexuality. I did not want to taste the sufferance of discrimination or the accusation of indoctrinating gay immorality, so the prison of silence shielded me again. Silence hetero-sexualised me, but my betrayal of the homosexual culture was about survival in a heterosexual world that sometimes defaced gays with the toxic label of paedophile. Silence was to conform in harmony to the different levels of tolerance and acceptance that society mirrored. My workload as an English Language Consultant increased more and more, roads diverged, other opportunity was seized and an abundance of tears fell from Audrey's eyes as she hugged me for the last time. My insight into the industrial world now enriched the tutorials that I gave on marketing strategy, meeting enactment, presentation techniques and statistic analyses in the Business Management University. Intense societal discrimination was deeply ingrained in some minds, but I openly disclosed my homosexuality there. Certain judgements dehumanised gays as promiscuous fuckers, certain myths homogenised queers as effeminate creatures that worshiped Madonna more than god and certain hostility affirmed that homosexuality were a form of social contamination. I was not a gay militant, but I needed to enlighten the world that being "a queer fucker" was normal among all the different social classes, colours, cultures and religions. Coming out of the dark dusty closet of silence was not a rebellion, but a manifestation that homosexuality was not intrinsically immoral.

In the book of Genesis there was Adam and Eve; "fuck, reproduce and conquer the world" were the words of the almighty god and the fruitlessness of homosexuality was created. As I aged it got harder to be a prisoner in the silence of my dream, but Philippe wasn't ingrained with the same passion that silently devoured me. My desire to father a child faded away with some tears of regret, but there was the fruition of other reveries to console me. Catholic Ireland still believed that I was too queer to be godfather, but did society condemn my immorality forever? It was my brother's last chance when Caelian was born in July 2005, but the brutality

of the sermons still contaminated him to believe in the immorality of homosexuality. Perhaps he thought that in total despair I would implore him again, but there was absolutely no sufferance that he dishonoured me for the fourth time. In revenge something had changed; Joey had fertilised Maarika with love and in her womb she nourished my amazing godson. From the first time I tenderly held him in my arms there was a sensation of euphoria that I had never known before. His brown eyes opened as I kissed him on his forehead in the hospital room and the ocean of love that I had always wanted to give was liberated forever. Vladimir Murray was born on August 27th 2005 and was most certainly all of my dreams come true. I solemnly promised to enrich him with the core values of social behaviour, to cultivate him with tolerance, liberty and a sense of morality, to strengthen his emotions and to believe in his dreams. I definitely didn't give him spirituality, but he tasted the abundance of my love instead. When feeding the ducks in Jardin Le Coq one day I smiled because he nibbled on the majority of the bread and forgot all about generosity. When his Easter egg melted in the warmth of the sun I wiped away the tears of woe that fell from his eyes. Being overly strict his parents didn't believe in junk food, hence it was clear that his first taste of Mc Donald's was with me. I was an atypical godfather; in my belief he needed to be able to confide in me without fear of judgement, which gave forth to profound trust and an eternal friendship blossomed between us. I didn't know that time went by so quickly until I saw myself aging in the changes of his life, but climbing trees in my garden with him immortalised my youth.

The Promise Of Silence

The Desolation of Secrets

Carols that celebrated the naissance of Jesus Christ blissfully resounded in my rural catholic home and I admired the multitude of rich colours that adorned each branch of the Christmas tree with the sentimental decorations that my mother dearly treasured. It still tearfully enraged my father that I didn't worship his catholic god in Saint Joseph's Church on Christmas day, but I didn't want to be contaminated by the intolerance that was preached during the pulpit sermons. My holy father gave a bottle of whiskey to the beggar on the church steps and enriched the collection plate with a one hundred euro note that year. Both acts of almsgiving enhanced the social reputation of his sanctity and certainly reserved him a seat in the kingdom of heaven, but his excessive generosity also incited my mother's rage. He silenced her emotions; after all she needed to be more politically correct in the presence of Sister Mary Magdalene. The nun, in her habit and starched white wimple, blessed the abundance of food on our table in thanksgiving to the almighty catholic god and I still rebelled against Amen and closed her prayer in total silence. I ravenously ate the mouth watering Brussels sprouts, which had been cooked in the salty ham water especially for me, not knowing that all the happiness in my life was ephemeral. After the delicious meal he sang a harmony of hymns with the virgin bride of Christ and his masquerade of holiness totally repulsed me. It was my last Christmas in rural catholic Ireland; my father betrayed me and the forgotten sufferance of 1987 resurrected. The changing colours of so many seasons had seduced me since, but the fruit of his erections was liberated from the dark dusty closet of silence.

On December 27th 2005 my father disclosed to me that his sperm had created a certain Alice and Sabrina and that in the silence of his thoughts he had loved them for years. I learnt that he had fondly observed them as young children playing in the street and that he now wiped away their tears of sufferance with a tenderness that I had never known. I turned my eyes to

the crucifix on the pale egg shell coloured wall as he implored me to be clement in my judgement, but the green eyed monster certainly consumed me in rage. Forgotten sufferance was unearthed and 1987 resurfaced to crucify me again. I re-felt the barefooted touch of the carpet on the stairs. I re-heard the pleas of his fucked whore wanting to conquer the eternity of his love. I re-tasted the despair that emotionally destroyed my poor mother. I re-saw the vase fall to the floor and break in violence during their physical struggle. My eyes involuntarily turned to the corner of that room to now understand that the two crying babies had resurrected from the silence of the past forever. Since the beginning of time Dean had cherished, defended, loved and treasured them in the belief that he was their genitor, but in a drunken rage the bitch slurred that it was the sperm of another man that had really fertilised her. Her husband's name had been immortalised on their birth certificates, but she disclosed to all that they were the forbidden fruit of her adultery. Her indelible words created so much destruction and she savagely ravaged everyone in the ruination of silence. In their hour of need Alice and Sabrina voraciously entrenched their claws into my father's affection. I hated my fucking father with so much rancour and I didn't have the serenity to ever grant him my pardon. Normally the last few minutes of my every visit were alone with my mother, but in fear of my betrayal of the solemn vow of silence he certainly did not abandon her side. Silence was now my battle to save her emotions from another slaughter and my life was never to be the same again.

1987 had gloriously resurrected and I battled to survive the changing tides that shaped the first months of 2006 with the total destruction of my emotions. Something died in me forever and an ocean of desolation consumed me. A profound depression followed in the months after and I faded away in the silence of my sufferance. The reflection of a ruined man stared back at me in the mirror. For the first time in my life I didn't have the force to battle for my resurrection, but Philippe loved me more and more. Joey and Maarika also wiped away my tears and loving Vladimir strengthened me in my moment of profound despair. My father implored me to love them in silence, but I didn't want to hear their voices or see their faces. I coldly disclosed that I didn't want to know them; after all did I have to pay for the sins that his penis had committed? My defiance enraged him, he begged me not to discard them, but I still refused to reap the devastation that he harvested. My silence fuelled their fury, but I didn't want to betray my mother. In revolt they solemnly threatened to enlighten her of everything if I didn't accept them into my life. My father besought me not to enrage them further. He certainly didn't want a coming out of the

closet for his immorality. My hand trembled as I composed the thirteen digits of their phone number. A foreboding sensation of immense destruction engulfed me. After a moment of silence I heard their tears, but I didn't feel any emotions and a sensation of deep regret already devoured me. I was definitely made in the cold image and judgemental likeness of my catholic mother. I did not step into the light of tolerance, but judged them as belonging to the lowest stratum of underclass of a certain urban Cork area. From that moment on they encrusted their toxicity into my life and consumed me like a parasite ripping into my flesh and soul.

My father begged me not to liberate his silenced sins, but unable to survive in the prison of sufferance I enlightened my brother. He had also felt the barefooted touch of the carpet on the stairs and had seen the vase fall to the floor and break in violence. 1987 resurrected and enriched with a profusion of tears he vividly remembered so much more of each second of the destruction than me. Her voice was still deeply embedded in his head. "The fucking whore" had ravaged his world by disclosing to the fifteen year old boy that they were the fruit of his father's sperm. My brother always believed that silence was not eternal and contrary to me he had even envisaged such a resurrection. In his caustic judgement he didn't want to ever know them. A few pints of Guinness later he reverted to the world of silence and I battled in the desolation alone again. My father flaunted his affluence, probably to seduce their forgiveness, but he also gave them something different that he had never given me. They conquered the taste of his profound love, but was it the green eyed monster that liberated my rage or my desire to defend my mother in cold revenge? An abundance of sufferance had destroyed my emotions since the age of eleven and her fallen tears were still deeply engrained in my mind. Their dream was to know the eternity of my love, but I needed to destroy them and in the silence of my thoughts I wanted to create their sufferance. They implored me a million times to return to rural catholic Ireland to meet them, but I certainly didn't want them to become tangible. I did not envisage ever meeting them, but I contaminated their ears with the reverie that they longed to hear. I falsely promised to liberate all of their desires, but in time the flattery of my words seduced them less and less. They rightfully began to disbelieve in my sincerity and threatened me that if I didn't collude with their demands that my mother's tears would taste their destruction in punishment of my betrayal. In the belief that my mother was strong enough to survive another storm of emotional brutality I liberated my enragement in her honour.

I really didn't know that I was capable of causing so much destruction, until I unleashed the revenge within me that I had never known before. I really needed eternal freedom from the sufferance of 1987, so I abandoned all the social values of life. Their tears implored me to love them forever, but the coldness of my emotions gloriously resurrected and I enriched them with "fuck off" instead. I revolted that they repulsed me, I destroyed all of their dreams and I cast them out of my life perpetually without a sentiment of catholic morality. Enragement enriched the background and I clearly understood who that screaming voice was. My father's whore was certain that it was not the sperm of her catholic marriage that had created them, but the fruit of her adultery. If Dean's penis had been sterile, it would have enforced her theory with a taste of truth, but of her five children she was merely adamant in her belief that only two belonged to my father. It was certain that there was a strong physical resemblance between twenty one year old Alice and my brother that I was unable to deny, but twenty year old Sabrina was definitely made in the image and likeness of her three younger siblings. My judgement rebelled that DNA finger printing would unriddle the mystery forever, but she categorically refused the paternity test that I requested. I retorted that if two men had passionately fucked her in succession it was her fucking problem if the bastards were born in sin and not in love. She enlightened me that in punishment of my betrayal and insolence that more tears were to fall from my mother's eyes. "Fuck off you fucking bitch"; naturally dispersed from my enraged mouth and her telephone handset was directed back to its cradle in silence. My two fingered gesture of revenge had liberated me, but they now paraded in the direction of my holy catholic mother to reap the havoc that I had fuelled.

It was an ordinary night reading from the discoloured gilded pages of her aged bible in her catholic home, but in the hours that followed my mother tasted their revenge and 1987 resurrected from the forgotten silence to destroy her again. In her battle alone she prayed to her almighty god for the strength to survive. My righteous father implored her forgiveness and another gold and diamond ring glittered before her holy blue eyes in temptation. She didn't want to revert to poverty and his affluence certainly conquered the eternity of her love. My contemptuous judgement was said in rage, but I really believed that he enriched her catholic marriage with an abundance of tears. I wanted to liberate her, but she didn't revolt against her eternal sufferance. Rather than forsake him for freedom she kissed him with passion and rather than abandon the prison of his love she punished me for my insolence. He escaped scot-free; but in the months that followed a profound depression totally consumed me. I was totally ravaged by the

ruins of desolation and I lamented that something deep within me had died. I believed that the immortalised happy smiles in every photo of my childhood were all a myth and it was a long road before my resurrection. Philippe had fallen in love with an Irish warrior, but I was now completely defeated by despair.

There was no emotion of love when I returned to rural catholic Ireland in May 2006 and my betrayal had not been forgotten. He held Colm's hand with a tenderness that I had never tasted. In the silence of my thoughts the green eyed monster consumed me. I wished that the small hand in my father's palm could belong to me, but it belonged to the young boy that lived next door. I really hated my father, but why did I still battled to conquer his affection? I desperately wanted to believe that somewhere in the forgotten past it had once been different, but sometimes even dreams needed to be abandoned in despair. My mother kissed him passionately, but there was more sufferance than love underneath the holy appearance of their catholic marriage. If the kingdom of heaven condemned the immorality of heterosexuals I believed that she needed to crucify him. Sometimes she actually forgot that I was gay; that was when she loved me the most, but those moments were very ephemeral now. Nothing had changed; my righteous parents still prayed to hetero-sexualise me, church candles still burned begging the almighty catholic god for my repentance and they still slaughtered me in punishment for being "a queer fucker". My father implored me to believe that he had forsaken "the bastards", but judging by the insincerity that glittered in his blue eyes I knew for certain that he was a liar. A few minutes later when he was under the shower I roamed through each message on his mobile phone; indeed he had silenced that they were still an active part of his life. I never granted him my catholic forgiveness and I never loved him again.

Naomi, Sorcha and Darius sang before thirty candles, which flickered on a chocolate iced cake. Caelan, who was embraced in my cuddles, looked just as surprised as me. I suddenly understood that the multi-coloured abundance of balloons that decorated the kitchen were in my honour. Enriched with their affection Philippe and I had the freedom to love them that day, but had Dublin really changed or was my dream ephemeral again? My brother did not know how to love his children with the tenderness that I did. The beauty of their births had slaughtered his liberty and imprisoned him in a catholic marriage that he still didn't want to belong to. He did not have the patience to be a loving father; whereas I played toys on the

carpeted sitting room floor and liberated their imaginations, he shouted that they made "a fucking mess". Whereas I energetically jumped on the trampoline in the garden with them, he bemoaned that he was "too fucking tired". Whereas I ballerina danced from room to room and enchanted them with laughter, he bellowed with rage that Darius resembled "a fucking queer". His virile heterosexual stereotyping judgement didn't really accept the effeminate sport that Billie Elliot practiced and he denuded Darius of Sorcha's pink tutu. It enraged me that he didn't appreciate the four beautiful children that the catholic god had bestowed on him, after all I aged in the sufferance of my eternal forgotten dream and mourned in silence that homosexuality condemned my sperm to be unfruitful. He still eyed me with suspicion; perhaps homosexuality was learnt and I really wanted to indoctrinate them with a passion for the homosexual culture, to enlighten them with the corruption of gay promiscuity and to contaminate them with the desire to become "queer fuckers"? Homosexuality was legalised in 1993, but the kingdom of heaven still outlawed homosexual love and Ireland still discriminated against queers in 2006.

The dark dusty queer closet of silence was still my eternal prison of solitude in rural catholic Ireland. I didn't parade my homosexuality, but many had seen love glitter in Philippe's profound ocean blue eyes and still society hetero-sexualised me. Aunty Mary had spoiled me with penny sweets and cream donuts from her grocery shop since the beginning of time and it was certain that she had an abundance of affection for me. I dared not have a coming out, but she led me to understand that she wanted me to enrich her with the truth. She certainly enticed me to forsake the promise of silence, but was there a righteous judgement waiting to destroy me in despair? There was no wrinkle of abhorrence, no flinch of aversion, no frown of repugnance and no sentiment of repulsion to contaminate me with a taste of intolerance. Rather than condemn me to be crucified, she kissed me on the cheek with the strongest emotion of catholic love that I had ever known. For the first time since the catholic creation of my immorality I felt truly accepted, but was there a Judas Iscariot lurking in betrayal behind her kiss? She knew all the scriptures off by heart, recited her prayers in mass with reverence, had faith in all the myths in the holy heterosexual bible that she read, but she deluded me to believe that the sermons hadn't contaminated her with a passion to hate queers. She rebelled that "those kind of people" were made in the image and likeness of god and also belonged to the kingdom of heaven. She nourished my dream of homosexual freedom, but in the changing colours of the seasons her hostility resurrected and I tasted sufferance. Underneath the surface of

her facade of tolerance homosexuality was indeed a social contamination and I was "a queer fucker'.

Forbidden fruit had polluted my world with a dark cloud of sufferance. I loathed that Philippe had seen the deep fragility that devoured me, but he certainly loved me more than anyone had ever loved me before. When rage and rancour consumed my emotions he enriched me with the catholic virtue of morality again. It was in his profound ocean blue eyes that I found my resurrection; I now had the serenity to rise from the destructive ashes of 1987, but I had changed forever. Holy carols certainly echoed in the background as she embellished the Christmas tree in December 2006, but my catholic mother was alone to admire the abundance of rich colours, which glittered in the flashing luminosity emitted by the fairy lights. There was sadness in my eyes too, but I didn't desire to return to the destructive taste of her ephemeral love. I didn't want my father to implore me to celebrate the holy birth of Jesus Christ in Saint Joseph's Church again. I didn't want to be contaminated by the harmony of hymns that he piously sang with Sister Mary Magdalene. Whereas my holy mother had the clemency to forgive him, hate was deeply engrained in me. In the changing colours of many a season my sufferance withered away, but there were other emotional battles to betray me. I rebelled against the pulpit sermons, but my mother firmly believed in the immorality of homosexuality that was preached by her righteous religion. There was no resurrection of tolerance and her almighty catholic beliefs ravaged me. There was no repentance for "a queer fucker" in the kingdom of heaven and she needed to forsake me. Aunty Ellen enlightened me with the bitter taste of her revenge too and that was the desolation that further destroyed me. My brother unearthed his perpetual brutality and Naomi, Sorcha, Darius and Caelan became weapons in his ruthless last barbaric judgement of me. The wrought iron nails that crucified me like Jesus Christ destroyed me more and more, but perhaps such sufferance was a stepping stone towards my eternal freedom?

The Promise Of Silence

The Infliction of Social Intolerance

Fields of sunflowers danced before my eyes in August of the year 2007. It was certain that dwelling among the anonymousness of a city had offered us protection against animosity, but our home was now in a rural village in Auvergne among the strict rigours of a heterosexual agricultural world. We did not need to parade in the street for queer pride, have a rainbow coloured flag flaunting our homosexuality outside our house in the wind or harbour in the dark dusty closet of silence either; because two men living together did clearly signify to everyone that we were gay. In the beginning Philippe was devoured with a sensation of fear, but I believed that there was no difference between a heterosexual and a homosexual mortgage. If heterosexuals did not need to justify their heterosexuality I certainly did not have to justify my so called immorality. The history of homosexuality was engrained with great sufferance; the gay culture had been crucified with pink triangles in the holocaust and the holy sermons still contaminated society with the loathing of queers, but the homosexual revolution had liberated me in appearance. What if homosexuality was to be forbidden again and if there was a resurrection of intolerance to come? I merely wanted my homosexuality to flourish in a balanced harmony of social acceptance, but I learnt that to cultivate homosexual freedom also enhanced certain aversion.

In appearance nobody in the village had distaste of our homosexual corruption, but in the changing colours of the seasons I tasted intolerance. A wooden fence separated our gardens, but rather than silence her abhorrence the catholic woman next door dehumanised me. She believed that homosexuality was a choice, but I kindly retorted that my passion for men was innate. Her bible preached that mankind needed to "fuck, reproduce and conquer the world"; hence the fruitfulness of homosexuality was a sin, but I certainly rebelled that I did not believe in the kingdom of heaven or in the other myths of her demoded religion. With total

conviction she further lectured me that I needed to revert to heterosexuality in repentance to god for my immorality. I defended that I had sucked so many cocks that even her almighty god wouldn't envisage the clemency to forgive my promiscuity and my insolence enraged her. Rather than cultivate her intolerance in silence, other barbaric judgements fell from her lips. Nobody had the right to crucify me with a catholic opinion, but she cast yet another stone that condemned me as being "a queer fucker". Homosexuality was largely no longer envisaged as a symptom of mental disorder, but the social injustices that discriminated against pink love were deep engrained in her. Reveries sometimes needed to be abandoned, but her profoundly embedded prejudice definitely wasn't going to make me abandon my dream of eternal homosexual freedom.

Anita Foulet lived directly across the road in a stone facade house. She was a woman of catholic virtue, but there was no crucifixion of queers in the scriptures in her holy bible. The sermons on the Irish pulpit fuelled my catholic mother to believe in the wrath of god and the sin of homosexuality. Anita prayed with the same reverence to the same almighty catholic god, but homosexual liberty was in total harmony with her catholic beliefs. Perhaps her tolerance to befriended two homosexuals betrayed god, but the fag hag believed that there was nothing immoral about our homosexuality. Surviving with a hefty mortgage enhanced our normality and it was no secret in our rural village that we were gay. We lived our homosexuality overtly, which granted them the liberty to condemn us if they wanted, but the majority of inhabitants didn't believe in the hostile judgement of god or the social myths that discriminated against queers. One day as I admired the flowers that bloomed in my garden another close located neighbour had the barbarism to inform me that I was "a fucking queer". He further disclosed that my "perverted immorality" should return to the "country of my origin". "Arse fucker, bender, fag, faggot, fairy, nancy, poofster, queenie, queer and sissy" had oppressed me since the beginning of time, but it was certainly his attack of racism which shocked me more than his homophobia. Many years in France had enriched me to master the language of Molière, but rather than defend myself with the politically correct words that I now bestowed, my fist closed in rage and I raised my middle finger to heaven in an upward position. He lowered his eyes in defeat; my "fuck off" gesture disconcerted him and my insolence silenced him forever. Perhaps others thought what he believed in, but if so, they lived behind the appearance of their cultivated smiles in silence.

The dancing queer that Philippe had seduced under the flashing disco lights no longer existed. The dust that whitened my hair was cement, the colours that stained my clothes were splashes of wall paint and for a man that had never touched a screw driver in his life, I had certainly changed. Tool shopping in Castorama or Leroy Merlin had become a million times better than clothes shopping in Gallery Layette. It was even difficult to believe that Philippe had originally met me in 'The George' and not gallivanting among the aisles of some DIY store in Dublin. Walls were demolished and other walls were rebuilt, a savage wild garden had become tamed and flowered in an abundance of different scented colours. I didn't ponder about anything else; creating my dreams consumed all of my time and I naturally forgot all about my Irish sufferance. French administration was a minefield of bureaucracy, but with a mountain of documents I battled the first steps to abandon my Irish nationality. A few months later Minister Brice Hortefeux's speech enriched me with the values of the French Republic. La Marseillaise, the national anthem of France, symbolically liberated me from the holy brutality that had destroyed me. The blue, white and red tricoloured flag became my heritage and my two fingered gesture of revenge on catholic Ireland. I had survived my Irish crucifixions, I had abandoned the hostile judgement of the Irish god and it certainly enraged my parents that I now belonged to the cheek kissing culture, liberty, equality and fraternity of secular France.

Rebecca Murray was born on March 15th 2008. She was only a few hours old the first time I met her and from that moment on I certainly believed in her dreams, nourished her emotions with my undying affection, cultivated her with tolerance, liberty, a sense of morality and taught her the social values of life. Year after year she blossomed in the abundance of my love and I saw myself age, not in the colours of the different seasons, but in the changes that the seasons enriched on her. Laughter filled the air during the vigorous effort of her first steps as the French marigolds that bloomed in my garden were flattened by her ass. She identified that the lion that I had seen in her drawing was actually a fox and her face glittered in delight when I overstated her artistic talent. During her sleepovers in our home her desire for breakfast was chocolate bars and of course I always indulged in the same childish pleasure as her. Catholic Ireland crucified me, Irish blood betrayed me, but Maarika and Joey legally appointed two queers to be the testamentary guardians for their children. They did not envisage that we would enlighten them with the corruption of homosexuality, indoctrinate them with a passion for the pink culture or contaminate them with the

"social immorality" to become "queer fuckers", whereas my catholic brother never liberated me from the intolerance of his holy judgement.

It was August 2008 and there was no rhythmical sound of factory productivity from the melting, rolling and forging machines in Les Ancizes metallurgical site. My clients journeyed to invade the beaches and the mountains of France for vacation, but I returned alone to rural Ireland to be crucified again. Nothing had changed; my holy mother still believed in the catholic god and prayed with brutality rather than reverence in her battle to hetero-sexualise me. Despair consumed me more and more, I needed liberation from her hostile judgement and the flashing disco lights of Dublin allured me. He had seduced me so many bygone years before, but there before my blue eyes was a face in the distance that I had certainly not forgotten. Robert was surrounded by the same social circle of friends, who still leeched him for pints of Guinness, but due to the smoking ban in Ireland there was no Dunhill dangling with virility from his mouth. Later that night his haggard deep sunken eyes glanced at me again, but not in total recognition yet. He took a few steps in my direction, but was still unable to identify me. Suddenly his flirtatious smile faded, his fist hardened into a clenched position, but I advanced towards him to conquer the few last metres that separated us and like Judas Iscariot my kiss betrayed him. The touch of my feigned affection on his cheek enraged him. I coldly informed him that I had resurrected from the ruins of his love, liberated all of my dreams from the ashes of his destruction and that the almighty god and I now had the clemency to forgive his brutality if he repented. Rage devoured Robert; "Fuck you and fuck the catholic god" his hostility retorted. Certainly enlightened by the devious revenge of Bette Milder, Diane Keaton and Goldie Hawn in the "First Wives Club" I riposted with serenity; "Abandon your sufferance my friend and flourish in the harmony of my forgiveness forever". I didn't believe in the resurrection of homosexuals in the heavenly kingdom of god, but with so much sincerity in my insincerity it was possible to think that a door to door Jehovah Witness had converted me to have faith in the bible again. I had tasted the fruition of my reveries, but the changing colours of the seasons had ravaged his beauty with great desolation. The ageing process had devoured him so much that there was nothing seductive left, but I still knew Robert more than he thought I knew him. Hate was engrained in the profound silence of my thoughts, but to display my enmity would have been his ultimate victory. To absolve my foe with catholic compassion certainly destroyed him more than if I had enriched him with my belligerence. I looked into his dark brown eyes, probably for the last time

ever. Slaughtered by my righteous morality he grabbed his coat with haste and absconded into South Great George's Street. I was liberated forever from the sufferance that I had forgotten.

Ireland was vainglorious and certainly too bombastic to elude the collapse of the economy and another great famine befell. The death of the Celtic Tiger now crucified the holy Catholics of Ireland in a plague of poverty. Irish prayers implored god for deliverance from such sufferance, but no almighty divinity had the compassion to save Ireland from the destruction that human greed had created. I discovered a desert in the abandoned streets that had once bustled with an abundance of frivolous shoppers and I saw the desolation that was reflected on so many ruined looking faces. The more the consumption society perished in the brutality of the recession the more the various nationalities that had invaded Ireland were condemned in the cold prison of Irish judgement. The immigrants that occupied the unbecoming jobs that the Irish had once pretentiousness boycotted with indignation, had enriched Ireland with the beauty of ethnic cultural diversity, but they were also the scapegoats held responsible for the economic destruction of the affluent nation. The holy Catholics of Ireland had forgotten the anti-Irish sentiment that had governed history and they overtly practiced the same persecution, discrimination and rancour now. In the belief that the Irish were savage and inferior, they had been colonised and crucified for being barbarically Irish, but the same immorality was now mirrored in the social crucifixion of another colourful race. A rise in racism nourished Ireland; perhaps catholic compassion was really only a myth?

"All civilisation that recognised and justified homosexuality as a normal lifestyle met decadence" was preached like a sermon from a catholic pulpit by Christine Boutin in the French National Assembly in 1999. She literally waved a holy bible and entangled her religious beliefs in a secular political structure, which was a shocking unconstitutional gesture. The creation of civil union in France was indeed a politically correct way to silence homosexual indignation, but was social equality to be closeted forever or did the gay culture need another bloody revolution for the freedom of marriage? The five minute PACS ceremony was in an austere office in the magistrates' court in June 2009. The civil officer coldly smiled and a sentiment of enragement consumed my thoughts in silence. Some dreams needed to be abandoned; Philippe casually wore a jeans and an aged T-shirt, both which reflected the colour of his profound ocean blue eyes and

there was no elegant gentleman's suit and tie, no flower girl scattering rose petals by my feet, no page boy bearing rings on a white satin cushion and definitely no "you may kiss the groom". My civil union was merely like a trip to the supermarket, but rather than sumptuously tasting caviar garnished blinis, ink immortalised our signatures on paper in a total anti-climax instead. The PACS contract was furnished with loopholes, but a visit to our solicitor in the days that followed consolidated our love with more legal protection. If death seduced me rural catholic Ireland wanted to bury me in a wet Irish grave, but Philippe now had the right to disperse my ashes among the flowers that blossomed in our garden. He became my sole inheritor; if rural catholic Ireland had the audacity to lament for a queer son, after their mourning their revenge was not empowered to enrich his life with sufferance or poverty. Homosexual union was legalised, but social intolerance still discriminated against "homosexual fuckers" and the conservative voice of Catholicism in laic France still battled to silence queers. Homosexuals didn't want a holy blessing from the almighty catholic god in the Sacrament of Marriage, but their love certainly needed the same legal recognition as straights. The Vatican condemnation of homosexuality was omnipresent during the Sarkozy reign in the belief that the morality of marriage was for heterosexuals and not for the pink market. Same gender civil marriage was not seen by politicians as a vote-getter and an illiberal president certainly wasn't willing to jeopardise his political career for promiscuous queers.

The fields of colours consumed her with tears of despair in August 2009. A profound sensation of total indifference devoured my mother as her blue eyes vacantly gazed through the sitting room window of my rural home. She certainly had no admiration for the abundance of nature that flourished outside and felt that the serene landscape that beautified my village was a barrenness of silence that tortured her mind. I knew that the sunshine scorched the limestone cobblestone paving of Place de Jaude and that the gentle wind that caressed the streets of Clermont Ferrand that day made the hot city air completely irrespirable, but judging by the exaggerated extent of her woe she definitely needed some retail therapy. She implored me with the same passion that she honoured her almighty catholic god with in prayer and rather than swim together in the fresh waters of the Gour de Tazenat volcanic lake as planned I showed kind forbearance and passively surrendered to her demand. Her dreams were now liberated in the consumption society that she loved to belong to. From shop to shop my holy father conquered her love and his affluence completely seduced her again. Philippe carried the plastic bags that contained all her booty, sweat

moistened under the armpits of his short sleeved shirt and her superficial demeanour enriched him with great repugnance. She explicitly set forth that she needed revenge on the poverty in Churchfield that had destroyed her childhood, but was her two fingered gesture on society really about that? I believed that his lovers' kisses were engrained in my mother's silenced thoughts forever and that she still punished my father for the sin of his forbidden passion. His almsgiving definitely wasn't about the solemn vows of a catholic marriage, but about his empoisonment to silence the sufferance that she was to never forget.

I thought that the cultural store FNAC wasn't the type of scene that would inspire a philistine like my mother, but she strangely insisted on going there. She paraded in a gallop fashion in the direction of the flat screen plasma televisions, stopped in front of an overly large sized one and charitably declared that she had loving bought the same model for my brother. He was certainly another entangled puppet for her to dangle in the web of her corrupt love, but I believed that with six mouths to feed in his one wage household that her affluence was needed for such luxury; after all he did battle in the ruins of the Celtic Tiger to survive with a hefty mortgage. She smiled that she wanted to bestow me with the same generous gift, but my soft words immediately declined. She retorted that mine was prehistoric and was correct in saying that it looked more like a microwave rather than a TV. In the silence of my thoughts I really wanted it, in the craving that glittered in Philippe's profound ocean blue eyes I saw that he wanted it too, but we didn't genuflect before her catholic god and certainly not prostrate before her money either. She always resurrected that she had housed, fed and clothed me for too many years and that she had sacrificed many a gold and diamond ring to finance my education. She also sang in self-praise that Molly still wiped the shit from her ass with the toilet paper that my holy mother as a good Catholic regularly sent to Dublin. I didn't want to be crucified in gratitude again or grant her the victory of buying my love, so I coldly refused to be contaminated by even a cent that came from her purse. I really wanted it, but I strongly rebelled to silence my materialistic desire and what she judged as my insolence enraged her. If the original 1970 pink flowered tiles still decorated the walls in my bathroom it was because I couldn't afford to change it yet, if the windows in my sitting room were naked it was because I needed curtains, if she incessantly crucified the impoverishment that lingered in my home so much it was because my dreams needed time to be built step by step. The house had been completely neglected since the death of George Dubois in 1997 and for ten years after his widow had bewailed in

despair without carrying out any maintenance. As she lamented in tears the paving stone driveway had become ruins, the garden was a deep overgrowth deglorified by the forceful brutality of time and the interior design certainly belonged to a long forgotten era. The dark salmon coloured patterned carpet in my bedroom was well worn and displayed the sufferance of its old age, a grotesque tapestry wallpaper still decorated the sitting room with an encrusted layer of dust, but rather than admire the many changes that we had already made, my catholic mother criticised and belittled absolutely everything. I wanted her to be proud that I struggled with a homosexual mortgage, but she mourned that I didn't have a modern looking television and her hard judgements destroyed me again.

Each golden daffodil that gently danced in the March winds, each hand-like-painted iris that gloriously flourished after the April rains and each different flower that enriched my garden with splendour year after year coloured my life with so much gaiety. All of my senses were aroused by the sight of a hedgehog roaming in spring among the debris of fallen autumn leaves, by the summer perfume of lavender, lemon thyme and honeysuckle, by the succulent taste of raspberries that grew in abundance, by the barefooted touch of grass that tickled my feet and by the symphony of hard laboring insects under the blazing sun. So many seasons aged me, but there was so much beauty in ageing in the sincerity that glittered in Philippe's profound ocean blue eyes. I survived in the passion of his kisses and I was salvaged from the ruins of destruction by the harmony of his eternal love. I was liberated more and more each day from the prison of my Irish sufferance, but as I blossomed in the liberty of my dreams, what was to become the last crucifixion in rural Ireland befell on me. Emotion devoured my holy mother's eyes when the wrought iron nails crucified Jesus Christ each Good Friday, but her rancour had been silenced for too many years and her intolerance was cold when she crucified me. Her catholic prayers did not hetero-sexualise me and it certainly enraged her that I didn't journey into repentance. The almighty god resurrected from silence, the catholic sermons devoured her love for her "fucking queer son", the immorality of homosexuality was condemned to perpetual tears and I was eternally forsaken. The climax of my homosexual sufferance was nigh, but was the zenith of queer freedom to be found among such desolation?

25

The Defloration of Ireland

It was the beginning of September 2010 in Ireland. The leaves were changing colour, some had already fallen in the gentleness of the wind, but rather than be liberated by a nostalgic love for the nation that I had completely abandoned I tasted the tears of Irish lamentation instead. The faces of the Irish were devoured with a sensation of woe. Their furrowed brows and pursed lips had clearly forgotten the glorious consumption days of the Celtic Tiger. Barrenness had resurrected, an almighty mass of unemployment ravaged and the ripples of the economic crisis ruined Ireland in a new wave of poverty. An abundance of Irish Catholics fell in the ashes of forgotten affluence. The repossession of homes had become an everyday Irish crucifixion that slaughtered human beings without compassion. In their dying dreams defeated holy men and women abandoned the power of catholic prayer and in the belief that death was deliverance suicides largely devastated Ireland. I had never seen so much desolation and so much despair, but I now had the strong impression that even god had forsaken Ireland. Needless to say that my catholic mother still flaunted her gold and diamond ornately decorated fingers to the world to revere and was it in almsgiving or still in repentance that my charitable father now tossed several coins to the many beggars that littered the church steps on the Sabbath day? There was certainly a resurrection for Ireland to come, but more imminent was the sufferance, the judgement and the eternal liberation of me their closeted gay son.

Naomi, Sorcha, Darius and Caelan were filled with gaiety the moment they saw us arrive. I was profoundly touched by the abundance of their affection towards Philippe and warmed by the sincerity of love that he showed them. Somewhere in my thoughts I still felt a silenced regret, but social intolerance forbid homosexual men to procreate and my dream was forced to fade away in the eternity of such despair. My nieces begged their father for permission to travel the four minute drive to Lidl in my car rather than

in his, but it was strictly forbidden for them to be alone with two queers. Sorcha didn't want discord and hesitantly relinquished, but Naomi fastened the rear seatbelt and became amused that a French steering wheel was on the opposite side. My brother roared "get your fucking ass out immediately", but she simply acted deaf as if she hadn't heard him. Sorcha retorted that it was better to silence his rage than ever revolt against him. He warned Naomi that she knew him well enough not to rebel further, but in cold defiance she shunned his threat. Then, tears fell from her tender eyes as he physically removed her with brutality. He still believed that I wanted to enlighten his catholic children with the corruption of the homosexual sin, to indoctrinate them with a passion for the homosexual culture and to homo-sexualise them with "queer fucker immorality". I should have defended rather than abandon, but I gently kissed her on the forehead and lowered my eyes in defeat. She whispered that she knew why he hated me; perhaps she had unriddled the mystery alone? My passengerless car followed his for the 2.2 kilometre journey; Catholic Ireland had certainly crucified me again.

Pushing a trolley in the supermarket wasn't exactly the ideal place for a coming out, but Naomi and Sorcha inquisitively liberated the words that my brother never wanted to hear. He was highly enraged by their insolence, but I battled in the belief that they now needed to know the truth. He really wanted to imprison my homosexuality in the dark dusty closet of catholic silence forever, but I solemnly promised not to betray them in the name of an illiberal Irish god. He aggressively retorted that it was my "fucking problem to justify such a sin". There was no politically correct manual to explain how to disclose homosexuality to my teenage nieces, but even if one had existed I didn't have the reactive time to read it. An ocean of nervous tension devoured me. I forced a loving smile in fear that they would regard me with disdain afterwards. Then, I disclosed that indeed I was homosexual and confirmed that Philippe certainly was my boyfriend. I learnt that "The Simpsons" on television had made homosexuality banal for their generation. I remembered when the BBC broadcasted ungodly images in our catholic home and my outraged mother sprinkled me with holy water, but Ireland had changed and liberated homosexuals from biblical judgement. I surprising learnt that there was now compassion for queers in catholic Ireland. In their tolerance I tasted the ripples of homosexual freedom and years of sufferance suddenly disappeared. I believed that I had resurrected from the ashes of silence, but my coming out foreshadowed the agony of another homosexual crucifixion and the lamentation of Ireland that was to come. As the last leaves of

autumn fell my catholic brother destroyed me in banishment forever. Before the cold colours of winter arrived I tasted his almighty eternal revenge.

The river Lee flowed with passion and the charming bells of Shandon at Saint Anne's Church echoed in the near distance. My catholic mother forewarned me with brutality not to betray the silence of my homosexuality. I sarcastically retorted that I had forgotten my rainbow coloured queer flag, my gay pride T-shirt and my pink effeminate sparkling handbag, but the glance of rage in her eyes immediately silenced my insolence. The store was highly reputed; certainly the best quality blind makers in Ireland and my mother knew the shop assistants relatively well enough to converse with them in idle gossip. The abundance of patterns and designs that decorated the showroom seduced me in awe and Philippe in virile admiration. My taste in colour coordination was a certain eyesore, hence I desperately needed him to harmonise the made to measure roller blinds with the colour scheme in our guest bedrooms, but for some unknown reason he was now seated at the far end of the store alone. My righteous mother glared at me with repulsion and even seemed enraged that I beckoned him over. I still didn't understand that her holy judgement had condemned him to purgatory. A moment later she physically pushed "the queer fucker" away from my side to isolate him further again and in total obedience he began to abandon me. I had no tolerance for such a crucifixion. I revolted that there was nothing immoral about homosexual love and that the shop didn't really care if the colour of queer money was pink. She enlightened me with severity not to flaunt my "fucking homosexuality" in her catholic world. I rebelled that no almighty god was ever to contaminate Philippe with tears or sufferance. She silenced her hostility, his profound ocean blue eyes glittered with serenity beside me again and I unknowingly became another step closer to homosexual freedom.

In the belief that homosexuality was a catholic sin my holy mother bemoaned the beauty of our gay love, but I didn't repent for the immortality of loving Philippe. There was clearly no tolerance for queers in catholic Ireland and in the hours that followed her animosity savagely destroyed me more and more. She dehumanised me with so much repugnance as if something had changed in the level of her hostility. Little did I know that my brother had enlightened her of my coming out and that her brutality justified her revenge on my betrayal of silence. I had never

been so slaughtered by her before and in the abundance of her sufferance she wrathfully enriched me with her eternal aversion of homosexuality. In need of freedom from such despair my car followed the road to nowhere. The waves raged in a cold wind in Ballycotton, an Irish drizzle began to fall, which clouded my spectacles with a layer of mist, but Philippe and I were now liberated from the desolation of her deep rancour. In the inn by the harbour delicious salmon sandwiches conquered our ravenous hunger. Philippe politely nodded; he certainly hadn't understood the quick paced undulating utterance of the friendly Corkonian barman that served the creamy headed pint that had just settled. Indeed he was "a queer fucker" as my mother had earlier said, but he savoured his Guinness with as much heterosexual virility as all the other men around us. I didn't particularly feel a desire to return to that rural catholic home, but the stars in the night sky forced us. There was a cold and caustic silence as neither my righteous father nor my pious mother faltered a word. She glanced at me in total disgust, lowered her eyes in repulsion and I was devoured by a foreboding sensation of doom. In the profound silence of my thoughts I feared that those blue eyes never wanted to regard me with love ever again. It was common practice that I revolted against the bible, but this time my holy mother decided to revenge me.

Catholic Ireland had decriminalised homosexuality in 1993, but for years her intolerance nurtured me with brutality. My mother begged in prayer to hetero-sexualise me, but her dream was always silenced by the Irish god. She implored me with tears in her eyes to abandon my immorality, but I didn't repent. I was the "fucking queer" that destroyed her heterosexual reveries and her sufferance clouded my freedom in a prison of perpetual silence. Was social aversion of the homosexual culture so profound that she really needed to forsake me or was her catholic reverence the almighty force that inspired my cherished mother to pink triangle me? God frowned upon homosexuality, queers were condemned to banishment from the kingdom of heaven, the sermons immortalised my sin and she crucified me with biblical wrought iron nails, but unlike Jesus Christ there was no resurrection after my crucifixion. The son of god had forewarned the denial of his disciple Peter, but he didn't admonish me of my mother's intolerance beforehand. Before the rooster crowed Peter had disowned Jesus three times and after having turned the discoloured gilded pages of her aged bible the next morning she destroyed me. Rather than stone a homosexual sinner to death, she banished me from the eternity of her love. Rather than crucify me on a wooded cross with a non-repentant queer on my right-hand side, she deported me from her rural catholic Irish home

forever. In the repentance of Peter he cried bitterly, but no emotional tears of regret fell from my mother's cold eyes. She certainly loved the mythical god more than she loved her "fucking homosexual son".

Dawn enlightened the crucifix on the pale egg shell coloured wall. I saw the first morning ray of sunlight penetrate through the curtains. Its gentleness caressed Philippe's face and in the silence of my thoughts I admired how it enhanced his absolute beauty. There was complete silence for a few minutes more, the stairs then creaked as my father descended for his habitual tea and toast breakfast and I heard the softness of my mother's voice praying alone with reverence in her room. The discoloured gilded pages of her aged bible turned as she knelt in prayer. She revered her almighty god; not in the regret of crucifying her homosexual son and certainly not in repentance before she crucified me again. I distinctively heard the stairs creak for a second time and after that there was the familiar faint sound of the radio from the kitchen below. Philippe now awoke and kissed me, but the eternity of love that glittered in his profound ocean blue eyes didn't liberate me from the emotion of despair or from the foreboding sensation of sufferance that devoured me. I feared the brutality of another crucifixion, but he thoroughly believed that her wrath was ephemeral. As I opened the bedroom door she appeared from nowhere; my catholic mother certainly had been waiting outside to ensnarl me in her catholic judgement. She lowered her eyes to the carpeted floor and coldly disclosed that there was no more tolerance for queer fuckers in her holy catholic home. I implored her to be clement, but her brutality resurrected and the eternal lamentation of Ireland began. I begged her not to practice her intolerance in haste, but her words rebelled to passionately slaughter me for my "fucking immorality" again. Homosexuality was the veneration of Satan and she could not love me in the silence of my irreverence to god anymore. She justified that there were no "fucking queers" in the kingdom of heaven and no more "fucking queers" in her fucking catholic home. I forewarned that she would never see the ageing process destroy my fading youth if she didn't repent, but she didn't liberate any sentiment of penitence and her aversion crucified me for the last time. I was forsaken forever, but was eternal freedom to flourish in the sufferance of my tears?

Medium beige foundation invigorated her complexion, a resplendent rosy coloured blush enhanced her cheekbones, eye shadow, eyeliner and mascara brought depth, dimension and harmony to her cold eyes, a touch of pale red lipstick made her even more alluring and an abundance of

lacquer stiffened her blonde highlighted hair. Glittering gold and diamond rings immortalised her beauty as my tears fell in total despair; it was the last time that I ever saw my catholic mother. I didn't repent for being a "fucking queer" and I certainly didn't pray to the almighty god to battle for my homosexuality, but I implored my righteous father to defend me against her injustice. I forewarned that he would never see the impact of time wane my vigour if he crucified me, but he savagely liberated his rage. He also justified that the immorality of my homosexuality needed to be punished by eternal banishment and enriched me with even more sufferance. Philippe wasn't cultivated with the language of Shakespeare, but judging by his reaction he had clearly understood everything. In silent revolt he handed my house keys to my intolerant catholic father. Such silence was not his acceptance of defeat; Philippe was enraged, but he did not betray the beauty of our homosexual love with insolence or a two fingered gesture of vulgarity. It was not with the habitual time consuming delicacy that Philippe packed our suitcases, but with great haste and disorder. Then, dragging our luggage without a drop of water to quench our morning thirst my "fucking queer lover" and I were deported. My emotional eyes looked in the direction of my holy father for the last time. My glance of woe begged him not to forsake me forever, but he still displayed no sign of repentance. I besought Philippe to be strong in my hour of need and he promised with sincerity to love me forever.

My car stopped outside the local grocery shop; so much had changed since the light-hearted days of my childhood when I used to skateboard there to spend all my pocket money on white chocolate mice, milk teeth, sherbet filled flying saucers and fizzy cola bottles. I knew the taste of every penny sweet that existed in Ireland, but dyeing my tongue by sucking Black Jacks was a long forgotten pleasure. An ocean of tears devoured me and Philippe was contaminated with the same emotion. Each tear of sufferance that fell from his profound ocean blue eyes enriched me with eternal wrath against my mother. If she had crucified me alone I would have tolerated her brutality and been clement, but I didn't have the catholic compassion to ever forget that she had crucified Philippe too. My forgiveness didn't resurrect from the ashes of such destruction and I certainly never loved her again. I now learnt that the promise of silence was a barren prison of desolation; the doubled edged sword had shielded my pompous mother from the social shame of having a queer son, but it had completely enforced my isolation from the world. The years of silencing my homosexual immorality in the dark dusty closet of rural Ireland suddenly betrayed me. In my moment of need there was absolutely nowhere to go

and a great sensation of complete solitude enhanced my sufferance even more. I succumbed to despair and the revenge of silence totally ravaged me. I didn't disclose to the owner of the Bed and Breakfast that we were forsaken homosexuals, but Mrs. O' Bryne must have understood. My red puffy eyes were carefully concealed behind dark sun glasses, but it was certainly obvious that I had been crying. Ireland didn't discriminate against the colour of gay money and Cobh harbour became immortalised in my profound grief.

Early the next morning I walked along the water edge alone. The sharply pointed roofed Victorian Houses, which normally seduced me in admiration, gave little or no pleasure to my eyes. On the steps of Saint Colman's Cathedral I heard the church bells pealing over the sea. My tearful prayers implored the almighty catholic god to liberate me from the sufferance of my Irish crucifixion, but the abundance of god's revenge resurrected in silence to crucify me again. The sun fell between the gaps in the clouds and the cold sensation of the moist air on my face was replaced by a subtle feeling of warmth, but I was still conquered by the emotion of despair. Philippe didn't want my catholic virtue to be consumed by an ocean of eternal tears and later the same day he found the serenity to forgive my mother. He thoroughly believed that a holy Catholic would be enlightened by god's compassion, but in her biblical judgement the forbidden immorality of homosexuality was a perpetual sin. I did not repent for being "a fucking queer", but I tragically implored her to nourish me with her love again. There was a moment of silence, perhaps she was touched by a sentiment of regret? There was a second of hesitation as if she really desired to seek my forgiveness, but there was no resurrection into repentance. She solemnly swore that I was "fucking dead", her telephone handset was directed back to its cradle and I lamented in the eternity of silence. It was with such coldness that she destroyed my emotions for the last time. If I had been alone that day death certainly would have allured, enticed and seduced me. Requiescat in pace would have been engraved on a marble headstone in Saint Catherine's Cemetery and my catholic mother would have publicly mourned in crocodile tears. The intolerance of rural catholic Ireland would have silenced my homosexuality forever, but the love in Philippe's profound ocean blue eyes gave me wings of survival.

The Promise Of Silence

26

The Affection of Judgement

In my battle to survive I had no choice but to accept my emotional sufferance. What destroyed me created me; I resurrected from the ashes of her holy judgement, but there was no emotion of revenge in my coming out. I needed to be liberated from the dark dusty closet of silence, but was homosexuality a prison of eternal tears? My mother had completely deluded me into believing that there was no tolerance for "queer fuckers" in rural catholic Ireland, but in the betrayal of silence I now discovered that catholic compassion wasn't a myth. It enraged Aunty Annie in abundance that my mother tasted the body of Christ in hypocrisy after she had crucified me. Aunty Eucharia believed that my mother had brought great shame on a religion that preached the love of god. Sitting on the sofa her gaze was downturned, replete with a combination of remorse and self-reproach. She lamented in despair that I would not forgive all the years that she had not waved a rainbow coloured flag to liberate me. I learnt that day that the world had loved me in the silence of my homosexuality, but in reverential fear of her vengeance nobody had ever rebelled against my mother's savagery. Catholic Ireland didn't crucify homosexuals in barbaric repulsion and they both had the serenity to regret that they had never battled for my homosexual freedom. They implored my forgiveness, indeed their silence had destroyed me to a certain degree, but there was no need to lament in tears for my forgotten sufferance. Profound thoughts of how my life could have been different surfaced, but there was no turning back time. They now granted me liberation; from their repentance beauty bloomed, from their acceptance I tasted true love and the freedom that I had always desired was immortalised in their clement judgement.

Everyone believed that in the prison of her silenced thoughts that my mother still profoundly loved me, but her brutality had forced me to abandon all belief in her affection. I was certain that it was the catholic sermons that had enriched her with eternal disdain against homosexuality

or was it the pointed finger of social judgement that she really feared? Aunty Annie rebelled from silence in a heroic fashion and attempted to shield me from eternal tears. She enlightened my mother that nobody wanted to crucify her, but she was silenced by the liberation of her rage. Parading catholic pompousness was certainly more important than the beautification of homosexual freedom that Annie preached. My holy mother retorted in lie that she didn't know that I was "a fucking queer", but Annie hadn't smoked me out of the closet. There was no resurrection of love and her telephone handset was directed back to its cradle in the creation of my perpetual sufferance. It completely astounded my aunts that I didn't know about Thomas and it certainly stupefied me to discover that my younger cousin by a year was also gay. My mother had cunningly silenced my immorality, but she had candidly loved Thomas. She had crucified me for my homosexuality, but she had nourished him with tolerance. Her catholic judgement had slaughtered me, but she overtly pardoned that he denuded men. She knew that rural Ireland totally condoned his homosexuality, but she didn't grant me the same fate. Thomas had flourished in freedom, but in despair I had battled in the dark dusty closet of silence and solitude alone. My catholic mother had destroyed me, but she had always displayed her total support for him. There was never a glance of disdain or disgust in her blue eyes to crucify him, but my sufferance was immortalised. Regret was now deeply engrained in me, the green eyed monster even contaminated me and I mourned the years of liberty that I had never had. I didn't want the sensation of hate to devour me forever, but I now believed that there was no forgiveness of her sins.

Ireland hetero-sexualised me, but with serenity I faced judgement after judgement and lived so many coming outs in the harmony of my liberation. My godmother was euphoric that I liberated the truth and enlightened me that she regretted that the perpetual prison of silence had condemned me to so much sufferance. Like all others, she was enraged that a homosexual eviction had been practiced and she believed that if my catholic mother destroyed me with no degree of repentance that there no forgiveness for her in the kingdom of heaven. Brigitte lovingly kissed Philippe in abundance and tears of freedom now devoured my eyes. I was liberated from the chains of silence and the social brutality of the dark dusty closet as she touched me with a sensation of true acceptance that I had never known before. My coming out was nourished with great compassion, but I was also enriched to understand that hostility was sometimes masked behind the appearance of tolerance. A gasp of horror in the immediate

seconds betrayed my godfather. I then distinguished the minuscule wrinkle of distaste that marked his forehead in total disapproval of my immorality and a nervous twitch as his body stiffened in repugnance. Being politically correct Ronald hugged me, but his mechanical emotions were extremely cold and under the surface lacked sincerity. He didn't overtly disclose his hate, but his body language certainly unfolded his aversion of "queer fuckers' and his holy bible resurrected in silence. Indeed, there was no homosexual crucifixion practiced, but he repetitively referred to the gay culture as "those type of people'. His catholic belief of the homosexual sin was not tangible, but it was transparent that his opinion of me had changed forever.

I learnt that my silence had crucified Ann Casey and indeed the dark dusty queer closet had been a prison of sufferance for her too. Silence had betrayed everyone; in my silence she had believed that I didn't want to liberate my homosexuality, in her silence I had believed that the almighty god hadn't bestowed her with tolerance and as the truth enlightened us our tears fell in profound regret. Catholic silence had deluded me to believe that it hetero-sexualised me, but she had deduced that I was a queer; after all I was more sensitive in my emotions and more sincere in my affection than a heterosexual man. Being homosexual had naturally enhanced our platonic closeness, it justified why her husband had tolerated me without suspicion and Terence retorted with a laugh that I could flirt with him now instead. So many seasons had changed colour, the solitude of so much brutality had destroyed me in despair and it enraged me to understand that I had silenced my homosexuality in complete error. They believed in homosexual freedom and their teenage children had no holy judgement either. Indeed Ireland had abandoned the biblical intolerance that the pulpit sermons preached. I had the right to be a homosexual and I flourished in their acceptance of my immorality. My betrayal of silence immortalised my freedom; I was eternally liberated from the prison of sufferance forever.

From the Pont Aven promenade deck I saw the multi-coloured houses that lined Cobh harbour disappear from my view. A moment later catholic Ireland faded away into the horizon. An abundance of different emotions fell from my eyes and I was consumed by despair, wrath and rancour. She had crucified and forsaken "a queer fucker" and I had become the forgotten fruit of her love, but did I have the strength not to lament in the prison of eternal sufferance forever? After the silence of many emotional days I

desired to believe in a resurrection, but had the boundless mercy of god contaminated my holy mother with repentance? There was no social judgement of disgrace brought upon her catholic home, but she judged that my treachery of silence was unforgiveable. Her regret did not resurrect in the changing colours of the seasons either and the tenderness of my kiss on her cheek didn't beautify her life with affection ever again. I dreamed in silence that she still loved me, but did she light a candle in Saint Josephs Church with a secret thought for her homosexual son or was I perpetually banished from her prayers too? She certainly continued to turn the discoloured gilded pages of her aged bible with reverence, but many now believed that that would not ensure her passage into the mythical kingdom of heaven. I revolted from the prison of silence that had enchained me for years and there was certainly no reverting to be "a fucking queer" in the brutality of her holy catholic judgement. I abandoned her intolerance and in the ruins and ashes of time she aged in solitude without me. Indeed if the exorbitant price of my homosexual freedom was the eternity of her silence I wanted to mourn in the tears of such silence.

Clement judgements had immortalised the tolerance of a changed Ireland, but my enraged father believed that my coming out was betrayal. I begged him to have repentance, but there was "no fucking redemption for queers in the kingdom of heaven". He bowed with reverence before the altar in Amen, but the divine body of Christ on his tongue was a myth of compassion. "Homosexual immorality" was forbidden by god and his biblical judgement condemned me again. I was "fucking dead", but Requiescat in pace was not engraved with my name on a marble headstone in Saint Catherine's Cemetery. He certainly did not repent, but his telephone handset was directed back to its cradle in the creation of my perpetual sufferance. He tossed coins to the beggars on the church steps on the Sabbath day, held the narthex door open with a virtuous smile for an elder, closed his eyes verily in prayer, but it was with such coldness that he crucified me for the last time. A dark thought seduced me, but who would feed the singing birds when a blanket of winter snow covered my garden? Who would nurture Philippe with love if I didn't exist? I didn't walk into the shadows of the valley of death, but resurrected in tears instead. Autumn denuded the trees; the pious Catholics of rural Ireland had perpetually judged "a queer fucker". My dream of homosexual freedom flourished in the emotions that fell from my blue eyes, but if sufferance was the punishment that liberated me from the prison of intolerance I accepted my eternal sufferance.

27

The Revolution of Revenge

Aunty Ellen wanted to love me in the battle to survive my emotional sufferance and invaded my world after years of silence like a parasite ripping the flesh from its host without pity or remorse. She had delicately held me in her arms a few days after my birth and admired my beauty, but she had forgotten to love me throughout all the years that followed that. Suddenly, she profoundly wormed her way into my homosexual life and began to consume me in the revolution of her revenge. Her efforts to befriend me repulsed me more and more, but she further encrusted herself in the bricks and walls of my fragility. I saw certain hypocrisy in the transparency of her holy appearance, but she still deluded me to believe that she practiced sincerity. She disparaged my enraged mother, but she didn't have the catholic value of love or forgiveness when cocaine had corrupted her heterosexual son. My cousin Ciarán had implored her help in his moment of need, but was cast into the wet streets of Ireland and abandoned by her in perpetual silence. Ellen didn't understand that I still loved my mother and even if the bitch had forsaken and destroyed me I still defended her from belittlement and judgement. I now hesitated to believe that Ellen was a good Catholic; she flaunted in abundance her sparking gold and diamond rings and gossip burned her lips with toxicity as she backstabbed friend and foe alike. The catholic religion preached not to throw stones, but I had the impression that she threw shit instead. Tears fell from the eyes of some, others lowered their heads in shame after having been slaughtered by her captious remarks, but she pompously held her head high to the world without repentance. Religious indoctrination had taught Ellen that gays would not inherit the kingdom of heaven, but for a Catholic she didn't have "a real problem with queers". With compassion and tolerance she supported my homosexual freedom, but she certainly had faith in all the social myths of homosexuality too. I hated the mannerisms and affectations that straights adopted to dehumanise "those kind of people" and she audaciously wanted to know was it Philippe or me who was arse fucked passively in the bedroom? What factor determined the

balance of effeminacy in homosexual couples? It was clear that she understood nothing about the homosexual culture, but I believed that some thoughts needed to be silenced in grace. Ellen certainly didn't master the art of being politically correct and her social ignorance contaminated me with a feeling of more and more repugnance.

My father made the sign of the cross and knelt with reverence before god in prayer, but Ellen disclosed in rage that he wasn't a good Catholic. Years of dust had silenced what should have been forgotten forever, but she coldly divulged that he who preached the righteousness of god had seduced and fucked before marriage. In her next breath, she caustically stated that the passion of his erection had even given rise to an illegitimate son nine months later. Since the beginning of time Irish homes enforced high catholic principles and social moral values and the immorality of bastard births was closeted. There was no harmony between the love of god and the savage treatment of promiscuous women in holy Ireland. The brutality of sufferance must have fallen from her eyes; in repentance that woman returned to the grace of god and another catholic adoption masked the inhumane treatment that the almighty god of Ireland practiced. It bewildered me that Ellen revealed with fury what god had silenced. I hated my father with all my strength, but in his moral defense I impugned the injustice of such a rumour. Her words attacked without catholic compassion again, but this time she was irrefutable because she knew with factual accuracy all about the factory women that he had fucked too. I didn't understand what source had rightly informed her, but I knew that her husband was also renowned in rural Ireland for his betrayal of the Seventh Commandment. It was not catholic on my behalf to throw stones in judgement, but I retorted that she knew the destructive taste of adultery too. It was certain that my insolence enraged her, but it was her revenge on the silence of another sin that empowered her to destroy me further.

Indeed, "hell hath no fury like a woman scorned". Underneath the surface appearance of her virtue was the forgotten sufferance that resurrected in Ellen's revenge. She was unable to love me, because in my eyes she saw the savage eyes of the man that had destroyed her. She needed to liberate the sufferance of her unforgotten tears from the prison of silence and I then heard what a son should not know about his father. It was the first time that she was ever kissed and she didn't understand why god had punished her. She struggled in disgust, but his wet lips kissed her stronger again and again. He lowered his pants in lust, but she was too catholic and too young

The Promise Of Silence

in age to understand his erection. He then covered her mouth to silence her resistance and the oily smell of industrial machines that was embedded in his hand became ingrained in her mind forever. She obeyed his unholy desire and with terror in her tearful eyes she touched his erect penis. In her battle to survive she had completely forgotten if he had ejaculated or not that day, but she remembered his heavy breathing and his moans of pleasure. In the changing colours of the seasons he denuded her, fondled her adolescent breasts and her panties were lowered to her feet. She had memorised the flower coloured wallpaper of the bedroom. For over forty two years Ellen had survived in the prison of silence, devoured by chronic depression, phobias and anxiety attacks, but I found injustice in the liberation of her sufferance.

If her wrath was against my father, why did I have to taste emotional destruction? I didn't want to be ensnarled in the prison of her sufferance, but in agony my tears fell in abundance. Then, she contaminated me with even more desolation, but I didn't want to believe that he had destroyed some of the other sisters too. My telephone handset was directed back to its cradle, but Ellen didn't understand why I abandoned her in the creation of everlasting silence. The encrusted parasite had crucified my soul in the regurgitation of her crucifixion and indeed I needed to coldly cast her out of my life before she ruined me even further. I had to know for certain if my holy father had committed such an unforgiveable sin or not, but I didn't want to resurrect the sufferance of others either. If they had the serenity to lament in silence, perhaps I needed to worship silence too? I really wanted to forget, but he had preyed on Ellen at the age of my nieces and I certainly didn't want them to become the disposable toys of his lust too. In the hour that followed, another aunt liberated what she had never wanted me to know. She was highly enraged that Ellen had abandoned the solemn pact of eternal silence that they had all made. In her judgement it was an injustice that Ellen's revenge had contaminated my emotions with his immorality. For a few minutes she also tearfully relived her profound sufferance before reverting to the prison of silence again. Her story was identical to Ellen's. I didn't have the clemency to forgive him and I now hated my genitor forever. Two roads diverged, to pray to god for perpetual silence or in despair to liberate the intangible truth.

On the surface of silence they had forgotten; I really wanted to close my eyes in silence too, but what if his immorality resurrected? Could I forgive my silence if I learnt that my holy father denuded and fondled in the

creation of such sufferance again? Could my blue eyes reflect in the mirror with sincerity knowing that I silenced such a monstrosity? I really wanted the serenity to forget his sins, but what if he liberated his erection again? What if the oily smell of the industrial machines in his workshop, where they frivolously played alone, was to become ingrained in my nieces forever? What if his hand silenced their mouths and he lowered their panties to their feet too? I didn't want them to taste the tears that had crucified Ellen, but Molly didn't want to believe me. She certainly thought that I was enriched with revenge; after all I was a forsaken "queer fucker" and he flaunted his catholic virtue to the world and prayed to the almighty god with true reverence. My brother believed in my betrayal, swore that I was to reap the harvest of his wrath and be contaminated with eternal sufferance. His real foe was his catholic father, but he judged me with brutality instead and his deep rancour punished me for the last time. His children became entangled in his enragement and in his war to destroy me he forbade them to love me ever again. I implored him not to estrange me from their emotions, but their innocence became his weapons in the creation of my perpetual tears. Naomi, Sorcha, Darius and Caelan faded away; it was now certain that catholic Ireland had forsaken me forever. What lies did he nourish them with to enlighten them that I didn't love them anymore? Had they already forgotten the blue colour of my eyes? Perhaps they even lamented in the belief that I was dead? I survived the changing colours of the seasons in despair; the cold days became weeks, the weeks became months, the months became years and the years became an eternity of silence.

Aunty Bernadette had nurtured me with so much love as a child, but had rebelled in defiance against my mother in an argument in 1985. Like many others, her punishment had been eternal banishment from our catholic home; hence it had been an eternity of seasons that I had not seen her. She certainly had not forgotten me and in my moment of need she resurrected from the ashes of silence to enrich me with the strength to battle my tears and to survive all of my emotional sufferance. Enraged that my catholic mother had abandoned me she befriended me in a harmony of perpetual affection and in her clement judgement she loved me with almighty sincerity. She liberated me to blossom in her tolerance, my dreams flourished in the freedom of her acceptance, but brutality resurrected again. In her need to revenge my coming out my holy mother implored everyone to ostracise "a fucking homosexual". Some lowered their eyes in silence to avoid her wrath, others like Judas Iscariot kissed me on the cheek in betrayal, but Bernadette wanted to enlighten her with the true grace of god.

The Promise Of Silence

The pulpit sermons had too deeply contaminated her to believe that "thou shalt not mother a queer" and there was absolutely no repentance from the woman that turned the discoloured gilded pages of her aged bible in prayer. Bernadette tasted the liberation of her fury, but she still waved a rainbow coloured flag and immortalised her profound love for me. In the bible the rooster crowed as the apostle Peter betrayed Jesus three times, but "fuck off" Bernadette revolted and did not bow before my tyrannical mother in silence.

I rediscovered my Christmas decorations as if it was the first time that my eyes had ever seen them. In tears I unboxed the crib that my holy mother had given me; I certainly hadn't forgotten how she had venerated it with so much awe and reverence each year. My home became a multitude of rich colours, but there was an abundance of melancholy in the silence of my thoughts. I remembered the hymns in the background as she sang glory to her catholic god and the child-like glance that glittered in her eyes when she admired her sumptuously embellished tree. So many forgotten memories suddenly resurfaced to destroy me with a sentiment of nostalgia, but the profusion of her love had abandoned me forever. I didn't believe in the resurrection of my emotions, but on December 5th 2010 Pasha Murray was born. Loving him enriched my life with so much beauty that I forgot my sufferance. Irish blood had betrayed me and forbidden me to love, but he liberated me from the eternal ruins of such destruction and from my profound despair he gave me the strength to believe in my dreams again. Philippe nourished him with an ocean of affection and cultivated his morality. In the changing colours of the seasons the profound complicity with his godson developed, but I still mourned that I was fruitless in a righteous society that preached the immorality of homosexuality. Intolerance from the heterosexual catholic pulpit engrained the world to believe in the injustice that queers should be fatherless. Ageing forced me to find the serenity to silence my regret, but the battle for homosexual rights had just begun for other queers.

Vladimir, Rebecca and Pasha Murray were the greatest treasures in our lives. The ephemeral beauty of their purple, white and pink bouquets of Lilac seemed to dance in the Chinese cloisonne vase that Marie Therese Passavie had bequeathed to Philippe in her last will and testament. Much to my delight the summer fragrance, which distended from such splendour of colours, perfumed the entire room. The flowers withered, but my mind immortalised everything from the sweetness of the sun ripened raspberries,

after they had denuded each bush of its fruit, to the autumn taste of the gathered walnuts, that had fallen on the succulent coloured leaves. In the silence of my thoughts they were the children that we never had. We wiped away their tears with our kisses, faded away their fears with our hugs and protected them with all the strength of our affection from the harshness of life. Year after year they flourished in the abundance of our love and I saw myself age, not in the changes of the different seasons, but in the changes that the seasons enriched on them. Each Easter they hunted for the hidden chocolate eggs among the flowers and trees that blossomed in my garden. Each birthday a delicious cake with candles illuminated the youth that marked their faces with exultation. Each Halloween was the celebration of Irish traditions; monsters for trick or treat had become a common practice in our village and Pasha tearfully gripped Philippe in fear as the demonic story I created utterly frightened him to death. They endeavoured with their hands behind their backs to fish coin-filled apples with their mouths from a plastic washing up basin. A river of water flooded our tiled sitting room floor in the process, but bobbing was certainly an Irish culture that they needed to know. Every Christmas Day Philippe appeared in a white fur trimmed robe. He had forced his feet into my leather boots, which judging by his awkward walk were clearly at least one size too small. A black buckled belt held the cushion in place, which enlarged and rounded the shape of his stomach. A white pompom red hat descended over his ears and covered his forehead. A fluffy synthetic beard severely aged him. Awe glittered in their eyes to see him, but especially the toy-filled coal bag. Even if they didn't believe anymore, for those few minutes everyone forgot that it was Philippe disguised and really believed in Santa again. In 2015 it was Pacha Clause; so much laughter resounded in the gaiety of our home as the five year old, dressed in the same outfit, called out our names and distributed each present. They were the beautiful children that we did not father, but we certainly cherished them as if they were ours.

Was my catholic mother to crucify me again or was her holy brutality silenced forever? Her gold and diamond embellished fingers still turned the discoloured gilded pages of her aged bible in prayer, but her wrath resurrected with vengeance and brought shame on a religion that preached the righteous social values of god. I didn't ever think that her vindictive spirit was so resentful, but money was certainly the contamination of her soul and in July 2011 I unknowingly reaped her rancour again. For birthdays and Christmases my parents had nourished a savings account for my brother and another one for me in the local credit union. The fruit of my father's hard labour additionally enriched each son with five or ten

pounds a week too. I don't remember if I was encouraged or pressurised, but even my communion and confirmation money was safely planted there. In time a generous nest egg had developed, my brother had used his as a down payment, but not in need I reserved mine in prudence for a rainy day and had almost even forgotten it. Throughout many years my catholic parents had befriended the staff there, which facilitated their revenge and justified the fraudulent release of the balance and the unauthorised closure of my account without me knowing it. Those that absorbed the holy sermons with passion had abandoned the morality of god. Perhaps they justified in prayer that my homosexual coming out had betrayed them, but would the almighty catholic god of Ireland have the compassion to forgive "thou shalt not steal" in their last judgement?

The colourful leaves of autumn 2012 had fallen when I learnt all about their silenced revenge on their homosexual son. It bewildered me that the credit union employee wanted to silence me into believing that the closure of my account was totally normal and she pushed this belief forward in an overly strong way. A sensation of injustice devoured me, but even if I began to question her sincerity I accepted my defeat. I even thanked her for her valued assistance before bringing a polite conclusion to the phone call. The light of dawn contaminated me with a sentiment of deep injustice and each Google page enlightened me more and more with my legal rights in the days that followed. It enraged me that the Credit Union Director wanted to silence me too, but his firm efforts to cast my reclamation aside were not victorious. His incessant insistence to discard me enhanced my rage with passion, but I still revolted in a courteous fashion. It was made very clear by his condescendence and arrogance that he did not deign to discuss the matter with me further; but little did he know that I never abandoned in despair. In appearance I was passive, but his dismissive attitude had only fuelled me with a need to battle even more.

The switchboard operator in the Financial Services Ombudsman directed my call to a dynamic masculine voice, which resounded with the vigour of a man that I imagined to be in his late twenties, but perhaps he was more mature, certainly not more than his early forties? It was typical that I pictured in my mind a face that I hadn't seen before, but the more I listened to him the more he aged. He didn't need to deliberate for long before disclosing that all my banking rights had been violated in abundance. I didn't want to bow in silence before the brutality that crucified me for being "a queer fucker", but in my search for justice was I creating a storm

of rage? No, my parents had sinned and needed to reap the shit that they had harvested with so much hate. The Credit Union Director was now au courant of my follow-up and he immediately changed his attitude towards me after that. He apologetically affirmed that the release of capital from my account had indeed been "a fraudulent error" and a few days later I was enriched with the sum of 9,300 euro and some cents. I signed a terms of settlement to waive my right for legal action and waited for the wrath of Ireland to fall upon me again. After the silence of more than two years my holy father phoned me. The booty that they had pillaged had become his crucifixion and there was the resurrection of his fury. I heard tears of desolation wailing in the background; my mother certainly mourned for the money, but she should have been lamenting for the loss of her homosexual son. All his fuck words cursed me for my so called revenge, but I believed that the holy Catholics of Ireland had been rightfully punished.

I lamented reading each hand written letter knowing that it for the last time. Those were the tangible treasures that had once immortalised my mother's affection, but it was now certain that I was never to taste her cold love again. A match was struck to reduce her words into ashes. It was not the flames of my enragement that destroyed them, but my solemn need to resurrect from destruction like a phoenix. All the photos of her were boxed away in my basement and became dust covered for eternity. I didn't want to look at them in despair anymore. The signs of ageing betrayed me for the first time, but my catholic mother didn't see the sunshine glitter on the enlightened colour of my silver-greying blond hair. Some dreams were ravaged, but in the changing colours of the seasons other dreams flourished. With serenity my homosexuality came out of the dark dusty closet of silence forever. My pink triangle was forsaken, my rainbow coloured flag paraded the streets and I was liberated from my sufferance.

28

The Seduction of Perpetual Immorality

Philippe's profound ocean blue eyes glittered; in the silence of a glance it was so unmistakable to anyone observing that he sincerely loved me. His perpetual love had liberated me from the brutality of catholic judgement, but he now needed me to resurrect him from the profoundness of his silenced sufferance. All along the road a foreboding sentiment of death engrossed my mind, especially when passing through the village where John and Colette resided. It was an atypical practice to find Philippe home from work before me. A glance later it was certain that he had been crying, but in the days that followed I did not see him lament. His emotions were enraged and he savagely revolted in the eternal regret of his father's intolerance. I implored him to liberate his woe, but he hadn't forgotten my crucifixion. It was engrained in his sufferance that John had judged my "social immorality" and banished "an arse fucker". I didn't feel any profound sadness either, but I beseeched him to mourn with serenity rather than have his goodness be devoured by his rage, however Philippe had certainly not forgiven his father. He unearthed the deep thoughts that he had silenced in his mind for years and I understood that he hadn't granted his pardon. It was too late for John to resurrect from the shadows of the valley of death in repentance.

Throughout the years of my banishment I hadn't seen the ageing effect of the changing seasons on Colette. It was certain that she had aged, but Philippe had silenced that the rage of time had blighted her with so much destruction. Perhaps he didn't want to see that age was destroying his cherished mother or did he know that it was just the beginning of his sufferance? Her legs trembled feebly as she battled each one of the twelve steps that led to our front door and with a haggard look on her face she smiled as I kissed her. The vibrant woman that I had once known was completely gone. I held her withered hand tenderly and found the awkward words needed to give my sincere condolences. It was at that precise

moment that I understood that time had severely ravaged her mind too. Her profound ocean blue eyes revolted in tears of despair; she had already forgotten that John was dead and reacted as if she had just learnt about the tragedy of her life from my lips. She implored me that it was not true, but a moment later she had completely forgotten it again. A few minutes later she questioned where John was? It was with the same disbelief and woe in her eyes that she lamented ephemerally again. Indeed Philippe didn't have the time to mourn for his father; all his emotions were devoured by his sufferance for Colette and the uncertainty of what needed to be done next.

I did not sit in the front row next to Philippe in the crematorium, but in the second row just behind him. That was close enough to comfort him with a discrete gesture of love if needed, but it was certain that there was no coming out of the dark dusty closet for him that day. I felt many eyes observe me in silence; probably trying to identify who the man that displayed so much tenderness for Colette was. She seemed so absent as if she still didn't understand, but I dared not mention again that John was dead. There was no emotion in my eyes as I looked at the photo on the flowerless coffin, but there was no cold resentment in my thoughts either. Even if I didn't believe in the almighty catholic god, I still believed in the biblical parables of forgiveness and I didn't feel any hostility towards John. Nineteen year old Mickael certainly didn't bestow the social grace of respect and his absence at his beloved grandfather's funeral did not go unnoticed. It thoroughly enraged Philippe and other tongues wagged in disgust of such irreverence too. An abundance of crocodile tears fell from his sister's eyes; certainly not genuine tears of woe and lamentation. The coldness and insolence that Amelie had always displayed towards John was too deeply embedded in me to believe that a sentiment of love had resurrected within her. The thirty minute non religious ceremony came to an end and as flames consumed the corpse a long line of people offered their condolences. Some did it with real compassion, others with tears, but I especially became aware of those that did it with so much hypocrisy. In appearance they seemed sincere, but my judgement was right; in the days, weeks and months after the funeral they totally forgot to console Philippe in his hours of need. There was a lot more solitude in death than I had ever thought.

All the tears that consumed the beauty of Philippe's profound ocean blue eyes were his sufferance for his ageing mother. Colette was fading away more and more into a world that silenced her emotions, that imprisoned her

forgotten thoughts forever and each colour of the changing seasons further ravaged her mind and body without remorse. Philippe battled to survive as his mother withered away, his face thinned with worry and in the weeks that followed I didn't see him much. Our paths merely crossed with a discreet kiss of affection as we changed shifts in our struggle to ensure that Colette wasn't alone. It was perhaps at that moment of time that I began to learn who Colette really was. I listened attentively to the parts of her history that she still remembered. Her far away memories were more deeply engrained in her mind than yesterday, but the savagery of time was to betray that too. She freed all the emotions of her journey of life and I relived the sufferance of her birth in 1929 and tasted the vibrant passion she had felt during the Liberation of Paris in 1944. Philippe led me to believe that I even knew things that she had never disclosed to anyone. In the sunshine of summer 2012 we laughed together in harmony, but in her forgetfulness it seemed that she was ageing before my eyes. I knew that certain smiles were ephemeral, but Philippe still didn't want to see the truth. Indeed a cloud of powder and a touch of blush enhanced a healthy colour to her pale white cheeks, a pink salmon lipstick contoured the beauty of her smile and delimited the wrinkles around her mouth, but no make-up was able to conceal the profound cracks of her fragility that surfaced more and more.

Philippe and I battled alone to care for Colette, while her other son drank coffee and puffed passionately on a cigarette in an idle fashion outside in the garden. His touristic appearances in her home thoroughly enraged me; but in the belief that nobody ever needed to know I silenced that I had denuded her and washed the faeces from her legs a few hours earlier. Another fall had blacked and blued her delicate face. A glossy covered nursing home brochure was strategically placed by Philippe next to the TV remote control in the hope that Colette's eyes would befall upon it, but a few days later she still hadn't touched it. It was beyond his emotions to turn the pages with her, but my gentle flicking through it allured her interest. Indeed, I needed to liberate Philippe from the dark circles which completely enhanced the sunken look of his profound ocean blue eyes. Her positive reaction flabbergasted him and his eyes watered in relief, but such deliverance from his sufferance was short lived and a few minutes later she had completely forgotten everything again. A day later I hovered and mopped the white tiled sitting room floor, while Colette browsed through the brochure that I had placed under her eyes on the kitchen table. Her fears of the stereotypical reputation of a retirement home surfaced, but were the beautiful photos it contained a myth or was it not really a prison?

During the ten minute journey to Effiat she admired the magnificent colours of the sunlight that glittered on every flower and every tree. Everything was more glorious than what she had just seen before. I struggled alone to seat her in her wheelchair, which then rocked as I pushed it on the uneven surface of the pavement. A few steps later the automatic doors opened in despair. In the core of the foyer there was a fountain, the waterfall like sound appeased me as we neared. The plants around it thrived in the natural luminosity that descended in a heavenly fashion from the glass roof above. The elderly faces around seemed content; it was a beautiful world, but a deep sensation of betrayal devoured my mind.

A clinical fragrance was encrusted in the long corridors and each wing of the building was clearly identified by a different coloured wall. Nurse Catherine disclosed that the negative myth that many envisaged was totally untrue. She didn't direct her conversation towards me; it pleased me that her smile and gentle words were forthrightly to Colette. The sound of elderly voices singing distended in the air, songs of Colette's generation echoed from the common room and much to my surprise she began to chant the words of "Les Champs-Élysées" that she had not forgotten. Photos of smiling residents lined a wall, each one certainly manifested that happiness was to be found among the age of death. A week later her vacant house was on the rental market and a room in Effiat was decorated to Colette's taste. Her mind and body were ravaged more and more by the destruction of four more years. She aged before Philippe's tearful eyes; each treasured moment was the profound love he had for his mother; each fallen tear was the solitude of his emotions and I battled to conquer his sufferance in great despair. It was an October 14th when Colette faded away into a world of eternal silence. With her aged hand in mine her journey into the shadows of the valley of death began. Colette had liberated her cherished son from his sufferance.

I had never seen Colette not clothed in blue and nearly everyone that attended the crematorium was dressed in her favourite colour. I sat in the front row with Philippe directly on my right hand side; that was close enough to comfort him with a discrete gesture of love if needed, but much to my surprise his hand embraced mine in public. The five minute eulogy I had written was gallantly recited like a poem. It impressed Philippe that I had learnt it off by heart, but like the beautiful flowers that decorated her coffin I wanted everything to be perfect. Colette believed in the almighty

catholic god, so some holy prayers were uttered. Philippe's mouth was stationary. I didn't know the words of "Our Father" in French either, but "Ár nAthair, atá ar neamh, go naomhaítear d'ainm. Go dtaga do ríocht. Go ndéantar do thoil ar an talamh mar a dhéantar ar neamh." suddenly resurfaced from nowhere and what was engrained in me in the Irish language simultaneously flowed. Each smile of the 87 years of her life traversed on an electronic photo frame. I didn't liberate my tears of woe, perhaps the world believed that I was cold in my emotions, but my lamentation was in the months of severe solitude afterwards. As the flames consumed the corpse the mourners offered their condolences to Philippe. I believed that a fraternal bond was to resurrect from Colette's death, but it enraged me to learn that her last will and testament was the unique thing that linked two men. I implored him, but his brother simply didn't want to know Philippe anymore.

Sarkozy frowned upon homosexuality in an illiberal fashion, so in the belief that François Holland was the liberator for queers, pink votes fell into the transparent ballot boxes in abundance on May 6th 2012. It was the glorious resurrection of a gay culture, a revolution for the dream of homosexual marriage, but it was the liberation of many barbaric judgements too. In a profound catholic righteous minded society the streets were overwhelmed with holy heterosexuals preaching in uproar against homosexual immorality. Queers danced under the flashing disco lights of urban gay clubs in harmony, some militants walked the streets in revolt against biblical homosexual intolerance and if there had been passion in the crucifixion of Jesus Christ there was certainly rancour in the crucifixion of homosexuals. Thou shalt not have compassion for "queer fuckers"; some pious heterosexuals battled to banish gays from the kingdom of heaven in a pacifist way, whilst others resorted to gay bashing without repentance. The sudden increase in physical attacks that ravaged the gay community nourished my profound fear of wearing a pink triangle. The holy heterosexual Catholics that practiced the same promiscuity as queers judged my sin and their pantomime of homophobia enraged me. Another glass of whiskey liberated the truth and in sufferance I learnt that a heterosexual that I had befriended didn't believe in the homosexual battle for liberty. Gilbert lowered his cold eyes in distaste of queers and his drunken mawkish words betrayed me. In his hostile holy judgement homosexuality needed repentance and not civil equality. I certainly battled to cultivate him with tolerance, but the righteousness of catholic sermons were too savagely embedded in him to silence.

The almighty catholic god was eternally silenced in France on May 29th 2013 and Vincent Autin and Bruno Boileau were the first queers to espouse in the secular sacrament of a pink civil marriage. The immortalisation of their love by media was the positive dissemination of homosexual propaganda, the dream of liberty for homosexuality that I had always wanted, but as some queers made the solemn promise of eternal love, in other parts of the world homosexuals were condemned to death. Highly tolerant societies granted homosexuals right after right, reveries for some had even become tangible, but the rainbow coloured gay pride flag was still silenced worldwide. The universal war to liberate all persecuted homosexuals from intolerance and suppression in heteronormative cultures had just begun. No gold ring glittered on the digitus quartus manus of my left hand. I loved Philippe, but marriage was the prison of sufferance that had destroyed my catholic mother. What had been forbidden for years was now my liberty, but I needed more time to decide. Homosexual immorality was deeply embedded in society, but the preservation of catholic family values had certainly crumbled in France. Same-sex couples had the legal right to adopt, but my desire to father was an eternal dream. I had an ocean of love to give, but there was so much destruction in the heterosexual culture that I belonged to. Perhaps I didn't have the strength to battle the regard of society again?

It was while renting a seaside apartment in the summer of 2014 that I befriended Babeth Ochoteco. Her glorious smile glittered with so much vivacity, but underneath the deep surface of her gaiety she silenced her woe. Perhaps the rimple that traced her forehead in a horizontal fashion when she stopped smiling was the clear sign that she had suffered, but had she not disclosed her story to me, I would have simply imaged that such a wrinkle had been tailored by time as she aged. So many years of living in France had enriched me with the language of Molière, my Irish accent had softened; some were seduced by its charm, but others still discriminated. Babeth loved different cultures and hungered to know about the acceptance of homosexuality in catholic Ireland. I certainly didn't want to unearth the journey of my life, but Irish brutality resurrected to betray me. An ocean of emotions fell from her eyes as she listened. Each tear liberated the perpetual sufferance that was engrained in her. She mourned for Vincent; the almighty catholic god had given death to her beloved heterosexual son and it enraged her that my holy mother had abandoned me, "a queer fucker". Babeth proclaimed that she would have done anything in the world for his resurrection, but the injustice of his death was her eternal lamentation. Two parallel paths of desolation crossed, our bodies embraced

and from the ashes of tragedy a profound friendship blossomed. In the changing colours of the seasons my pious mother ungraciously aged. Much to my despair she still displayed no repentance and I didn't have the clemency to ever forgive her. Her intolerance for queers was my everlasting sufferance, but if eternal sufferance was the key to my homosexual freedom I merited such sufferance.

Was the vulgarisation of marriage the unleashing of perpetual immorality in Ireland? On January 18th 2015 the Irish Minister for Health publicly disclosed his homosexuality. Leo Varadkar's heroic coming out was a major stepping stone to encourage equality for Irish homosexuals as the debate on a pink sacrament of marriage for Irish queers neared. Two roads diverged, either catholic Ireland would continue to silence homosexual love forever or the liberation of homosexuals would silence the catholic judgement of Ireland. On May 22nd 2015 Ireland emancipated homosexuality from the almighty barbarism that religion practiced. In a historically reputed pious catholic country, 62% of holy voters in the referendum rebelled against god's intolerance. The once mighty Catholic Church was so ravaged that the homophobic influence it had exerted on Irish society, morality and political culture was gone. Homosexual marriage was certainly the absolute defeat of god in Ireland, but the real victory was the birth of hope for all of humanity. An ocean of emotions devoured me that day and Alexander's desire of loving me forever fondly resurfaced in the silence of my thoughts, but his tragic death had sealed our fate. Ireland had liberated my revenge on the promise of silence. Queer love was freed from the prison of injustice, the bereavement of the Irish god began and as each tear fell from my blue eyes I flourished. The intolerance of a catholic Ireland had destroyed me, but I now granted a serene Ireland my forgiveness. Irish homosexuals were liberated from the slavery of silence forever. Irish queers didn't have to battle for the freedom to love anymore. A harmonious voyage into the new horizons of tolerance began and I resurrected from the ashes of despair that had traced the history of homosexuality in Ireland. My Irish sufferance had created me, but I now tasted the freedom of my dreams in the beautiful dream of others.

From the Pont Aven promenade deck I saw the multi-coloured houses that lined Cobh harbour. The splendour of the sunlight penetrated the dark clouds and glittered divinely on Saint Colman's Cathedral. Some Corkonians on the mainland waved in a friendly fashion to the ferry; the

gloomy weather hadn't dissuaded them from giving such joviality to the passengers that waved back. An abundance of emotions devoured my blue eyes on that 28th of August 2016 and each tear denuded me of my sufferance. There were delicious sandwiches and chocolate covered biscuits with a nice cup of Lyons tea in the homes of some. Others, with zeal had accepted my invitation for a pint of Guinness in the Kingsley Hotel. The true friends that had never abandoned me, the loyal aunts and uncles that had not forsaken me, the amazing cousins and cousin-in-laws that I hadn't seen for donkey's years and the many second cousins that I had just met for the first time; all knew that I was a fucking queer, but each one had tolerance and loved me for me. My holy catholic mother had perpetually entombed me in silence and still had no repentance, but I tasted the eternal affection of those that didn't give a damn about my homosexuality. In their total acceptance I was liberated from my sufferance forever. I aged for eternity in the love that glittered in Philippe's profound ocean blue eyes; my glorious dream of freedom had flourished with serenity.

This is the immortalisation of my reveries and my revenge on the promise of silence was certainly the most emotional journey of my life. My immorality came out of the dark dusty closet, my tears unearthed my deep despair and my betrayal liberated my profound sufferance to you. I resurrected the social myths of queers, rebelled against the barbarism of the catholic religion, painted the real promiscuity of the homosexual culture and dreamed of your harmonious voyage into the horizon of tolerance. You tread on my dream of homosexual freedom; your judgement is now the perpetual crucifixion or the eternal liberation of queers.

THE PROMISE OF SILENCE

The persecution of queers in the name of god is still practiced worldwide and the universal battle to liberate all homosexuals has just begun. I am certainly not a gay militant, but I have a dream that the heterosexual and homosexual cultures can live and flourish in harmony hand in hand...

Wave your rainbow coloured flags, come out of the dark dusty closet of your silence, liberate homosexuality from sufferance and injustice, immortalise your tolerance and battle for FREEDOM with me now...

Please feel free to contact me: **the.promise.of.silence@gmail.com**

Be the word of mouth for "The Promise Of Silence".

Have a nice day. Marshall.

The Promise Of Silence

Made in the USA
Middletown, DE
31 March 2018